WHERE DID I GO RIGHT?

WHERE DID I GO RIGHT?

HOW THE LEFT LOST ME

GEOFF NORCOTT

monoray

First published in Great Britain in 2021 by Monoray, an imprint of
Octopus Publishing Group Ltd
Carmelite House
50 Victoria Embankment
London EC4Y 0DZ
www.octopusbooks.co.uk

An Hachette UK Company
www.hachette.co.uk

ISBN 978-1-91318-343-1

A CIP catalogue record for this book is available from
the British Library.

Printed and bound in Great Britain

10 9 8 7 6 5 4 3 2 1

Some names and identities have been changed

This FSC® label means that materials used for the product
have been responsibly sourced

This **monoray** book was crafted and published by
Jake Lingwood, Liz Marvin, Pauline Bache, Juliette Norsworthy,
David Eldridge, Claire Rollet, Ed Pickford and Pete Hunt.

To my brilliant mum and dad.

Without them I wouldn't be here, but more importantly, this book would've been light on anecdotes.

A NOTE TO THE READER

This is a memoir which follows the formation of my political character, and in particular, looks at my voting story throughout the tumultuous and highly charged 2010s. While I was writing the book the pandemic happened and the book was sent to the printer whilst we were deep in the second (or was it the third?) lockdown. Whatever happens in this crazy and distressing period may or may not affect my voting choices in the future, but this is not a book about the pandemic. Instead it begins (and ends) with the General Election of December 2019...

CONTENTS

PROLOGUE

FALL OF THE RED WALL

It's 12 December 2019, the day of the general election. I'm at Riverside TV studios in London, waiting in the wings of the television programme *Channel 4's Alternative Election Night*. We are all waiting for the exit poll to give us our first big pointer for the outcome of the general election.

This feels like something of a gathering point for the so-called 'metropolitan elite'. If Remainer Central was a stop on the District line everyone would get off here. As a working-class Conservative, I once again find myself in the wrong 'neighbourhood'. However, I grew up in a politically diverse household so it's nothing new. Mum and Dad loved a 'lively' debate. I'm comfortable around differing views but often find that, in this world, people aren't comfortable around mine.

There is a profound sense of electoral suspense hanging over the day, a feeling Britain has grown accustomed to over the last few years. We've become jaded veterans of many a bruising political campaign, from the divisive Scottish independence referendum of 2014 to the surprise Tory majority in 2015, the political earthquake of Brexit in 2016 and the twist of a hung parliament a year later. It's been an oppressive sort of London day building up to this moment. The tight anxiety the nation is feeling seems to be matched by the pressure per square inch in the sky above. Throw in the added fug of London pollution, particularly around the Hammersmith flyover, and there's an awful lot bearing down on this day.

As a Conservative-voting comedian, I've appeared in this sort of context before, but never on a flagship show on election night. It feels like a big moment. And yet, on arrival at the studios, my general sense of discombobulation is exacerbated by the fact no one seems to know who I am. This isn't uncommon. I'm not massively well known and my usual attire of jeans, polo shirt and bomber jacket makes me look like a cross between an electrician and a ticket tout. Tonight, though, the crew querying my presence triggers something in me. 'Should you be here?' seems like a valid question, professionally and politically. Being working class drives a non-stop stream of internal heckles in situations like this. When I arrive to appear on grown-up shows like this and *Question Time*, there's always a part of me inclined to say, 'You know what, mate, you're absolutely right – I *shouldn't* be here. I'm off to eat some Spam and do a conga.'

By the time the seventh crew member fails to understand that I am actually supposed to be on the show, I realise I am starting to get a bit testy, which doesn't suit me.

'I'm *Geoff* Norcott,' I tell her.

'Jez Norcroft?'

'Geoff.'

'J – e –'

'No, G – e . . .'

At this point, a drunk bloke behind recognises me and tries to get a selfie. I'm not one for grand showbiz gestures but I hope the fact a perfect stranger wants my photo might make this lady reconsider. I throw her a look as if to say '*See*?' – possibly the wankiest thing I've ever done. As I impatiently spell my whole name, a runner finally clocks who I am and takes me to the backstage area. I am cross but maybe I should be blaming politics for the way it's drawn us out of our normal characters. Tonight, it feels like we've spent three and a half years in a state of political PMT.

This isn't where anyone thought I'd end up. My dad was a proud union man. I remember him singing 'You don't get me, I'm part of the union', and thinking it was a cute song for kids – until I realised he was trying to indoctrinate me. Mum wasn't a Labour voter but if she was still with us there are two things she'd have been appalled to see me do: take sugar in tea or vote for the party who gave the world Margaret Thatcher.

It wasn't so long ago that I was an English teacher tucked away in rural Bedfordshire; staring out of the window thinking there might be more to life than pretending I knew how to use a semi-colon. And it has only been a little while since I was a fixture on the weekend comedy-club circuit, plying my trade to a sea of stags and hens. It's fair to say that I had not envisaged a role for myself in political comedy when I was getting an inflatable penis thrown at me at a Butlins gig.

This campaign has been exciting, but the last days leading up to the vote itself have made it clear some people are suffering from a form of democratic PTSD. One day, when things return to 'normal', there might be a recognised condition called 'Brexit shellshock', with homes for people who still scream out Andrew Neil's name in the dead of night or dive behind the couch at the opening strains of *Newsnight*, but for now the condition remains undiagnosed and these damaged souls wander around paranoid and glassy-eyed. (If this all seems a bit dramatic, remember these are different times. It was pre-coronavirus, back when we allowed ourselves the playful delusion that leaving the EU was the most dangerous thing a country could go through.)

I enjoyed the disarray of 2016 to 2019 in the same way perverse way Churchill once admitted to feeling invigorated by war. The cut and thrust of modern politics even began to replace sport in my psyche. Earlier in this tumultuous year, I left a pub so I could get signal on my phone in order to find out the results of the midweek 'indicative votes' held to establish which of May's Brexit plans had the most support. I exited with the kind of trepidation I used to reserve for checking the cricket score during an Ashes series (and just like Ashes cricket, my hope for a positive outcome was quickly dashed).

And who could forget the box-office appeal of 'Super Saturday' on 19 October 2019? The first time the Commons had sat on a Saturday since the Falklands! If it had been on pay-per-view I'd have forked out £14.99 to watch it (the debate that is, not the Falklands). Although, in the end, 'Super Saturday' turned out just like all the crap boxing matches I've paid good money for: a total non-event.

There was also the time I pulled over into a lay-by because I'd got too excited listening to Geoffrey Cox's response to the eleven–nil Supreme Court judge ruling against the government. It was defiant, loud and sonorous – like nothing I'd heard in my lifetime, as though Mufasa had survived his fall and was tearing the Labour front bench a new one.

He boomed out: 'THIS IS A DEAD PARLIAMENT . . . THE TIME IS COMING WHEN EVEN THESE TURKEYS WON'T BE ABLE TO PREVENT CHRISTMAS.'

I punched the air, and not just because this is a man who spells 'Geoffrey' correctly. He gave a voice to the frustration and inertia we'd all felt for so long. The combative tone probably wasn't helpful but fuck me, it was exciting. I looked at the bloke in the car next to me – clearly he was listening to the same thing. We gave each other a little thumbs up.

Like I say, it was an odd time to live through.

It's been an odd polling day too. Talking in the green room before the broadcast, it seemed no one was contemplating the idea of a big Tory majority, which is odd, given it's within the margin of error. The most likely outcome tonight is a narrow Conservative majority, a squeaky political one–nil. This won't be enough to be sure of 'getting Brexit done' or much else over the next five years. Despite the Tories having led throughout the campaign, there is once again a rising belief on social media that Corbyn could upset the odds and heroically lose by slightly less than he did last time. Indeed, if you go by social media, Labour are probably heading for a one-hundred seat majority. All day long, I've read stories of queues outside polling stations in trendy London districts. Only on Twitter could a few hipsters standing outside a primary school in Crouch End herald a new socialist dawn.

I glance around at the studio audience, main presenters and array of TV types circling in the wings next to me. Everyone seems nervous. I look down at my palms: they're sweaty. It's not just the result I'm anxious about. Not long after the exit poll is announced, I'm required to go and bring the funny at the comedy desk, which *Alternative Election* has set up as a counterpoint to the more conventional electoral analysis. This section of the show might work if the result is still in the balance but if it seems clear the Tories are going to win I could be the clown at a cancer diagnosis.

I'm due to be on with the father of the current prime minister, Stanley Johnson. I'm not sure sticking two Tories on together moments after announcing the exit poll is a good idea. Stanley has been all right in the green room but it's late, he's drinking red wine and in person seems a lot older than he looks on telly. I'm not sure how this is going to pan out.

The narrative around this election has been a familiar one. The Tories are either a hard-right, far-right or fascist regime. This election has come down to the same childish principles as the last few. It's a battle between good and evil, right and wrong.

The NHS is – for the seventh time in my life – 'moments' from extinction. (You have to hand it to the NHS, it's like Batman in the old Adam West sixties TV show. 'Is the end for the caped crusader?' Of course not. Batman never dies. Deep down we all know that but the delusion and the jeopardy that the NHS could cease to exist has become intrinsic to the soap opera of British politics.)

I, like many people, have lost friends over politics. Sometimes very shortly after making them. Shortly after the surprise Conservative majority at the 2015 election, I performed my stand-up set at the Manchester Comedy

Store. Afterwards, I got chatting to a young couple in the bar and we went out on the piss together. We were getting along famously, then I casually mentioned the fact I'd voted for the Tories.

I felt the air go out of the room. The girl's effervescent smile dipped into a look of murderous reproach. She very deliberately took her phone out of her handbag and tottered off to the ladies' toilet on the kind of heels that must make dads and podiatrists weep. Her fella looked mortified. I got the sense he was a leftie too but that this wasn't the first time a social event had been soured by the shock news someone had voted in line with a large swathe of the country. He furrowed his annoyingly smooth forehead. Then he got a text from his missus, shrugged apologetically, went outside to join her and they left.

This kind of tribalism doesn't really suit Britain, it's made us uneasy. We've all had social gatherings where the conversation has slowly drifted uncomfortably towards politics. You hear those coded phrases people use as political markers. From Remainers, it's 'People didn't know what they were voting for.' A right-winger might throw in a 'Well, you can't say anything these days.' A leftie could equate Conservative party membership with being part of the SS. Before you know it, you've shifted through the social DEFCONs to mutually assured destruction, where the only thing that can pull it around is watching that clip of the American woman making tea in a microwave. Badly made tea remains one of the few things with the power to unite warring cultural and political factions in Great Britain.

In the studio, I'm now trawling my Twitter feed and it seems like a lot of celebrities who've spent the last few years 'despairing' over Corbyn have voted for him anyway. I know this because I'm seeing the word 'Labour' coming up time and time again on my disproportionately luvvie timeline. I later find out this was a co-ordinated attempt by the Labour campaign team. They'd been direct messaging any cool young slebs they presumed were onside and thought they could get this simple, one-word idea trending.

I only found out because they hadn't done their research and messaged a couple of Lib Dem comedians who promptly outed their cunning plan. Some comics expressed anger that these lads had gone public but it belied yet another lazy presumption of the Left: that if you're young, cool and a comedian you must vote for them.

In some respects, that episode underlines one of the problems the Left have faced of late. They want elections to be won on the smartphone not the doorstep. Progress on social issues online has been huge but elections haven't gone the Left's way for some time. It's a convenient and appealing idea to think that you could reshape British democracy with a kick-ass meme. However, if elections were decided by likes and retweets Russell Brand would've been prime minister since 2015.

I look at the clock. The show only started broadcasting five minutes ahead of the exit poll, which is a short lead-in to such a big moment. Krishnan Guru-Murthy is anchoring and my friend Katherine Ryan seems impressively ice cool in the face of history.

And this *will* be historic, however the dice land. The stakes couldn't be higher. An inconclusive result won't simply yield a replay later that week, this is a whole country stuck in a holding pattern while air traffic control accuse each other of Russian interference. If we have a hung parliament or a small majority the uncertainty continues. If we have a large Tory majority Britain will definitely leave the EU. Boris has gambled and gone for the car. Will he be like those people on *Bullseye* who win the speedboat? Or will he be left waving gamely at the end, having been given his Boris Bus fare home?

I haven't been sure about Boris during the campaign. He's not my kind of politician. I can't tell how seriously he's taking it, whether he really wants to lead this country or if this is the final victory over his bullies at Eton. Voting Tory when you're working class always involves a bit of nose holding. The more Latin they speak the harder you have to pinch. It's not just the fact that Boris sometimes uses noises instead of verbs, for the first time since 2010 the tone of this campaign had me briefly doubting if I could vote Conservative. I wasn't considering voting Labour – or Lib Dem for that matter – but there's something about seeing your prime minister hiding in a fridge that gives cause for reflection.

Krishnan does a quick re-cap on how we got to this point, democratically speaking. Politics has often felt like it's needed that over the last few years, an HBO-style 'Previously on . . .' At least with *Game of Thrones* they had time off between each series. The Brexit saga has been more like *Eastenders*: high octane drama at least four times a week with no chance to fully digest which poor bastard got mowed down last week.

I see an on-screen image of Theresa May looking peak Theresa May: tired, confused and lacking in red blood cells. I feel bad for her; if Brexit does happen a lot of her work will still be in the Withdrawal Bill. She gave it her all. She faced down the Left, the Right, the media . . . she even got trolled by a conference back-drop and her own throat. She will have – in cricketing terms – opened the batting, taken knocks and left the field for a doughty but unmemorable 27. Boris, however, is coming in after tea, the bowlers are tired and he's been slapping the ball around for fun.

Back in the studio, I look at an audience member in the seats to my left. He raises his thick black glasses like Eric Morecambe and does a semi-comic grimace. I don't know if it's the tension of the moment or he knows my angle and is empathising as I'm probably going to die on my arse.

Krishnan says the exit poll is now in and we switch to the huge screen stage-left. Everything seems to stop for a moment, like that weird pause in time between dropping your phone and hearing it smash on the floor.

All I really see is a blue colour. It says: 'Conservative majority'. I notice the words but the blue is the thing I realise I'm subconsciously seeking out. It suddenly occurs to me just how much I like the colour blue. Is that what all this boils down to? I'd like to think my politics were a rational synthesis of the world around me but maybe I'm just like someone's nan picking her Grand National runner because she likes the name. Perhaps we all are.

Perhaps that's the point of this book.

As I get older, I place more importance on the emotional and psychological drivers of our political views. Like everything else, the way we see the world is largely born of our early life experiences. Right-wingers weren't hugged often enough while socialists were arguably cuddled far too much. This book will, figuratively speaking, be my attempt to work out where hugs or the lack thereof have put me on the political dial. You might read parts and think 'That's a bit biased.' Indeed. The fact I am biased is a given; the real question is where it all came from.

One thing this election has done is tested the old class loyalties. The Labour party have been slowly losing touch with the working classes, which seems quite an oversight – like Wetherspoons neglecting older men who like drinking one pint while taking seven hours to read a paper. In the run-up to the election, I was on a stand-up tour and had plenty of discussions with punters in the so-called 'Labour heartlands'. One night, I had post-gig beer with a group of people who were so hilariously diverse they might've been invented by a BBC panel. There was Diane and John who were from the north-east, another couple who were essentially metropolitan Remainers living up north and two lesbian women who seemed less exercised about Brexit and more interested in getting shitfaced.

If the Labour Party had wanted to do some useful field-work leading up to the election I'd have urged them to have a pint with John and Diane. Diane was the kind of working-class woman I've always warmed to, partly because she reminded me of my mum: blunt, smart and with a wicked tongue. You know the type – women who, when they're on *Question Time*, savour holding politicians to account. They sniff the air and straighten their bra straps so their tits are facing the minister down like two cannons. Diane could hold her drink too, so within a few rounds of Jagerbombs she had us splayed out over the couches like we'd been spiked with Novichok.

Speaking to Diane, I got a sense of just how remote the modern Labour party seemed to someone living in Stockton. Some of the policies appealed to her but the 'brand', she said, felt like a middle-class pressure group. Diane and her husband also didn't like the 'victim obsession' of the party in its current guise. Not every working-class person wants to think of themselves as living a shit life and in need of saving. Diane wasn't planning on voting Tory, however. No, she was lining up to vote for the Brexit Party and Nigel Farage. She was excited by her democratic right. That's one of the appeals of politics. The idea that every so often you get a chance to exercise agency. Maybe that's why a slogan like 'take back control' was so popular with the working classes. The polling booth is one of the only places we have true equality.

So Diane went purple but, from what I'm now seeing on screen in the studio, many working-class people in the north must've gone blue. Just how many is the next thing to appear on the screen.

It shows an expected Conservative majority of 86 seats.

Even I'm in shock now. If I'm honest, outside of the Brexit paradigm, I quite like governments with small majorities – it keeps them in check. The coalition years sometimes felt like a sweet deal: the solid economic house of the Tories with a Lib Dem granny flat of compassion. Tonight, Boris has ended up with a mansion all to himself.

A comedy promoter waiting with us in the studio wings looks like she's been bereaved. She surveys me through accusatory eyes and says, 'Do you have kids?'

'Yes.'

'Well, their future's FUCKED.'

I'd like to say that I immediately responded with, 'No, love, *your* future's fucked, I've actually invested very wisely,' but I just stare back trying to work out how hammered she is.

Her barb isn't my biggest concern right now. I was already anxious about having to go on to do comedy so shortly after the exit poll but that was in anticipation of a small Tory majority and an unclear outcome on Brexit. However, it looks like it's game, set and match to the Conservatives. And not only have the Labour voters in the audience lost spectacularly, everyone in the room now knows that at last Britain will definitely be leaving the EU.

It's a lot to take in.

The live panel are already talking about the swing to the right from working-class voters, especially in the north. Many of us have been predicting this for a while but not even I expected such a violent lurch. Asking people in former mining towns to vote Tory isn't like someone from the south making the same switch; they are literally going against the voices of all their ancestors. The ghosts of their forefathers would've been pulling their hands back to the box on the poll card into which they'd usually put their cross. For many people, voting Tory is like putting a cravat on the Angel of the North.

The floor manager readies me and Stanley. The father of the newly elected prime minister is happy. The red wine seems to have mixed with a good mood and the possibility he'll be doing even more bizarre slots on celebrity TV shows. As I walk across the stage, the view of the audience is something I'll never forget. There are boos for Stanley, some for me too. The show and Channel 4 subsequently got a lot of stick for supposedly not having any Tories in the audience. The truth is they did, but the Conservatives in the room were in shock like everyone else and looking over their shoulders in case it all kicked off.

Matt Forde kicks off the comedy section of the show with his excellent Boris Johnson impression. He hands over to me and I try to make a point that Boris needs to make good on his new alliance with the north. I attempt a metaphor using *Game of Thrones* but if I'm honest, this doesn't feel like the right time for comic analogies. As the short section progresses, it becomes increasingly painful, like trying to ride a unicycle at a wake. It's not just that people aren't laughing, they aren't even listening. They're still staring at that giant screen with bug-eyed astonishment, like a collective comedy pause in a Pixar film. The director wraps up our section pretty sharpish.

Back in the green room, I'm in a mixed state of mind. I'm pleased about the election result but disappointed at how my bit with Stanley went. You never want to play to virtual silence but I'm philosophical enough to know that, in comedic terms, it was like tickling an injured bear. I find lots of people from the comedy industry milling about. I try to be magnanimous. It was one of the first things my mum ever taught me: 'Be magnanimous in victory and magnificent in defeat.' Well, I've already won and lost tonight, so it'll be a balancing act. Despite my views on magnanimity, I wouldn't mind at least one person to have a silent fist bump with but it seems I'm totally alone. No one is in the mood for drinking.

I decide to stay in the green room when I'm not needed on set. By the time I'm back on stage at about 3am, the show is now has moved to more straightforward political discourse and this time I'm glad to be able to make my point about the idiocy of ignoring your working-class voter base. The studio audience has slimmed down to a hardcore of about 100, mostly lefties. It's like they're holding on, postponing the moment they have to step out into the reality of five more years of Tory rule and the final inevitability of Brexit.

For me, the night has been yet another experience of feeling politically isolated. Given my solid working-class background and performing arts job, it's obvious to everyone I meet that I should be Labour through and through. I'm a comedian who grew up on a council estate with two disabled parents, and my dad was a trade union man. But that's not how I voted. I grew up to vote Tory.

Here I am, leaving the studio alone, having got into bed with the so-called 'baddies'.

How did it get to this?

1

I SHOULD NEVER HAVE BEEN WORKING CLASS

In truth, I should probably have been a Conservative all along – certainly if my family's trajectory is anything to go by. The Norcotts had been on a gentle, upward curve for many years by the time I was born in December 1976. Mum and Dad are no longer with us but anyone who's lost both parents by the age of 40 will know that losing the second one brings with it a certain clarity as to who they were. I can see now that, for the most part, in terms of social mobility, they were doing no more than pushing a car up a hill.

My dad's plaque is in St Mary's Church, Wimbledon. If you go there you'll be able to find it because he had the exact same name as me. I don't *mind* the name but 'Geoff Norcott' isn't such a belter that you'd give it another outing. My mum's labour with me wasn't especially long, so I can't even put it down to fatigue. As a Christian name, 'Geoffrey' is a bit strange. The shortened version, 'Geoff', sounds like a Scouse plumber, while the longer version, 'Geoffrey', sounds like a guy who owns a Jaguar dealership. Maybe that duality explains a lot; even my name is sitting on an awkward precipice between two social classes.

St Mary's is a posh church, adjacent to the finery of the All England Lawn Tennis Club. You've probably seen it during the sweeping shots the BBC does of the grounds during its coverage of the tennis. It's a fancy place to worship. The surrounding bucolic aesthetic reflects most people's idea of Wimbledon. There's no shrapnel rattling around in *their* collection tins, it's all notes, thank you very much.

In my experience, people tend to think anyone living in Wimbledon has got a few quid. If you go up north and say you come from Wimbledon, people often repeat the word back to you in a mocking posh accent, '*Wimbledon*'. Living on a council estate in the same town as the world's premier tennis tournament doesn't get you much in the way of working-class credibility. No one thinks it could've been a bad experience either – it's like announcing you have cancer of the toe. However, anyone who knows the area – particularly in the late seventies and early eighties – will know it as a schizophrenic sort of place. Yes, you have some of the world's most expensive real estate in the village but, down the hill – in a pretty blunt metaphor for wealth and class – the town wasn't so different from anywhere else in south London. I always thought of the hill leading up to Wimbledon village as an apt metaphor for the location itself. Elevated and with great sight-lines, it gave folk with money time to roll out barrels of hot tar if the great unwashed ever got a bit restless.

The area around South Wimbledon tube station is still dodgy to this day. Local estate agents call it 'Southern Wimbledon'. The more they dick around with semantics the more you know to exit the tube station at a brisk pace. The parade of shops leading down from the tube station to the next stop on the Northern line, Colliers Wood, is a bizarre assortment of those specialist shops you pass and wonder if they make any money. Lamp shops, Hoover-repair shops, places selling nothing but sinks. Maybe there's a contractual deal that comes with being on the Northern line. Those decrepit grey tube stations and the line's jet-black coding dictate that even the surrounding businesses have to imply perennial decay.

To sum up the area's bipolar relationship with wealth, when I was growing up, Wimbledon had both a Grand Slam tennis tournament and a greyhound racing track within a mile of each other. You could pay a tenner for strawberries or have a whole night out, including carvery, for the same price.

It was strange living in an area that became a focal point of the world for two weeks out of every year, on account of a tournament which brought conspicuous wealth to the town, like a sporting version of Davos.

Tourists would sometimes take a wrong turn on to our council estate and ask directions to the tennis. One day, a couple who I considered very old (so probably in their fifties) wandered aimlessly towards us kids playing in the street. They were American.

'Excuse me, is this the way to the tennis?'

We all clocked how loud the bloke was speaking. We also looked around and behind us, as if to say, 'Does it look like the way to the fucking tennis?'

I'd never understood how health could be 'rude' but this guy's was. His suntan was offensive. I'd never seen teeth so straight. His wife was unlike any woman I'd ever seen either. Her hair looked like it had been built off site and lowered onto her head by a crane. I was intrigued by him though; an American accent will always seem exotic to me.

There was a long period when it was distinctly uncool to be into American culture but I never stopped loving the sound of that accent. It was the voice of *The Goonies*, Han Solo and Elliott's mum in *ET*. It was exotic. Now we have curve TVs and streaming platforms, it's hard to explain what it felt like to consume American culture on the big screen during that time. The family films of the eighties were waking dreams.

My sister and I visited North America in 1990, though sadly the closest we could get to the promised land was Canada. Mum wisely invested her divorce settlement in buying me a video camera and paying for us to both go on a holiday. They were trusted family friends, so we travelled alone. The money came from my dad's redundancy. He was obliged to pay Mum a percentage, which she promptly spunked up the wall like *Brewster's Millions*. She'd have been the first to admit she didn't like having money – the only person I've met who took the words 'disposable income' literally. So, despite having a school uniform full of holes and budget versions of everything from Coke to mince, I also had a video camera and tickets booked to Canada.

It wasn't the most conscientious use of the windfall Dad received. He must've been pulling his hair out. Having lost his job heading into a recession, he then found his son opening the door of his ex-wife's council flat filming him with a £600 bit of high-tech kit. These days, I could tell him I was creating content for a monetised YouTube channel. Back then, I was just carrying a bit of his redundancy around on my shoulder and talking with an inexplicable American accent.

In Canada we stayed with family friends to keep the cost down.

'What do you want to do?' asked my adopted uncle, Mike.

'We want to go to a shopping mall,' said my sister.

I concurred.

Seeing Niagra Falls would've been impressive but we lived in south London and so returning with a banging pair of LA Gear trainers was the mark of a man truly well travelled. Walking around that mall felt like shopping in the future. In my mind, I was Marty McFly, except I'd only travelled forward in time a couple of years and instead of saving my parents I just wanted some cheap Nike Airs.

Eventually, Wimbledon got its own shopping mall. I was doing work experience at the time for the *Wimbledon News*. At the grand opening of 'Centre Court' (unimaginative names are a feature of the area), a brand new piece of modern art was unveiled. The reporter I was with was under instructions to gauge the public reaction to the new installation. However, he had to come up with his own description because practically everyone he spoke to concluded the pair of female figures looked like 'two fat lesbians', which sounded less a work of art and more like a fictional pub in *Viz*.

This was a less politically correct age and in Wimbledon 'meet you at the two fat lesbians' became a common plan for a rendezvous. I can't speak for everyone in the area but in the current climate, I've revised my language to: 'Meet you at the two strong women of no obvious sexual orientation.'

So, back on the council estate, with his American accent, this Yank had my attention. He had the earnestness Americans have and Brits generally don't. He already thought I was his 'buddy'. I've never fully bought into the British cynicism about Americans. I quite like their upbeat disposition and open celebration of success.

Maybe it is a bit fake but it's also fake to pretend to be miserable when you're happy – or that you're not trying to earn a few quid. The British relationship with money is fundamentally dishonest. We're all out to get it but act like it's this accidental consequence of the way we've organised our lives. It's never more acute than in the comedy industry. There's nothing quite like watching a left-wing comic bank yet another million quid for their most recent deconstruction of capitalism.

I don't even buy that Americans don't get irony. If you've seen the best American comedies of the seventies you'll know how ironic it is to think that. I think they get irony, they just don't *like* sarcasm. I understand why, but sarcasm is under-rated. Encapsulating a terrible experience under the mocking pretence of hope is about the most British thing you can do. There's no doubt that sarcasm has helped me through my darkest times. It's an ember of humour glowing in the blackness. It's congratulating Alanis Morissette on her understanding of irony.

I regret what I did next with the American.

He asked how to get to 'centre court' so I told him, but my directions were to the two fat lesbians.

Technically I was being honest. Morally I was not.

'I hope you're not leading me on a merry dance,' the guy said, sensing the mood.

'Course not,' I replied, avoiding his gaze like he was CIA.

Well, at least he got to experience some of the real Wimbledon. Not many tennis tourists get the opportunity to take a photo in front of two strong women of no obvious sexual orientation.

So to live in Wimbledon was to straddle a class divide straight from the get-go. Dad would drink in the low-rent boozers down in South Wimbledon but, as he got into late middle age, also played a full part in refined church life up the hill. A congregation member once said of him: 'Geoff Norcott is truly a man of both sides of the tracks.'

Dad liked this idea, so when he died in 2015 the family thought those words should go on his commemorative plaque. I was in the church grounds on Father's Day recently and, reading it again, saw how open that phrase is to misinterpretation. In isolation – and without any accompanying notes on the class connotation – 'both sides of the tracks' seems to suggest the family wanted the world to posthumously know my father was bisexual. It made me laugh, such an odd thing to declare. Graveyards are depressing places, so maybe we could all do with revealing some sexual preferences to add a bit of levity.

'George Treverau. Died 1886. Liked it rough.'

With two disabled parents, my family always took solace in that kind of mordant wit. For Mum's cremation in 2009, we were deliberating over what song to play as the casket went between the curtains. My stepdad, Roe, suggested the song 'Feeling Hot Hot Hot' by The

Merrymen. There was a brief pause before we all pissed ourselves laughing. She did love the song and would play it to get herself in the holiday mood on her bi-annual trips to Bognor Regis. I respected but never understood Mum's attachment to Bognor. I'm all for defending the great British seaside but Bognor didn't have much to do and the sea looked like bum gravy. However, Mum approached holidays there in the same way middle-class people would savour a week in Provence.

So it seemed right to send her on her next journey with the song that always accompanied her favourite one on earth. However, the connection between the lyrics and the act of cremation were hard to ignore. We asked ourselves, 'Would Mum appreciate the joke?' and the answer was an easy yes. However, we might have done well to also consider whether our fellow mourners would see the funny side. As her coffin made its final journey towards cremation it's fair to say that, once they'd clocked the significance of the lyrics, most did not.

Mum had also stipulated she wanted everyone in bright colours for the service, which was a nice touch. She requested that the pall bearers, rather than the usual stuffy formal wear, turned out in simple blue jeans and white t-shirts. It just so happened that the pall bearers on the day all had shaved heads. As my mate Mick observed, 'It looks like they're burying a member of Right Said Fred.'

*

Something holds this family back once we get a glimpse of the promised land of being solidly middle class. It's the social mobility equivalent of a diver getting the bends. We come up too fast, our noses start bleeding, then we choke on a piece of sushi. It's a shame, because over the generations a lot of work went into hauling us up another rung. My great-grandfather Frank Norcott (where my middle name comes from – we love continuity in this family) was a notoriously hard-working bus conductor in south London. My grandparents Reg and Peggy (is it just nostalgia or did that generation simply have better names?) also had a solid work ethic.

I didn't know Grandad as well as I'd have liked. He was one of the many gentlemen horrified to find themselves holding a rifle when the Second World War began. He served in North Africa and then knuckled down to hard graft upon his return. My nan, unlike many women of her generation, also worked, the net effect being that they were rare in their social circle in owning their own property. The property was in the arse end of Mitcham and worth less than a garage in Wimbledon but it was theirs.

That homeowner status got to my nan, who put on airs and graces and reminded me of a cross between the Queen and Maggie Thatcher. There was something very proper about her – even her roast dinners were modest but immaculate. Always served at one o' clock on the dot, the beef was good quality, but you didn't get much of it, and the veg was lined up with military precision.

She also nailed the Yorkshire puddings every single time (as much as feminism has advanced in my lifetime there has remained a unique envy among the women I know at anyone who can serve up a perfect non-soggy Yorkshire).

Mum and Nan had one of those simmering understandings which sometimes exists between alpha females. Mum referred to her as 'the old battleaxe' and Nan eyed Mum the same way I imagine the Queen first surveyed Diana. I'd say that domestically, 90 per cent of this kind of family conflict I've known comes from the women. A big shout, I know. I'm not excusing men, they start wars and crash economies, but the emotional territorial land-grabs by women in our family have the same legacy as the great global conflicts. Even the names of Norcott skirmishes sound like historical events. 'Christmas Boycott '97', 'Eastergate' and 'The Battle of Brewers Fayre'.

These days, our Christmases are organised with the kind of forward planning usually reserved for the Olympics. The jockeying for hosting got so intense we had to bring in the 'May Moratorium' whereby no one was allowed to speak about Christmas until after the May Day bank holiday. There are World Cup bids conducted with more transparency than how we decide the location of a family gathering.

When my parents got divorced, Nan, the supreme traditional matriarch, cut down contact with me and my sister. You always got the sense Grandad wasn't fully onboard with the diplomatic hostilities but had grown used to following orders. Like many men of that era, he was expert at seeing which side his bread was buttered and went along with it for a quiet life. He was a good-looking man, my grandad, over six feet tall – a galling reminder that the height gene passed from my dad to my sister (I'm five-ten but people helpfully inform me I look a lot shorter). My grandad looked like a better-looking version of Charles Hawtrey, the friendly looking bespectacled bloke from the *Carry On* films.

Like many men who'd been through it, Grandad didn't like to talk much about the war, but I remember one story in particular about his time stationed in North Africa, which underlined the gentle, enquiring spirit he possessed.

'I'd been in Africa a while and my regimental sergeant major called me in for a chat. He asked how I was getting on with the natives. I'd been sharing a tent with two African chaps and told him we got on well enough. There was one thing though.

'My sergeant major said, "Yes Norcott, spit it out."

'"Well, they'd don't half stink."'

As a teenager hearing this story, I was already cringing at what other dodgy stuff Grandad was going to say. He continued: 'The regimental sergeant major laughed and sat back in his chair, "Well, I'm afraid you're too late, Norcott. They made the exact same complaint about you and have asked to move tents."

'Turns out white people have their own smell and my new colleagues reckoned it was something like off milk.'

This anecdote might still make the modern liberal wince a bit but I'd argue that a working-class man from that era acknowledging any kind of bias represented some sort of progress. Imagining he didn't have his own smell is akin to people from the south-east imagining their voice represents 'English' and anything else is an 'accent'. It also underlines a theme of the twentieth century: whatever principles led racial integration, it was working-class people who were more often than not on the frontline. He was learning how to work, live and get on with people from very different backgrounds. I'm glad my grandad was able to laugh at his own parochialism and return from Africa with attitudes to race a good deal more enlightened than those held by many in Britain at that time.

War left him wise but anxious, and in constant need of a drink.

Much has been said of the impact of the two world wars on British men and their sons. It definitely had an effect on my old man's dealings with me, as a result of the relationship he'd had with his veteran father, but, as he once said to me when watching yet another Second World War documentary, 'Hitler fucked up my dad. However, now I'm retired, I do appreciate the documentaries.'

*

Mum and Dad continued the family's gentle creep forwards in social standing, but in the mid-eighties, as Dad was reaching for the higher echelons of his trade union and drinking more, the whole thing came crashing down with the Norcott family's first ever divorce. In truth, the breakdown of my parents' marriage wasn't strictly due to immediate circumstances but psychological booby traps laid long ago.

At the start of their relationship, everything had been moving in the right direction. Dad had sought to acquit himself in the tech boom of the early seventies and achieved good success as a draftsman in aircraft engineering. His Labour loyalties initially came from an association with Harold Wilson's aspirational brand of tech-savvy socialism. Dad was forever in awe of big infrastructure. He loved transport too. Not especially a fan of visiting actual places, he'd often do the journey for its own sake.

He once rang me from France: 'Hi son, I'm in Lille.'

'OK. How?'

'I took the Eurostar.'

'How did you find it?'

'*Very* slick.'

'What are you going to do in Lille, Dad?'

'Nothing, I'm heading over to the other platform to wait for the train back to London.'

He'd gone to France just to see what the train was like. As far as I know, it was the only time he ever visited the country. His lifetime experience of French cuisine was limited to a croissant from a platform vending machine.

He repeated this trick with the bullet train to Stratford during the London 2012 Olympics. A Londoner his whole life, with the Olympics more or less in his back yard, still he didn't give a shit about archery, the velodrome or even just visiting the Olympic Park. What he wanted to do was to see if he really could get from central London to Stratford in eight minutes. If he'd gone with Darwin to the Galapagos islands it would've only been to see how the *Beagle* coped with the return trip.

Possibly Dad's greatest transiting achievement, however, was in the car. I was living with him briefly in the late nineties. He was normally up, showered and drinking coffee by 5am latest so I was surprised to find him surfacing at about nine.

'What happened to you?'

'I drove round the M25 last night.'

I didn't take him literally and presumed he had to do something for a friend so carried about my business.

'Right round it. Always wanted to.'

I'd had my back to him but I now stopped and turned to face him. 'What? *All* the way round?'

'Yes,' he said proudly, looking at me like he'd ticked something major off the bucket list.

I stopped eating toast and stared at him. I loved the bloke but in truth I never fully worked him out. He was one of the most off-the-wall people I've ever met. I asked him how it felt to drive all the way around the M25.

He said, 'Like driving on a normal motorway but you end up back in the same place.'

Dad's success as a draftsman was all the more impressive since he only had one arm. He was born with two but lost the right one in a motorcycle accident in his twenties. We Norcotts love the story of how it happened, for morbidly comedic reasons.

It was the sixties. He'd been doing the sixties thing of getting drunk with his mates and driving motorbikes up to a café in Box Hill, Surrey, to be a bit sexist and smoke fags. Dad had just snagged himself a new 'bird' who I believe was called 'Carol Darden'. I never saw a photo of her but imagine she must've been incredibly beautiful. Just the name alone implies it, 'Carol Darden'. She sounds like a cross between a girl next door and a French film star. I don't know if she wore a headscarf and Jackie Onassis shades but let's take that creative licence. She got into the sidecar of Dad's bike and off they went. He was drunk, driving too fast and hit a vehicle coming the other way. He lost his arm that night and spent some time in a coma.

You might now wonder why I previously said that my family loved the story; as anecdotes go, it's not got an obviously comedic pay-off. What we love is what happened to Carol Darden.

The impact took out Dad's bike but Carol's sidecar

was fine. It detached quite neatly, in fact. The road was long, very straight and on a slight incline. Over the years some creative 'VAT' has been added on to just how long Carol Darden carried on in that little sidecar before it came to a natural halt. I don't know if it's all those *Some Mothers Do 'Ave 'Em*-type slapstick sequences of the era, but we always imagined her trundling apologetically by while some old duffer trimming his privet bush had to wipe his glasses because he couldn't believe his eyes.

Yes, Dad lost his arm and wore the psychological scars for the rest of his life, but CAN YOU IMAGINE THE LOOK ON THAT OLD GEEZER'S FACE?

(This is how the working class cope with sad stories.)

Being not only disabled but culpable for his own misfortune was a burden my dad put great effort into overcoming. He knew that a USP is no bad thing so becoming 'one-armed Geoff' was a hindrance physically but it made sure people remembered him. He was known for turning up at fancy-dress parties as a 'one-arm bandit'. At one party, a particularly persistent piss-head kept tugging on his arm asking 'Have I won? Have I won?'

My dad said he needed to give him a quid before he could tell him.

The guy gave him a quid and my dad said, 'No, you haven't won,' and punched him in the face.

Despite only having one arm, he was a powerful swimmer. On one family vacation, a holiday camp in the Isle of Wight, they were holding a swimming competition for the dads. Mine had been in the bar most of that holiday but heard the announcement that the competition would begin shortly. He put his pint down purposefully and made his way poolside.

Dad dived in fully clothed and beat all the two-armed dads by some distance. Me and my sister were screaming with laughter watching him whizz past the other competitors still wearing strides and a collar. It was a tumultuous holiday, my parents' marriage was on the edge, but there was something about my fully clothed father showing all the other dads a clean pair of heels that momentarily brought us together. As Mum commented wryly afterwards, 'Well if that doesn't sober him up, nothing will.'

He wasn't the only one playing to the gallery on that holiday. At eight years old, I'd entered a 'Best Cowboy Competition'. Instead of rustling cattle and throwing lassos, it basically involved young lads dressing like cowboys and going out in front of the assembled parents and acting like Clint Eastwood. Most of the other boys were a bit bigger than me so I listened carefully to what they were doing and planned to mimic their actions as best I could.

However, the outfit they'd given me was way too big and, as I shambled on-stage, a holster dragging by my ankles, waistcoat falling off my shoulders and a Stetson starting to fall in front of my eyes, I was already discombobulated and could hear the parents giggling.

The host did the usual bent-knee schtick to ask my name. The boys before me had given the best cowboy-like name they could think of, like 'Chet', 'Wyatt' or 'Billy'. When asked where they came from, most of them seemed to say 'Texas'. I hadn't heard that quite right though, so when he asked me and I couldn't think of a cowboy name, I said, 'My name's Geoff,' which I followed with, 'and I come from Essex.'

Not exactly Butch Cassidy. The parents all laughed. I didn't know what I'd done or how but I knew I liked that noise.

As Dad spent more time in the pub than at home, Mum resorted to the old-fashioned trick of taking his dinner to him down The Sultan. I never understood that gesture. It was supposed to shame a man into accepting his responsibilities, however, as Dad put it, 'All it made me think was that if I got drunk enough, pork chops would appear.'

I think he drank because the extra effort of all that good humour and smiling gamely through physical challenges took it out of him. By the time he was on the verge of getting on the national executive of his union, Dad's drinking was becoming unmanageable. Mum took the right decision in bringing the marriage to an end, a decision vindicated when he immediately addressed his drinking. Coming second to his job and drink was never going to work for her. Not least because she needed someone to fill the black hole of attention that comes from being given away as a child.

Born in the fifties within the sound of the Bow bells to a single mother, she'd been left on the doorstep of a convent in Streatham when she was five (family history is a funny thing; I took that phrase 'left on the doorstep' literally until well into my early twenties, viewing her early life somewhere between *Annie* and *The Jungle Book*). Her mother, Margaret, was a single woman with three children out of wedlock. The other two children had severe disabilities so Mum, 'Jenny', was handed over into care.

Throughout her life, Mum had a lot of names. Jennifer at birth, she became Jenny, then Jen, but when she dated a bloke from Dundee he pronounced 'Jen' as 'Jan' and so she remained until she met my stepdad, shortly after which my stepsisters independently rounded it up to 'Janet'. Once she became wheelchair bound, Mum had a whole new set of monikers including 'Jan the Pram'. At Mum's funeral, I read all these out. With so many nicknames it sounded less like saying goodbye to a parent and more like I was bringing a veteran boxer to the ring.

The nuns who helped raise my mum were particularly strict. She was naturally left-handed, so they strapped it down and tried to force her to use her right. This seems like an odd thing to do but they saw left-handedness as a possible sign of the devil. Maybe that experience is why Mum got together with the old man in the first place.

She'd had her left arm strapped down and he'd had his right one taken clean off. Maybe it wasn't love at all but unresolved arm issues.

As she put it to me, they 'both saw in the other someone they could fix'.

Relationships like that rarely work out well (especially as they'd ended up with two left-handers). She was beautiful and vivacious; he was handsome and throwing out the high octane smoke-and-mirrors charisma of someone who doesn't want people to notice his missing limb.

Without any formative experience of the role, Mum tried to be a dutiful wife to a man making his way in the world. Like all women at that time who were married to men in the unions, there was a social scene she was duty bound to appear on. However, her early life had left with her with chronic social anxiety.

I remember once seeing her hand around a tray of vol au vents at one of Dad's soirées. Vol au vents are a stark symbol of putting on airs and graces. No one really liked them. Everyone would have been happier with a sausage roll but it was the 'done thing'. Even saying, 'Vol au vent?' made you feel like an awful wanker. It was training for the necessary self-sacrifice involved in social mobility. She looked desperately uncomfortable and resentful. It was the impostor syndrome so many working-class people feel when they try and 'level up'. As an adult, I probably looked exactly the same the first time I took my seat on the 'BBC diversity panel'. Luckily, feeling like I didn't fit in was the exact reason I was there.

There's a photo I often look at of my parents wearing their finest clothes for one particular union event. Dad's wearing a dinner jacket and Mum's wearing a beautiful oriental-style gown. Despite their glamour, the look in their eyes suggests she'd prefer to be in jeans working on the garden and he'd rather be down The Sultan.

If they were my age today, they'd have probably already reflected on how their traumatic life experiences had shaped them and learned to manage those hang-ups with medication, meditation and realigning their chakras. However, back then, with a solid working-class instinct for industrial-level denial, the default coping method was drink. My grandparents were pretty big drinkers too, but usually kept their shit together. Dad, when drunk, was loud, high-spirited and obsessed with buying everyone a round. A lot like me in fact – the one time I act like a socialist is when I'm shitfaced.

In the pub, Dad was fun to be with, but not so much when you're a mother of two and short on housekeeping. Despite being married to a go-getter, she was still struggling to get by. My mother didn't really drink, her drug of choice was nicotine. She always claimed she didn't smoke 'that much' but any family photo shows her with a cigarette attached to her hand like a permanent extra digit.

The country has been on quite a journey when it comes to smoking. My childhood was engulfed in cigarette smoke. At family meals, a 'fag break' would be called between every single course. Unlike now, they'd stay seated while me and my sister would dash to the garden, coughing like two Victorian old men in the final stages of consumption. Houses routinely became so orange that silhouettes were burnt into the wall like the aftermath of a nuclear bomb blast.

The culture is different now. When people smoke they often do so standing on a doorstep (which shows a fundamental misunderstanding of the way wind tends to work). Or they vape – a curious practice by which those who wish to smoke less have found a way of smoking more or less continually. It's almost certainly less harmful for the kids. They still go to school reeking but now they smell of pleasant things, like popcorn.

My parents were drinking and smoking hard, shooting for the big league, but showing the strains of trying to get there. Dad had the south London Del Boy spirit of the time but, instead of selling moody hi-fis, he saw the greasy pole to union top brass as his way out. He didn't just like the power and the money, he was attracted to the lifestyle. Unions looked after their own and he enjoyed being booked into fancy hotels. When I started doing stand-up comedy, he was more interested in the hotels than the gigs.

'Where are you son?'

'I'm in Cardiff, playing the Glee Club.'

'No *where* are you? What hotel they put you in?'

The real clincher, more than the calibre of the hotel, was 'Do you get a breakfast?' He seemed to think an inclusive hotel breakfast was the height of privilege. If I'd told him I had a residency at Caesar's Palace, all he would have cared about was whether I had to pay for my bacon rolls.

I wonder if part of my conservatism comes from those early experiences of lavish union weekends. All I knew from my mum was that the unions 'got paid by the workers and were supposed to look after them in return'. Even as an eight-year-old it struck me that the hotel they'd put us up in was exceptionally fancy. I was sure we could do it without four-poster beds and a bar tab.

The day they 'bombed' Dad from the union position he'd worked so hard to achieve is burned into my memory (the middle-class translation would be 'managed out'). I don't understand the particular arcane process by which Dad was removed but when I saw him looking desolate in our hotel room in Bournemouth I knew it was the unions what did it. He still had his day job, but it was the union work he was passionate about. He'd once sang 'You don't get me, I'm part of the union', but in the end it was the Union who 'got' him.

So if you ever see me climbing into Len McCluskey on Sky News, there's a chance it might not be entirely objective. Part of my anger is because in 1985 we had to cut short an otherwise pleasant family holiday to the Dorset coast.

As the process of divorce stepped up, things became fraught at home. It seems mad to think now, but it was still a shameful thing in the mid-eighties for your parents to split up. Back then, divorce and cancer were both words you had to mouth in polite company, in the same way you'd one day tell someone you voted Leave.

I should warn you that there will be stories in this book about my parents that will seem outlandish or made up. Unfortunately for my mental health, they're not. They were two unique people, social mavericks. Mum especially was never one for doing things the expected way.

I was acting up at school but, like all mummy's boys, was reporting that I was in fact being victimised by one particular teacher, Ms Read. Mum had already taken against her the moment she knew Ms Read wanted to be known as a 'Ms'. It's fair to say that if Mum was alive today, she wouldn't have much time for the 'my pronouns are' brigade. It's not that she wasn't liberal in the general sense but she always felt moral crusaders tended to be privileged enough to have the time to worry about such things. I remember the first time she was served a vegan meal by one of my Dad's new middle-class leftie mates from the union. The encounter hadn't started well when the lady introduced herself to my mum as 'Beverley'. Mum was thrown by the fact she didn't offer the shortened version 'Bev', so curtseyed sarcastically. The moment Beverley left the room my dad read her the riot act.

'But what kind of women says all her syllables like that?' Mum protested. 'Why can't I call her Bev?'

Beverley busied herself in the kitchen cooking up something a lot more exotic than the meat and two veg we were used to.

She put the dish down in front of us. Mum took one derisive look at it and quoted the popular British lamb campaign of the time: 'Wot, no meat?'

We never dined with Beverley again.

Beverley and Ms Read were exactly the kind of women who would get under Mum's skin. One day, she dropped me off at school and I said goodbye to her at the gate. She made me promise to behave. My next memory is of it being well into the first period and I was once again in trouble for something I'd said. Before I'd even begun wriggling my way out of it, Mum appeared from the temporary partitions between the classrooms. It later transpired that, like a cross between a demented tiger mother and Special Forces, she'd waited until I was out of sight then snuck her way into the space, bedded in and waited to hear the evidence of this victimisation for herself.

I'm not sure whether what she heard corroborated my conspiracy theory or not but, knowing Mum, just the sound of 'that bloody feminist' Ms Read chastising me was enough to send her over the edge. Slightly wild in the eyes, she appeared in the classroom, grabbed Ms Read by the arm and said, 'You're going to see the headteacher, my girl.'

As someone who went on to teach, I now feel some sympathy for the teacher, but in that instant I was only aware of the rest of the class staring open-mouthed at me. I didn't really know what to do with their attention so made a face as if to say, 'Yeah, that's right, fuck with me and mad women start appearing out of walls.'

As the divorce proceedings progressed, Mum took the decision – against all advice – to let Dad keep the house and move me and my sister into a council estate on the border of Wimbledon and Wandsworth. Again, if anyone ever wonders why I'm a 'contrarian' I'd say a good deal of it came from having a mother who drove her own divorce lawyer to drink. 'Take him for the house' was a feminist mantra at the time. Mum, however, went for the slightly less favoured, 'Leave him with the house and move into a dodgy council estate.'

Not long after that, my dad's betrayal by the unions was compounded when he was made redundant by BT. Our family had gone from aspiring to be middle class to much more humble circumstances in the space of a few months. When your family doesn't have a proper financial safety net, any progress can fall away in a heartbeat. In some ways, Dad's peculiar circular transport trips were like the Norcotts' relationship with social mobility. We were destined to end up back at the same point eventually.

For a family like mine, when you're pushing that car up a hill, all it takes is one false step for everything to start rolling quickly back down again.

2

A LIFELONG FEAR OF DRESSING GOWNS

It's early in the morning, overcast and drizzly in Wimbledon. My mum puts the key into a door of a flat. The door looks like it used to be white. The paint is flaky and one of the frosted glass windows is smashed. Mum opens it. My sister and I hesitantly walk into our new home. It's dark, as some of the windows are still boarded up. The light we can see is hazy and punctuated by heavy particles of dust. The wallpaper is variously orange, awful or completely torn away. There's a smell somewhere between damp, tobacco and mouse shit.

'What do you think, kids?' says Mum, hope and desperation playing out in her voice and eyes.

We didn't carry particularly high expectations on the way here. Mum told us the place we are to live is a council estate not far from my dad's house in Wimbledon. It is called Pitt Crescent, which seems to carry with it the same duality of prospects as most other things in my life. 'Pitt' sounds like we're going to be poor. 'Crescent' sounds like we might be poor with a nice view.

My sister and I, using all the experience we've built up pretending to like crap Christmas presents, reassure our mother that it's . . . nice. She seems relieved but also loosely aware we're just being polite. Though, however polite my sister is, there's no getting away from the fact she appears to be walking everywhere on tiptoes.

'So are we sleeping here?' asks Joanna.

'Yes, I'll have it looking a bit nicer by tonight.'

'*Tonight*?' we both ask her to clarify.

It would be hard not to feel for my mum. This was the flat she'd been waiting on the council list for, on the other side of the brutal no-man's-land between filing for divorce and actually getting it. She and Dad tried to continue living together until the process was concluded but that worked as well as putting a bull in a hall of mirrors. Mum then tried living in a bedsit a quarter of a mile away. This created a frantic lifestyle where she'd have to get up, arrive at the house, get us ready for school and then get to work herself all within 90 minutes. It being the less enlightened eighties, Dad wasn't exactly helping out by tossing us a salad for our lunchboxes. Later, she would have to finish work, pick us up from school, make our tea and do a bit of cleaning before Dad got back from work at about half six.

But he didn't always get back from work. On one particular day, Mum was kept waiting very late for Dad to get back but his 'meeting' at The Sultan had overrun. She had to be back at her bedsit by 10pm, so at 9.45 tucked me and my sister into bed with the promise my old man would be home in no time at all. He did return shortly but was roaring drunk. There was no malice in his behaviour but he was chaotic so my sister and I, with no adults around, were forced to tend to him like grown-ups. Joanna sat him down and adopted the reproachful tones she'd heard used by other women in the family.

I decided to make him coffee because I'd seen people do that in films. What the films didn't tell you was that a cup of Maxwell House doesn't really touch the sides when you've done double digits on the Hofmeister. Stunned that TV and film had lied to us about the effects of coffee and cold flannels, we decided to get some help.

We went next door and our neighbour, Ferris, answered. He was what was known at that time as a 'yuppie'. This was an era in which young people having money was a surprise. It would become a surprise once again but for very different reasons.

'Hello?' he said, displaying the understandable caution of a grown man being doorstepped by two kids in their pyjamas.

'Our dad is really drunk,' said my sister, 'Could we get some advice?'

Ferris listened to our concerns and asked if there were any other grown-ups we could turn to (i.e. stop bothering him and piss off). He let us use his landline (or 'phone', as we called it then). We rang our grandparents, who told us to go back to our house and they'd soon be around to help. We thanked Ferris, who must've been relieved to see these weird kids exit his house. This was, after all, around the birth of Childline; he'd have been forgiven for looking down the street to see if this was a sting by Ezther Rantzen.

Nan and Grandad arrived. I had my suspicions they'd been drinking too, but with their wartime capacity for 'make do and mend', they attended to Dad then put us both to bed, with a helpful telling-off for bothering our neighbour.

Against the backdrop of this kind of drama, Mum would've probably had us happily living in a tent on Wimbledon Common let alone a dilapidated council flat. To be fair to her, she did have the house *feeling* clean by nightfall, thought it still *looked* like a smack-head's bedroom.

On our first morning in our new flat I went out to play. What I quickly noticed about these council-estate kids was they had an edge about them. They looked into you, not at you, and had no bones about asking very direct questions.

'Who are you?'

'I'm Geoffrey.'

'*Geoffrey*,' one responded, for the first time in my life making me aware that my name could sound fancy, the same way I'd one day hear people put invisible quote marks around 'Wimbledon'.

'We moved in yesterday.'

'Why do you talk posh?'

I hadn't had this accusation before. This 'poshness' was relative, a question of degree. I still talked a little rough around the edges, still wiped my mouth with the back of my hand, still dropped my aitches. The things that made me 'posh' were not smoking, not swearing and not spitting in public.

I also had a decent vocabulary, which Mum had always tried to expand. If I heard a word I didn't understand she'd challenge me on it, so by the time we moved into the estate I'd acquired weirdly extensive terminology for a nine-year-old. This meant I got the nickname 'Long Word Alert', which ironically is quite verbose (however, I quickly learned that that sort of pedantry would get you a dead leg). One of the oddest reasons I got stick for using long words was when Mum was in hospital. A lad from the estate called Darren asked where she was.

I said, 'She's in hospital, having a hysterectomy.'

He punched me on the arm, 'Stop using your fucking long words.'

I was confused. I didn't think there was another word for hysterectomy so I thought my only option was – instead of one word – to use all the words.

'The doctors are taking her womb out of her stomach.'

The lads all made various noises of disgust. 'Geoffrey, you are fucking rank!'

What I did learn during that time was diplomacy. There are only so many times you can get beaten up before you either learn to use your fists or your brain. One spectacular misunderstanding happened while I was being repeatedly bullied by a lad called 'Dukey'. He came from a very rough family who'd settled semi-permanently the other side of the industrial estate close to where we lived. For some reason, he just wanted to kick the shit out of me. I've since learned this is a completely natural occurrence in life. Sometimes faces are very slappable and sometimes the slappable face might be yours.

Sometimes I ran, other times I took the pounding. There was something about me that simply bugged the shit out of Dukey. Like I say, our family didn't have much but maybe my trainers had one less hole than his. On one occasion, Dukey, his brother and various other goons had me surrounded. There was something about the really tough boys, they seemed somehow older but without any of the wisdom. Their clothes had the kind of black marks which suggested their dads let them drive things they weren't supposed to. Dukey paused; I sensed in his eyes that he didn't have the stomach for it today. However, he was being egged on by his entourage. His brother, Steve, said, 'Use your head, Dukey.'

Like a fucking idiot, I honestly thought Steve had experienced a moment of clarity and reflected, 'You know what, lads, this is silly. Why are we beating up this kid just because he uses more syllables? We're all just young men trying to find our way in the world. Let's stop fighting and start *talking*.'

I sensed a moment when I could've legged it but thought this reconciliation could be worth hanging around for. Of course I'd misunderstood. What he really meant was that Dukey should literally use his head as a weapon. He stuck a nut on me but Dukey found out that I have a very hard head. (My son does too. Maybe I was bitten by a radioactive coconut as a child.) He snapped back, looking like he'd been tricked, scanning my forehead for illegal fighting aids like I was an old-fashioned boxer with a horseshoe concealed in a glove.

It wouldn't have taken him long to realise my balls weren't quite so well protected and he could've easily delivered one of his customary kicks to the plums. But luckily for me, a neighbour called Pat rounded the corner at that moment. Never underestimate how many kids an angry council-estate woman can disperse with a few swear words and a mention of 'your mothers'. She checked I was all right and suggested I too should 'use my head'. I still don't know if she meant be smarter at staying out of trouble or that my bonce was a neglected weapon.

Having the shit kicked out of you is a big part of growing up as a boy. It's not pleasant but the possible consequence of violence is a useful thing to keep in mind during escalating tensions. 'Will this get me punched in the face?' should be a reflex question by a certain age. Girls don't have this as much. I've noticed this in the way my wife responds to other motorists when driving around London. She gives the wanker sign back with the gay abandon of someone who's never been put in a head-lock.

The prospect of violence was something I eventually learned to manage. However, as a girl, my sister had different issues to face living at Pitt Crescent. It's fair to say we were very different people and reacted to moving to a council estate in our own ways. Despite my issues, I settled into estate life reasonably well. Joanna was that little bit older and perhaps wiser to the unusual way our parents' divorce had played out.

If you met Joanna and you might be forgiven for thinking we're not even related. It's not just the physical differences (she got the height and film-star looks), we also speak differently. I sound more common. I know 'common' isn't a politically correct word to use any more, but it's the best way of summing up the differences between us. Don't get me wrong, I'm not full-on Danny Dyer, but stick me next to Joanna and it sounds like she's chairing a panel on class on which I've been invited to speak. The posh 'Geoffrey' had his smooth edges roughed up a bit by council-estate life but Joanna sailed through the whole experience while never dropping her standards.

She already had the nickname 'Lady Diana' (one we dropped for understandable reasons after 1997). We called her that because even as a young kid she acted in a refined manner. Mum used to say someone had stolen the silver spoon out of Joanna's mouth (which was saying something because, as an abandoned child born within the sound of Bow bells, literally everything had been stolen out of hers).

One consequence of living on the estate was we were now adjacent to the main trainline coming in and out of central London. Sometimes the eleven-year-old Joanna would head to the end of our patch of 'garden' and stand there waving at the trains with regal poise. This was how she got the nickname 'Lady Di'.

I love working-class nicknames. I've got a mate who's still called 'Jobsy' because he was the first of us to get an iPhone back in 2007, so therefore found himself compared to Steve Jobs. Fourteen years later and that's still his nickname. Every time he gets a new girlfriend he has to explain it to a woman who'd otherwise imagine he has issues with his bowels.

Everyone on the estate seemed to know that Joanna was the closest thing we had to aristocracy and treated her with due deference. Mum, however, was always worried the deference wasn't going to extend to the teenage boys who had started looking at her differently. At that time, teen pregnancies were on the rise. Mum was obsessed with the idea that neither of us should become parents before our time. A fear not helped when several girls on our estate and the nearby Poplar Court had babies well before they were 16. One girl had two by that age and the circulating urban myth suggested the most recent dad was 13 but had nonetheless nobly 'manned up' by taking on a second milk round in order to contribute to his offspring's upkeep.

Mum took different approaches with Joanna and me. With me, she was reasonably liberal. She figured that boys will be boys and the best approach to sex was to take the mystery out of it. Indeed, she may have taken a little too much mystery out of it. Mum had a memorably visceral turn of phrase and once, when giving me a packet of condoms at the tender age of 14, said, 'I'd rather you did it under my roof with your wellies on than bare-back against a fence.'

I swear she was trying to associate sex so squarely with her phrasing that it would act like psychological bromide. The only way it could've embedded itself more in my psyche was if she'd ended that sentence by striking a tiny bell.

My sister was a different story. You might think of it as sexist in the modern era, but my mum saw her son as a key that would try and open lots of locks but my sister as a door that should mainly stay closed. She allowed my sister to have boyfriends but took great delight in grilling them. She'd use her no-frills language regarding sex to see how they handled the pressure.

'You thinking of going for a paddle, boy?' she'd say, watching them turn white as a sheet.

'You planning on doing a bit of brass rubbings on my little girl?' she'd ask, like a cross between Tony Soprano and Mrs Brown.

If Mum didn't succeed in making them uncomfortable it made her uncomfortable. One boyfriend in particular didn't flinch under her interrogation and it made her suspicious. One night he got a bit carried away and gave my sister a number of love bites on her neck. Mum was mortified and reacted with all the action-stations moral panic of a quintessential Victorian. She told my sister, 'You'll be going to spend some time with your aunty in Oxford.' Words which could easily have been said by one of Jane Austen's matriarchs.

My sister obliged and went to Oxford by coach (not 'coach' as in 'and horses', though in light of such antiquated parenting I can see why you might be thinking that – this particular journey was done by National Express). Joanna was spirited away from the estate under cover of darkness wearing several neck scarves. She looked like Michael Jackson leaving a central London hotel.

Joanna and I have never really discussed the effect of these weird episodes, but I'm sure a counsellor could write an interesting paper on our relationships with coach travel and fences.

In Mum's defence, she saw the council estate as shark-infested waters. The horny teenage lads on the estate were the predators and my sister's love bites would've been like throwing Chum into the water. After a couple of weeks, Joanna returned, chaste in the eyes of the estate, and the boyfriend never darkened our door again, or made eye contact with Mum on the occasions she ran into him. God knows what she said.

Despite the bullying, I enjoyed council-estate life. I liked the proximity of it. Yes, more people knew your business but equally, you knew theirs. It was like a bring-and-buy soap opera: entertaining so long as you weren't the main storyline.

Even the physical dimensions of our flat made privacy an issue. Our kitchen window opened out onto a landing walkway. It took a while to get used to people just banging on the window when you were standing there with wild bedhead and wearing just boxer shorts. I remember one of my mum's friends leaning through, chatting casually, then pausing mid-sentence to say, 'Your town halls are hanging out.'

I wasn't so familiar with rhyming slang at this point so after a painfully protracted misunderstanding, she said, 'BALLS, GEOFFREY. I can see your balls!'

Despite having little, in an immediate sense, we were still lucky to have more than most. We were the only ones on our block with a phone. My mum – ever the Pied Piper of dishing out free shit to strangers – told everyone they could use our number for emergencies. There must have been a lot of emergencies because we became unpaid receptionists for the entire block. It was a pain in the arse but also great for gossip.

The shape of the crescent itself added to the 'intimacy'. The three main blocks all faced in on each other. It made for people calling out of their windows rather than walking around to chat in person. I imagine now we'd have an estate WhatsApp group but then the only way to 'leave the conversation' was to shut the windows and go to the back of the flat. At night, noises could be heard even more clearly, as the sound bounced around the buildings in the quieter small hours.

Mum eventually moved in my stepdad to live with us. It's fair to say in the early days of their relationship they were pretty 'active'. It's also fair to say that my mum was pretty loud. I know this because I heard. The entire crescent also knew this because they also heard, particularly as we moved into summer and the windows were open. I can't describe to you the red-hot embarrassment of having neighbours knowingly remark, 'Say hi to your mum, bet she's having a lie-in after last night!' Or, 'Could you tell your old dear to keep it down, she woke up the baby.'

All of which must've seemed a little hypocritical to my sister. While she was being snuck out of Pitt Crescent like a disgraced vicar's daughter, my mum was broadcasting a sex noise pirate radio station proudly into the night sky.

I found having a stepdad around to be a positive thing. Roe was a good man and his work ethic made a massive impression on me. He started staying over shortly after we moved to Pitt Crescent and moved in permanently within a couple of years.

You might call it socially conservative but having a stable, employed man about the house had a positive effect on my attitude and discipline. It's primitive but as you become a teenage boy you're aware of your own growing strength and physical presence. It's quite useful to have someone who'll put you on your arse if you get too fresh. Roe actually never did but the possibility was a useful deterrent and we had a couple of 'Cuban missile crisis' moments.

My stepdad worked as a removal man, which was hard physical labour. His job involved a lot of driving long distances to put in short bursts of activity (something that may have had an inadvertent impact on my decision to get into stand-up comedy). Whereas my dad would've struck you as a very working-class guy, ultimately, his job – rooted though it was in the real world – was still done from a desk. However, Roe was a genuine grafter. He taught me a lot about just keeping going even when your mind and body say otherwise. In a time when we question whether such things are 'toxic', Roe didn't have that luxury, he had people depending on him. He wasn't paid for throwing a sickie. As well as providing for us, he also had our two stepsisters, Sarah and Lorraine, to look after. They often came to stay and were very much a part of our new extended family.

One value in particular that Roe taught me is why you should always offer workmen drinks. His theory was the more money people had the less likely they were to reflect on the fact that human beings generally need rehydration.

'And they talk about manners,' he would scoff.

Consequently, these days I overcompensate when we have manual workers in the house. However, while I found that it's easy enough to make the offer on arrival, there is something oddly emasculating about spending the whole day offering workmen drinks. There they are doing real men's work on *your* house while you show up every ninety minutes like a bored housewife, 'You fellas want a drink? Big strapping lads like you must be gasping.' I've learned through trial and error that a fanned-out selection of biscuits on a plate is too much. The only way to offer snacks and preserve the last shred of your own masculinity is to just give them the packet while doing a few pull-ups on the door frame.

Things were tight as Roe was supporting two households and Mum lost her job shortly after moving to the estate. She was also starting to have problems with her neck and back so the doctor suggested she claim incapacity benefit. The symptoms weren't severe at this point. She wanted to continue working but couldn't pass up the opportunity to keep a beady eye on me and my sister as we moved into a delicate age. With the various benefits and discounts, she was earning either the same or more than she would've been if she'd done basic clerical work. She could have been even better off still but chose to declare that Roe was living with us, which lost her her council-tax discount. Many at the time didn't declare they had 'live-in lovers'.

The estate, like many, was split between the working class and the non-working class. There were numerous households where no one had been in work for a couple of generations and you could see the listless effect it had on people. So, years later, when Cameron and Osborne started talking about the effects of being stuck in a life on benefits, it struck a bit of a chord.

It's easy to romanticise council-estate living. The middle-class view often imagines a supportive communal world where evil social services do their best to prosecute, despite a comradely wall of silence from within. Benefit-fraud prosecutions did happen but they had to get their information from somewhere and the vast majority of it came from so-called friends or neighbours. There was a lot of jealousy towards women who had working men living with them and they'd frequently shop each other to the council. The benefit of having an additional income without losing the council-tax discount is obvious, which would lead to the comical situation where women were trying to create the sense that a partner was in fact just a casual boyfriend. Some blokes would arrive at night and leave early. Some would shimmy out of bathroom windows at a knock on the door. I'm not saying shopping people to the social made us any worse; it was just the same as two posh people fighting a proxy war over creeping wisteria or planning permission. It was simply a different kind of keeping up with the Joneses – instead of being jealous of a double driveway, you were looking on enviously at a bloke with a job.

My sister and I started to worry that Mum was gravitating too far towards the non-working element of council-estate life. Without a job to centre her day, she'd started wearing her dressing gown later and later. We'd also noticed her vocabulary changing too. She now said 'fags' instead of 'cigarettes' and her moratorium on swearing had slipped spectacularly.

One summery morning, I left for school and mum and her mates were sitting on the stairs adjacent to our door, smoking and gasbagging. When I got back at 3.30pm she was still sitting there, still in her dressing gown. I was livid.

When you finally work out your place on the political dial, you can reflect on early life and see it was there all along (being 'livid' before hitting middle age was certainly a sign). It must be like realising you are gay and working backwards, looking back at moments in your life. In truth, reflecting on moments like my mum sitting on the stairs, I know I've always been a judgy little bastard and this may be my first memory of 'small c' conservatism.

It must've been written all over my face because one of the other mums said, 'You all right Geoffrey? We done something wrong?'

'Have you been sitting here *all day*?' I asked my mum.

The other mums raised their eyebrows. I looked around and saw the amount of tea cups on the floor around them and the brimming ashtrays.

The other mums reacted humorously to this telling off from an 11-year-old boy with a rucksack on both shoulders. One of them even held out her own hand and slapped it in mock contrition.

Mum, who always kept a sense of the divine right of parents, said, 'Yes, and I might do it again tomorrow. Now get inside, you cheeky shit.'

As I reflect on that episode, I think 'Who was I to be so judgemental?' I don't always feel good about judging people, I just think it's inevitable. Pretending you're immune from it is fundamentally dishonest. These are different times, however, and the activity of taking other people's lifestyles and decisions apart is a precarious activity.

The only remaining safe space left in which to judge others is within a loving and committed relationship. There's something about sharing a bed with someone at the end of the day which makes it impossible to hide true reactions. You must've had it with your partner. You're having dinner with some terrible people. You exchange that look which says, 'Well, this is awful, *they're* awful, but at least we can judge the shit out of them on the way home.'

Then, the moment you get clear you judge everything about them: their phoney socialism, their eco-hypocrisy, the fact they have African art all over their flat but not a single black friend. When people say, 'You shouldn't judge others' what they really mean is 'Don't do it to their face' or 'I'd rather you didn't judge me'. I'm not sure where tact ends and snide hypocrisy begins. Maybe the most honest thing you can do is share exactly what you think and, standing there judging my mother, I felt very strongly that she should've been showered and dressed by 9am, latest.

I'll be more honest still – that period of Mum taking a casual attitude to getting dressed has left me with a lifelong distrust of dressing gowns. And smoking. Both have come to stand for unproductivity in my mind. My view is you shouldn't be in a dressing gown after 9am unless you're ill or Hugh Heffner.

I knew Mum was smart, yet her current situation had allowed her to neglect her talents. Looking back, after a hectic early life and tumultuous marriage, she was probably just enjoying some absent-minded plain sailing, but I was struggling to keep effort levels up at my end and seeing her assimilate made me wonder why I was bothering.

The truancy rate on the estate was high and continuing to get dressed and go to school got harder as my sister and I moved towards our teenage years.

On one particular day, the quicksand of apathy was brought into stark focus. It was a bright, hot day and people were already sitting outside in dressing gowns, drinking tea, lazily eating toast and giving me and my sister stick. We were being called 'boffins'. That's where we'd got to: neither my sister nor I were doing particularly well academically but the very act of setting off for school had rendered us as try-hard nerds.

The school I went to, Southfields, was also a disincentive. I have no idea what its reputation is now but back then it was rough. Not only that, the school ethos itself was very liberal and laid back – a stark contrast with most of the pupils, who were noisy and often didn't have dads.

We did all the clichéd things you'd expect of a school where trendy teaching was encouraged. We did two hours of 'world studies' one day, where a couple of the teachers got together to 'team teach' and let the kids 'go where their instincts took them'. Unfortunately, the instinct of most of the kids was to stab each other with a compass. Southfields came under the jurisdiction of the Inner London Education Authority at the time, which was known for being particularly right-on.

One year, we didn't do any of the holy trinity of national sports: football, cricket, rugby. We did however do an indoor sport called 'uni-hoc' which I've never heard of since. It looked like the kind of office game played by wankers in Shoreditch. You know what they're like, they can't enjoy anything unless it's funky, vintage or miniaturised. I also remember prancing around with some ribbons for a whole term. I understand some people might find they have an aptitude for ribbon flouncing but I desperately wanted to kick a football.

I also had my first brush with diversity quotas at Southfields. My class wasn't particularly gifted in a sporting sense but we'd somehow made it to the final of the inter-class hockey tournament. My teacher, who Mum would've put down as another crazy feminist (mainly because she wore trousers) decided that we needed to have a girl in our team for the final. We complained but were told it was 'sexist' to have an all-male team. None of the girls in our class actually wanted to play but one of the mouthier ones – who'd actually raised the problem in the first place – was rewarded by being selected against her will. She then refused to run so we stuck her in goal.

The score was 1–1 coming towards the final whistle so it looked like we'd have ten minutes of extra time. Then the ball went rolling harmlessly towards our goal and I looked around to see Angela standing behind the goal chatting to one of her mates. The ball rolled in and we lost. I was furious but my leftie teacher assured me we had 'lost the right way'. She said that second place 'was a victory' which, even at 11 years old, sounded suspiciously like bollocks.

I started to become disenchanted with the school. None of the teachers could control the classes and I felt like I was in the wrong place. So I went down Mum's route and stopped going in. My mother, ever one for a crusade, decided that I wasn't just not going into school, I was 'staging a strike'.

It all got a bit out of hand. The local authorities came to visit and the head of year had to sit there while this absentee 13-year-old told him everything he was doing wrong. He had one of the governors with him, a tall posh bloke who seemed largely disinterested. The head of year was going through the motions and the governor seemed to be taking the view that I was just another truant. Mum, sensing I was losing the room, said, 'Tell him about the rugby.'

The posh bloke looked up.

'Well,' I said, 'last year I didn't play any of the main sports at all.'

'No rugby?' said the governor, now with skin very clearly in the game.

Suddenly I wasn't a snotty, recalcitrant kid bunking off, I was being 'let down by the system'. He listened attentively to all my issues with the school.

I left Southfields for another school a few months later, having learned that posh blokes can tolerate a lot of things, but not a world without rugby.

Despite the casual attitude towards work and education, I mostly look back fondly on the time we lived at Pitt Crescent. The amount of freedom we were given would make modern helicopter parents wince. A freedom I enjoyed with my best mate, Mick. I was lucky to find a friend for life while we lived there. He had a gentle soul and our friendship was one of the reasons I was able to get through the difficult early stages of living on a council estate.

Neither of us were bad boys, we had similar objectives in life: play football, watch football, play football computer games, talk about football. Mick was also a reminder of how my situation was relative. The eldest of seven, of which six were boys, his route to a good schooling was even more complicated than mine. I remember once going round his house to ask his mum if he could play out. She told me he was in his room doing homework.

I walked in to find an apocalyptic scene. Because of the rules on boys and girls sharing rooms, all six of the lads were in the one room. There were two captain's bunks and Mick was gamely trying to write an essay while all round him small boys were shouting or doing knee-drops on him from the top bunk. I have no idea how Mick emerged with any sort of formal qualifications against that back-drop. On the other hand, his family were and remain brilliant people to be around. There never was and never is a dull moment.

There was an industrial estate on the opposite side of the road from Pitt Crescent. One night we snuck in there. I say 'snuck' – the security consisted of one bloke in his late fifties who rarely seemed to turn up for work.

Mick and I found a particularly large skip. It was filled with small offcuts of bubble wrap. It seemed like an odd contrast, the harsh industrial reality of a skip against the light-hearted playfulness of bubble wrap.

Mick commented, 'It looks like a swimming pool.'

So we treated it like one and started diving in off the edge, trying to make each other laugh by doing the kind of exaggerated backstroke you associate with old ladies down the local baths. Then we switched from conventional dives to falling in like we'd been shot. For some reason, being able to do a convincing impression of being shot is a badge of honour among boys. That and talking in a crap American accent. Or simply being fast. Mum once asked why I'd made friends with a particular boy at school. 'Because he's fast,' I told her, like being able to run like shit off a shovel ranked alongside compassion or loyalty.

Being able to do sound effects is another big badge of honour among boys. I know we're not supposed to make sweeping gender assumptions now but I've yet to meet a girl who can do a good impression of a machine gun. Girls might live longer and be better at showing empathy but it all goes to shit when they try and impersonate an M16.

So there Mick and I were, randomly falling or diving into a skip. The industrial estate was close to the main road heading over Durnsford Road bridge, so it must have been an odd sight to motorists passing by, these two lads variously falling or diving into a skip, then emerging and high-fiving.

After our energy was spent, we just lay there for a while on the bubble wrap.

'This is the nuts,' said Mick.

'My mum wants to move,' I said, in the kind of blurty way boys finally get to the point.

'Why?' said Mick, arms outstretched in a comical pose like a bloke at a fancy all-inclusive resort gesturing towards panoramic views with his hands, 'You've got everything you need right here.'

Mum did want to move. Overall she'd been happier at the estate but as me and my sister became physically bigger the flat felt smaller. She started getting 'on' at the council. If you don't come from a working-class background, let me explain. 'On at the council' is more than just a complaint, it's a military campaign. If you want to move from a flat to a house, it's not just a case of asking, or going on a list, you have to pick someone at the council and make their life hell.

Mum was an expert at this. I know because, on my frequent days off school, I'd accompany her on visits. When she entered the council offices it was like an old Western; people would scatter and the receptionist would be like the barman making eyes as if to say, 'We don't want no trouble, you hear?'

While Dad was still a Labour-voting union man, Mum showed you didn't need to vote Labour to be a shop steward in real life. She also had a useful knowledge of local politics, having unsuccessfully stood to be a Liberal Party candidate a few years earlier. Like many Lib Dems, her hatred for the Tories could still be surprisingly visceral. One of my first memories of hearing her talk about the Conservatives was her saying, 'They don't give a toss about normal people.'

When Thatcher came on telly she'd use the kind of swear words normally deployed when you stand on a piece of Lego. By rights she should've been Labour – maybe she voted Liberal just to wind up my Dad.

Mum's campaign to get what she wanted – whether it be a new kitchen, new windows or indeed a new house – was always the same. She'd start with due process but then expand it out to multimedia and, in some cases, straight-up intimidation.

Behind the flats at Pitt Crescent was a row of small sheds where you'd put your rubbish. This became a hotbed of germs and eventually rat infested. Mum was rightly horrified that this open sore should be so close to people's front doors. So she started a campaign to get the council to move the bins moved somewhere safer. She wasn't getting anywhere so decided to get the local papers involved.

In south London, insulting someone's parents was already an Olympic sport, so imagine what I had to contend with when my mum's face was all over the local newspapers standing next to bins. Calling someone's mum a 'bin lady' would've usually been seen as a fictional verbal assault. My mates were holding photographic proof. Not only that, the headline next to her photo said, 'DISGUSTING'.

Mum knew getting a house would be her Everest, so deployed all manner of psych-ops for her weekly visit to the council offices. She'd often tell me to 'look depressed' (which, given Mum's nickname at my school was 'bin-dipper', didn't represent too much of a stretch). She had some genius strategies for exerting influence. One was bringing a big flask of tea and plonking it on the table once she finally got in the office to speak to someone. 'It lets them know I plan to be there for a while,' she explained.

She also went around the borough of Merton casually photographing vacant houses. Then when the council official told her they didn't have any available properties, she'd present her evidence, like a journalist handing a politician Polaroids of them wearing a gimp mask.

You might warm to my mum in these stories and I'm always happy to tell them, but the point is that she wasn't afraid to be unpopular if she felt she had a point and she got what she wanted in the end. Which she did. A three-bedroom house. Great.

'Only problem, kids, it's in Mitcham.'

3

YOU ALWAYS REMEMBER YOUR FIRST RECESSION

Getting a council house in Mitcham is another metaphor for my family's snakes and ladders relationship with social mobility. We stepped up in accommodation but down on location. If Kirsty and Phil were there, they'd have been talking about a compromise between 'floor space versus the sound of sirens'.

I'm not knocking Mitcham . . . OK, well I am. It's just a pretty rough area and I don't remember it ever being otherwise. To many people in south London, Mitcham is a place you drive through on the way to Croydon. Put it this way: in 2012 the McDonalds in Mitcham closed. When have you ever heard of a McDonalds anywhere closing down? It's like finding out a secondary school ran out of kids. It doesn't mean I dislike the place. If anything, Mitcham's lack of gentrification makes it stunningly unique.

The London Borough of Merton comprises three towns: Wimbledon, Morden and Mitcham. Wimbledon is the cherished first born, Morden is the tricky second while Mitcham is the third child who was more or less left to change its own nappies. Though it wasn't all rough. Like Wimbledon, Mitcham had its own split personality. From our new address, you could get into Mitcham town centre via two different routes. One would take you via the cricket green flanked by a country pub – actually one of the oldest cricket grounds in the world – and past the attractive red-brick fire station built in 1920.

However, if you went the other way – by the ironically named Love Lane – you'd run the gauntlet of some of the roughest families I've ever encountered. It went from *Midsomer Murders* to actual murders. You'd then make your way past the council estate where the chase scenes in the TV show *The Bill* were filmed. Which, if you live there, is a dubious honour.

'We want to film in your area.'

'Is it because of the lovely views?'

'No, it's because you have the kind of stairwells crackheads hang out in.'

But, despite some of the questionable elements of the new neighbourhood, and the fact that it was still a council house, we were effectively up-sizing in the middle of a recession.

This had been a rough time economically for the country. The recession had started in the second half of 1990, inflation remained stubbornly high and unemployment was starting a rise that would peak at over 10 per cent by 1993. Getting a house felt like a new beginning but at least we were on council rents. The people who owned houses at that time were looking at interest rates in double digits and rising.

Coincidentally, on the day we moved in, Britain sent a task force to fight the Iraqis, who were also trying to move into a new home in Kuwait. We listened to the news upon arriving at the house while Mum fired up the Calor Gas portable heater. As the blue flames licked around, I heard the news on the radio: 'British forces are currently engaged over land and sea.'

I've come to realise that I find something a bit sexy about war. I'm not proud of it, but even hearing that phrase 'engaged over land sea' with all its gravitas was a bit exciting to the 14-year-old Geoff Norcott. It was the first time in my conscious life that my country had been engaged in military conflict. I was told it was 'all about oil'. Everyone said that like it was a bad thing but it seemed sensible to me, as oil was something we all seemed use a lot of.

My bloodthirsty male teenage friends were excited by the idea of destruction. The more socially conscious were appalled by the prospect of civilian casualties. Whereas I was worrying what would happen to the country if we ran out of oil. I was not a normal 14-year-old.

Mum had a clean-up job on her hands in our new house. It wasn't as bad as when we first moved into Pitt Crescent but the state it was in still defied belief. In the dining room it appeared the previous incumbent had made several attempts to remove the wallpaper and ended up just leaving the wall torn and heavily gouged, like Andy Dufresne had abandoned his escape from Shawshank.

I have no idea what period of British history you'll be reading this in, but at some point people will try to make wallpaper a thing again. No matter who says it, or which celebrities eulogise about it in their glossy photo shoots, NEVER go back down this dark road. Wallpaper could work as a concept if people stripped the last layer every time they changed it. However, we all know that's not how human beings tend to work. 'Out of sight out of mind' is as true about wallpaper as it is about deep psychological flaws. Several generations of shit patterns later and there you are ripping out huge chunks of plaster, leaving the room looking like it got shelled during the Yugoslavian civil war.

The credit crunch of 2008 would eventually come to be the defining financial crash of my lifetime, alongside no doubt the fallout from coronavirus, but this was the first economic slump I was truly taking in. I knew that unemployment was rising, partly because my old man had been made redundant a few years back and still hadn't found work. In yet another family status drop, he was now doing a bit of minicabbing on the sly.

I also knew it because of the talk of rising interest rates. Such things didn't concern the likes of us on fixed council rents but I remember my Dad's then-girlfriend looking ashen-faced as she said, 'They've put them up to 12 per cent.'

I had no idea why 'they' were doing this when it seemed to cause so much distress and hardship. My dad explained to me it was to 'keep inflation down' but interest rates going up seemed like an inflation of its own. All I knew was that a lot of grown-ups were going very quiet when the news came on and Peter Sissons started talking numbers.

It's funny what filters through to you at that age. I remember house repossessions being characterised as 'having to post your keys back to the bank'. Just as with my mum being 'left on a doorstep', I took this in the literal sense. It seemed insane to me that keys had such economic significance, particularly as you could make a copy set for a couple of quid from that weird bloke at the station.

However, what really made the economic hardships hit home so quickly during that recession was inflation. Job losses, house-price slumps – they all take a while to filter through to the man on the street. Inflation, however, kicks the shit out of you every single month. Nothing demoralises normal people quicker than coming back from the supermarket with less in their trolley. I knew, loosely, from Dad, that the Conservatives were trying to get inflation down but 'didn't care who they hurt doing it'. It occurred to me that anything that stopped Mum looking in disbelief at the rising price of the weekly shop might be worth a go but I kept it to myself. I can remember Mum, in her cockney accent, completely dropping the aitch and accentuating the vowels to say 'AHHHH much?!' These days that kind of reaction is reserved for train travel, then it was for milk.

The recession had started before we left Pitt Crescent. My dad's maintenance payments stopped when he stopped working (officially) so our financial situation deteriorated. Things became incredibly tight, underlined by radio stations dusting down Simply Red's version of 'Money's Too Tight (to Mention)'.

There are songs which will always be wheeled out for certain occasions. 'Three Lions' will always be the soundtrack to England doing passably well at football tournaments; 'Angels' will crop up as a horribly clichéd way of saying farewell to a loved one and 'Money's Too Tight (to Mention)' will always make sense when GDP is on the slide. It must be ironic getting rich off a song about poverty, especially when you didn't write it.

One big difference between being skint then and now is how much easier it was to fiddle various government agencies to work the margins. The early nineties was pre-digital by some distance and analogue blags were easier to execute. For example, back then, pretty much everyone used to fiddle the electricity meter. The problem was that a lot of us didn't consider doing it at a plausible level. We'd just drill it, or attach magnets, then forget to let the disc turn for a while and register a creditable level of use. I recall the weary gas man once standing there and saying, 'Right, so you've used pretty much no electricity whatsoever in the last quarter?' While we had the telly on and an electric fire going.

My mum, with a shit-eating smile, said, 'We bought thicker quilts . . . and draught excluders.'

Parents do their best to shield kids from the worst of the stress but when you're young you pick up on the mood and use that to ascertain what's going on. It would probably be better in some ways for your folks to say, 'We're skint. If the bailiffs call, hide in the cupboard.' It would be beat everyone seeming worried the whole time without explaining why.

One night, Mum, my sister, my stepdad and I were driving back from visiting friends in Clapham Junction. My stepdad had gone completely quiet and Mum was far from her usual chatty self. Apropos of nothing, we parked the car a mile and a half from our house and got out. Mum had a quick chat with my stepdad and we were briskly informed that we would be walking the rest of the way home.

'You kids could do with some bloody exercise, you're over-stimulated.'

Me and my sister exchanged a perplexed look. We were both teenagers by then and hadn't heard the 'over-stimulated' line since we were at primary school.

We had, of course, simply run out of petrol and my stepdad, an incredibly proud man, didn't want to talk about it, so Mum kept the home fires burning with a story that just confused everybody. It was a quiet and bizarre walk home. That feeling stuck with me and, in a broader financial sense, I've been worrying about 'running out of petrol' ever since.

I knew the pinch had started back at Pitt Crescent when Mum came up with an insurance blag to earn a few quid. I had got a BMX during the last year of my parents' marriage. Divorce is tough for a kid but if you play your hand well you can walk away looking like you did a trolley dash through Halfords. In some ways, divorce is like a big economic shock – despite the trauma and upheaval some cynics will do well if they play their cards right. Me and my sister were like brokers during the coronavirus pandemic. The family lost a marriage but I gained a bike.

I loved that bike. It was yellow and blue, like my beloved Wimbledon FC. The morning I got it was the usual cold 16 December that ushered in my birthday. Mum and Dad took me outside and there was a bike-shaped block of wrapping paper. I hadn't got adequately dressed so my fingers were freezing as I tore the paper off. Life shouldn't be about material things but no one can deny the childhood magic of getting the present you thought was beyond your parents' reach. If John Keats was alive today 'A thing of beauty is a joy for ever,' would be how he'd describe the packaging of iPhones.

Mum urged caution as I immediately tried to ride the bike, despite not having put on shoes or even socks. I felt the cold serrated edge of the metal pedal cutting into my foot as I tried to get going. The frustration of not being able to immediately enjoy my toy got to me and I had a little cry. Birthdays are a bit confusing; plus, I was a lot like my mum and having nice things felt a lot more complicated than having nothing.

Then one day I woke up to hear my mum on the phone, speaking in a hushed tone: 'Wayne, you need to make sure it looks like the chain was properly cut. Here's where it will be . . .'

She was in the process of setting up the insurance scam to get a payout on the BMX. I'm not sure she absolutely needed to go as far as getting a petty local villain to steal it at an agreed time under the cloak of night but she got a kick out of playing the system. Mum kept me updated on the whole plan, why she was doing it and how much money we'd get. I consented. I loved the bike but I also loved food and heating. The payout came and we were £70 richer, though admittedly down one BMX.

Several weeks later, Mum was out and I was sitting in the flat alone when the doorbell went. I opened the door to two police officers, which wasn't uncommon where I lived. They looked particularly pleased with themselves, which was also far from rare for coppers. They said, 'You Geoffrey Norcott?'

'Yes.'

'Well, young man, I think we've found something you might be looking for.'

I followed them down to the meat wagon and there in the back was my yellow and blue BMX.

Looking back, I feel for those coppers; this should've been one of those very rare days when everything went to plan. They'd probably started the day with a drugs raid, then had to help evict a pensioner, but thought, 'You know what, however many bacon-related insults people throw at us today, at some point we'll be re-uniting a little boy with his bike.'

Except my reaction didn't deliver. I just stood there, mouth open. All I was thinking was, 'Mum will be furious.' I had no idea how this would affect her insurance payout or whether we'd be in trouble. I knew that if I did the wrong thing I could land her in the shit, so I tried to think of a reaction that would throw them off the scent. I decided to give each of the officers a firm handshake. Nothing weird about an 11-year-old boy acting like an insurance broker who'd just closed a deal.

Luckily, at that point my mum appeared, striding towards us with two Sainsbury's bags in each hand and, somehow, a fag on the go.

'Ooh, officers, you found his bike. Look at my boy. He's in shock.'

'He shook our hands,' said the younger copper, still perplexed.

'He's like that,' said Mum. 'Very formal. He gets it from me.'

Then, with one of her most inspired bits of flattery

she said, 'Let me make you both a bacon sandwich. Big strong fellas like you, I bet you never get time to eat.'

I looked at the two policemen. On visual evidence alone, I wouldn't have said they were struggling to accommodate mealtimes but they looked flattered and who doesn't want a free bacon sandwich, even if she had folded in an insult.

The economic conditions of the early nineties weren't just apparent in our own house. It was the first time I'd seen large scale high-street closures. Places boarded up, closing-down sales – it felt like capitalism had simply packed up and moved on. There's something particularly bleak about a high street with lots of empty units, like a seaside town living in permanent November.

It wasn't all bad news, though, as the need for lower-cost alternatives eventually brought in supermarkets like Aldi. I distinctly remember a war over who could stock the cheapest cans of baked beans. It got as low as 3p. My mum had a whole cupboard full of them, which made it look like we were preparing for an apocalypse where the only power source would be methane.

She became a real wheeler-dealer of budget supermarkets and would go to specific shops for the best deals. In the town centre, you could easily walk between Tesco, Iceland and Gateway. Mum knew exactly which things to get from where. There was an almost military style precision about her weekly shop. She also had mates who would give her a tip on who was doing the cheapest bread, milk and eggs. She was a one-woman app.

Mum seemed to come alive in this economic drama. She talked with no small measure of glee about having to 'rob Peter to pay Paul'. However, knowing we were poor made me tense. It felt like a parlous way to live. What if this Peter bloke eventually got the hump and sent the lads round? And why is Paul such a priority? Does he have a gun?

Being poor didn't taste as nice either. Of all my friends at the time, we always seemed to have the cheapest 'cola'. This was a small but useful way to tell how well a household was doing. The families that had actual Coca-Cola seemed like landed gentry. And if you had *cans* of the stuff, well, I'd probably bow to your fridge.

There were several leagues of cola to indicate household disposable income. First Panda Cola, then supermarket own brand. Things hit a new low for us when we started buying a brand called Vogue Cola. The only sense in which this liquid was cola was that it was brown – but not the glorious rich brown of the real thing, a shitty, impenetrable brown, like the sea at Bognor. When mates came around, I tried to style it out and would attempt to discreetly pour drinks without them seeing the bottle. However, teenage boys from south London aren't massively alive to tact and sensitivity.

'What the fuck is this?' said my mate Leon.

'Is your Soda Stream broke?' chipped in Simeon.

Leon, being the more ebullient of the two, went straight to my fridge and held up the bottle.

'*Vogue*?' he declared in accusatory disbelief, like Poirot finding the murder weapon.

Simeon started dancing like Madonna and they both fell about laughing.

Being teenage boys, when Mum came in the room and asked them if everything was OK they resorted with beatific smiles, complimented my mum on the drink and said it was 'surprisingly tasty'.

This financially difficult period also gave rise to my deeply held conviction that women shouldn't smoke roll-ups. Before the feminists climb in, I should add that I don't have an issue with women drinking pints, so I don't think this is a case of me being an old fart. I didn't really investigate this belief for a long time, I just found that whenever I saw a woman rolling up I grimaced.

For a while it was an opinion I was able to share, then, as feminism evolved, I found myself increasingly on the back foot as I wasn't sure why I thought it and was unable to defend the stance. I'd spout platitudes like, 'It doesn't look right.' But once upon a time people said that about women in the workplace, or in trousers, so it wasn't helping. Like so many things masquerading as opinion, I'm pretty sure my aversion comes from life experience and in particular from this time when we had little money.

My mum smoked filter-tip cigarettes – much cheaper then than now but still more expensive than rolling tobacco. My stepdad smoked roll-ups. When things got really tight she'd hop onto the Golden Virginia for a while. I started to see it as a visual signpost that the money situation wasn't good. I don't like smoking as a habit but for me a woman smoking roll-ups is also an economic canary in the coal-mine . . . plus it really doesn't look right.

At that age, I didn't know anyone who had proper money. The real standout symbol of wealth wasn't just coke or cigarettes but where you went on holiday. We were definitely plumbing around the lower leagues, in the shape of a non-branded caravan park called New Beach on the Kent coast. It had a pool and clubhouse but it wasn't Butlins, let alone a Pontins.

It was called 'New Beach' because the beach was in fact new. Several miles of concrete, one of the biggest affronts to nature I've seen. On a clear day, you could see Dungeness nuclear power station in the distance. I don't know if it was psychosomatic, given the concerns about nuclear energy at the time, but the sea always felt unnaturally warm. However, you'd swim in that sea because the pool was one of those poorly attended bacterial hot-tubs you sometimes get on budget holiday sites. They appeared to have stopped filtering the water, so the plan was to keep adding chlorine, so much so it felt like swimming in Domestos. There was so much chlorine it would've made more sense for the exit signs to be in Braille.

However, like all working-class people, I've just told you a bunch of reasons why something was shit and I'm now going to tell you how great it was. And it was. Travel is relative.

Nowadays, particularly since the rise of the budget airlines, for many of us going somewhere just over an hour away and having a 'holiday' feels like an odd concept, but back then the Kent coast felt exotic, like a week in Cancun. I was aware some kids went 'abroad' every year. And during this era 'abroad' almost certainly meant 'Spain'. When I met my wife and told Mum that Emma used to go to Spain as a kid she gave me a wink as if to say, 'You're marrying up there, boy.' My one trip to Canada was the exception that very much proved the rule. It took divorce to fund that one and we knew that was a trick no mother could pull too often.

The only level above 'abroad' was 'America'. Where I came from, a kid going to Disneyland was something you only did if you were rich or dying. Both unfortunately and fortunately, we were neither.

By the time we'd settled into our new life in Mitcham, the money we used for the Canada trip had gone. I could deal with the Vogue Cola and the caravan holidays but one thing I hated was getting state handouts. When Dad's maintenance money stopped we slipped into the threshold for free school dinners. I don't know where in me this distaste for handouts came from but it was immediate and strong.

One positive of the move to Mitcham was the LEA looked at my school situation and got me into Rutlish, an all-boys school in Wimbledon. Southfields had been a bad experience and I still didn't fully understand why Mum had pulled me out of the Merton system to send me there. The only reason she ever gave me was, 'Your sister goes to Southfields. If there's a nuclear war I want to be able to get to you both at the same time.'

So I was burdened by the possibility of nuclear apocalypse but at least mum loved us equally.

At Rutlish, the free school dinner pupils were let into the canteen earlier than the paying kids and I felt their eyes on me, like they were talking about me. In fact I knew they were talking about me, because they *were* talking about me, loudly. There were a lot of good things about being at an all-boys school but lads can be brutal.

I'll never forget one lad humming the tune from the Hovis ad as we filed in, drawing attention to our humble poverty.

We also got school clothing grants. Unfortunately, they were only redeemable at certain clothing stores. Sherry's in Tooting was Mum's favourite. An old Bengali guy ran the store and Mum enjoyed haggling with him. I once got a pair of school trousers for a quid. This was long before cheap-as-chips clothing was widely available on the high street. The moment I put them on they felt very much like £1 school trousers. In fact, it started to feel like a rare occasion when Mum might have been ripped off. They were also tight, so the first day in school wearing them I was roundly cussed by the other lads.

'You can see his pulse,' one lad chipped in (a put-down for tight trousers I still use to this day).

I ripped those trousers in no time at all. Not surprising really. A modest teenage erection would've probably been enough to tear them but Mum insisted I'd have to make do.

I can't explain the feeling of going to an all-boys school with ripped trousers. It's not so much the insults once they start, it's the going to bed the previous night knowing what faces you the next day. There were a range of cusses sent my way. My favourite was a lad who used the fact the rips looked like claw marks and said, 'My man's been fighting LIONS.' He then followed up with some bang on the money sound effects of someone being mauled.

My attire continued to be a source of mirth. Even when we had a few quid, Mum just wasn't interested in spending it on clothing. In 1990, there was a trend for trainer boots with bigger tongues. I went out shopping with Mum and petitioned for a decent pair of British Knights. I still remember them – black and white, sleek, I'd have had in the region of six months' credibility – but no, Mum claimed the £15 Hi-Tecs she'd spotted were 'just as good'.

Not only were they not 'just as good', when we got home we realised the tongues weren't just big, they were enormous. England were playing the West Indies that summer, so my classmates claimed my trainers had built-in cricket pads. As I walked down the school's main corridor, boys jumped out screaming 'Howzat?' at my feet.

One of the worst aspects of being a boy isn't just the insults but having to act like you're enjoying them. The only thing worse than being the butt of humour is not being able to 'take it'. As we live in a more progressive, enlightened age, I wonder about how healthy it was. However, having ended up a stand-up comic, I look back on it like altitude training.

Ultimately, the crap trainers didn't bother me so much as getting stuff off the state. I felt embarrassed by it and couldn't explain why. Who was this 'state'? And what happened if they suddenly decided I'd had enough free stuff?

During that recession, I watched the news more than was healthy for a boy my age. It was worrying but exciting; the jeopardy was addictive. Just as the threat of nuclear apocalypse I'd heard about all through my childhood receded, this new abstract threat, 'poverty', was swinging into view. The economic peril seemed to reach its climax with the collapse of the pound, resulting in Britain leaving the European Exchange Rate Mechanism in September 1992.

I was doing work experience at the *Wimbledon News* at the time. For the first, and sadly not last time in my life, I saw a group of grown-ups crowding round a telly, which I'd learn is a sure sign that shit is about to hit the fan. The news was belching out dramatic phrases like 'crashed out'. A couple of the more alpha males made knowledgeable-sounding comments. The young reporter I was shadowing, 'Jules', ventured, 'Lamont's fucked it,' and looked around eagerly to see if his assessment had landed. It hadn't, but the prevailing mood was one of intense foreboding. I had no idea what the ERM was but could tell it was a big deal. They gave the day a name: 'Black Wednesday'. It was intriguing that money and politics could be given sexy names. 'Black Wednesday' sounded like a cross between a death-metal band and a horror film.

The newspaper's editor at the time, a Scottish bloke called Dave Buchan, simply said, 'Oh well,' and went back into his office. With all the grown-ups prophesying the end of the world, his jaunty irreverence impressed me. It's an attitude I've tried to emulate. For my whole life, the papers have been predicting utopias or dystopias. For most people, it's rarely either. So far, I've survived the threat of nuclear war, civil war, SARS, terrorism, austerity, coronavirus, four recessions, flooding, climate change. This might seem flippant and it's not to say some people haven't fallen foul of those things but they're so big and beyond the control of individual humans that you might as well just crack on, like Dave. To claim to give to a shit and do nothing is worse. My strategy is a healthy mix of optimism and apathy. I'd call it 'aptamism' but that sounds like a kind of spasm.

The economic problems of the early nineties illustrated that there are two sides to every economic coin. The interest rates the government had been raising in a desperate bid to keep the value of the pound high so as to stay in the ERM were now able to be relaxed. Eventually, the inflation that had peaked around 8 per cent also started to come down. So my first experience of Europe was that when you left a bit of it, it seemed like the end of the world but actually turned out all right (more of which later).

As this recession thing wore on, I became curious as to whether this level of economic activity was now a new reality we'd have to live with for ever. I knew that the economy had contracted before but everyone was convinced that this one was worse. Even though every recession in history had eventually returned to growth, this one was somehow 'different'. But then I started to hear another new sentiment: 'the green shoots of recovery'. As an 'aptamist' who always thinks things will get better but doesn't know how, I was drawn to the idea that someone somewhere would invent something or take a risk and we'd all start feeling better about life.

The 'green shoot' in Mitcham arrived in the form of the opening of a new Blockbuster Video store, bang smack in the middle of town. It seemed to just appear one day, like a spanking new blue-and-yellow spaceship, touched down in a retail unit, which had been empty since we'd moved to the area. Up until then, video rentals were common, but the business model was clearly unfit for purpose. For reasons I'll never fully understand, video rentals were handled by your local convenience store. You could get fags, Super Kestrel and a copy of *Bill & Ted's Bogus Journey*. They only ever had one copy of all the good films, so when *Rocky 4* came out I somehow saved up £35 and purchased it outright. I'd love to tell you this was an early capitalist venture whereby I then turned a profit by renting it out to friends and schoolmates. I didn't. I just watched it every day for about a year. However, my belief in the triumph of capitalism over communism may have been partly inspired by Rocky's improbable victory in the final round against the seven foot steroid-injected Russian Ivan Drago. As Rocky wisely says in his closing speech, 'If I can change, maybe everybody can change.'

Which at the time sounded like a fundamental shift in perspective but looking back meant a Starbucks in St Peter's Square.

Walking into that Blockbuster store was like stepping into another world. It smelled of new carpets and popcorn. They were actually making the popcorn onsite, just like they did in the cinema. They had multiple copies of the new releases. They had computer games too. And giant bags of Maltesers. On our first family visit we came home with enough viewing material to see you through a pandemic. This is one of the points about recession, it's not that everyone suddenly has no money. Like other people just about getting by, we still had *some* money but had become risk averse about spending it. We needed something new and exciting to get us to fork out. It's why I believe so strongly in morale. The liberal Left tend to mock phrases like 'believe in Britain' but to me it's just another version of 'consumer confidence'.

My dad explained consumer confidence to me like this: 'If people think the country's gonna be all right in the long run, they'll probably go ahead and buy that Ford Sierra. If they don't, they'll keep servicing the old banger.'

His analogy made me think of the old way of buying videos and the advent of Blockbuster video. I asked him how something like a new video rental chain comes about.

He said, 'Businessmen, son. They looked at a sector and saw a clear gap in the market.' For a supposed socialist, he seemed to get a glint in his eye whenever he spoke about money.

Up until this point, my only perception of 'business' was this dull thing grown men wearing grey suits were involved in. In my mind, they were all like Mr Banks in *Mary Poppins*, slowly dying inside as they waited on suburban railway platforms to spend their day filing away paperwork and their dreams. I never knew business could be this dynamic thing that could revitalise the high street and, more importantly, provide the local community with a sufficient number of copies of *Turner & Hooch*.

Blockbuster Video may seem an odd thing to focus on but in the grey midst of recession when normal people were finding it far harder to bounce back than GDP figures suggest, that video store lifted the whole town and everything around it. Meanwhile, at 15, I took on board how important the economy was. And I was to remain for ever wary of unemployment, high inflation and women smoking roll-ups.

4

THE TORIES AND A WORKING-CLASS BOY FROM BRIXTON

I'm on stage in front of a crowd of people and overwhelmed by nerves. It turns out the body's fight or flight instinct hasn't really moved on much from being chased by wild animals. I don't need to fight or fly, I just need to calm the fuck down and say something that makes sense.

But my mind feels wild. I want to touch my face for some reason, maybe just because it's so hot I want to check it's not actually on fire. My voice is strangled. My throat feels like it's swelling up. Maybe I'm allergic to public speaking and this is the anaphylactic shock. I can feel I'm losing the room. It's that horrible, almost ambient sense of failure familiar to anyone who has bombed on stage.

There's a reason why people fear public speaking. As Jerry Seinfeld once said of funerals, 'You'd be better off in the casket than reading the eulogy.' However, this isn't a funeral, or stand-up, and I'm not even an adult yet. I'm

15 years old and speaking in the Rutlish school mini-election running alongside the national ballot of 1992.

Am I standing as a Tory? Even given my pathological fear of poverty, surely that would be too young. William Hague didn't give his first speech until he was 16. Probably Labour, right? They say the apple doesn't fall far from the tree . . .

After my parents' divorce, the greater sense of kinship I had with my mother meant that politically I identified with her. So – if you're ready for the one true exposé in this book – I'm ashamed to say I ran on the Lib Dem ticket. However, things happened during my campaigning which may have been a sign of things to come.

To understand how someone like me could end up voting Conservative, you have to take into account one huge, looming figure. John Major. (I know, even his name feels like a disappointment after that kind of build-up, like promising someone a 'memorable jumble sale'.) As I first became aware, properly aware, of politics, that curious, mild-mannered, grey man was prime minister of Great Britain. However, the connection between me and John was even deeper than that.

John Major had also attended Rutlish as a boy, which, right from the get-go, challenged the prevailing narrative that the Tories 'don't give a toss about normal people'. This was an idea that had been reinforced at every opportunity by my mum and dad. They didn't agree on much but neither of them had any time for the

Tories. However, now the party had made someone with a similar background to me their leader. And they even had a successful ad campaign addressing that very issue: 'What did the Tories do with a working-class boy from Brixton? They made him prime minister.'

Though this was a slightly edited version of what actually happened. After the party dumped Thatcher in late 1990, they did their usual thing of avoiding giving the leadership to whoever wanted it the most. They didn't give it to Major because he was working class, they gave it to him because too many other Tories had beef with Michael Heseltine, whose view of Europe worried them and whose luscious hair and charisma made them jealous. Nevertheless, for the PM to have been a working-class guy from my actual school . . . it was an odd thrill to have such a solid connection between my life and the highest office of state. Though that's not to say I was exactly a Major fan. Like most people in Britain at that time, my view was that I didn't mind him. He inspired an almost ideological level of ambivalence.

The mini-election was designed to be a perfect microcosm of the national ballot. There would be debates, hustings and plenty of pressing flesh with the public. Rutlish being a boy's school, there were also lots of lads who thought we were wankers for even wanting to be involved. Clearly not all the boys felt particularly inspired by the fact that one of the candidates in the real election had been to our school. So the pressing of flesh was often concluded with someone removing their hand or 'spamming' you at the very last minute.

As my mate Terry said to me, 'Why you bothering with this when you could be smoking herbs with me and Darren?'

He had a point. Any great project is easily challenged by the idea that you could simply save yourself the hassle and do nothing. It sounds nihilistic but it's a legitimate philosophical position. My forgiving view towards politicians is partly driven by the knowledge none of them *had* to do it. Instead of getting grilled by Piers Morgan, every single one of them could be sitting watching *Bargain Hunt* stoned off their tits.

My campaign slogan was simple 'Norcott + Ashdown = Reform'. I was operating under the delusion that if I had a good showing in the Rutlish mini-election I might be offered a role alongside Paddy Ashdown in government. My basic poster was easily exceeded by the two lads running as Tories. Imran and Graham designed a poster showing a plane flying away from the camera with the slogan: 'How far would you go to avoid a Lib–Lab coalition?' They had an understanding of politics that was way above my level. I just thought you stood up and said things that made people feel good.

Just like the actual Tories, their message deployed a Saatchi-esque mistrust of Labour under Kinnock. Kinnock was an early life lesson that the brand of leadership matters as much as content. Whether you think they are superficial or not, there are certain things that make it harder to become prime minister of Britain. Among them are being bald, ginger or Welsh. Kinnock was all three. I'm not saying those aversions are morally justifiable but part of the Conservative mindset is understanding the public as it is, not as you wish it to be.

Kinnock had moved the party some way from its stroppy militant phase of the early eighties, but the strikes of the seventies and early eighties were still strong in the public's minds, particularly in the south-east. Rightly or wrongly, they were associated with Labour. However, Kinnock also seemed like a bit of a pillock. An impression not helped by the famous footage of him falling over in the sea with his wife Glenys. It wasn't so much the fall but his churlish 'up yours' gesture to watching reporters as he clambered back up that made him look like a liability. There are unwritten rules in Britain. If you drop a pint, everyone cheers and you bow. If you stack it in public you dust yourself down and roll your eyes as if to indicate 'what am I like?' The one thing you don't do is try to salvage your male pride by telling any observers to 'do one' while you go for an inexplicable little jog.

Another catalyst for public misgivings was the famous incident of Kinnock trumpeting 'We're all right!' at a needlessly glitzy and self-congratulatory rally in Sheffield ten days before polling day. Again, it wasn't so much the setting or the declaration but the fact he seemed to be saying it in a preposterous American accent. It was like he'd seen some of the glamorous Democratic conventions and thought he could get away with sounding like he was hosting *The Price Is Right*.

Someone randomly switching their accent has always been a trigger for mistrust. I knew a bloke from Nottingham called Stuart. Whenever he was in the company of someone Scottish, he fired up a pastiche of a broad Glaswegian accent. I'm not talking the odd word; he would literally talk like Rab C. Nesbitt until the person had left. The moment they did, he'd continue in his East Midlands tones like nothing had happened. It was like being mates with a dialectal version of the Incredible Hulk.

Whatever the average man on the street thought of Kinnock, popular culture seemed to have little time for John Major. His nice-guy persona was seen as an effective stick to beat him with. The trendy leftie comics of the time climbed into him for his peculiar gimmick of standing on his soap-box to deliver speeches on the election trail. I didn't know much about actual politics but from the direction of fire on satirical shows like *Spitting Image* and *Have I Got News for You* it seemed impossible that this boring, grey man could win.

Major had already visited our school the previous year. We were getting ready for Speech Night when the school was descended upon by plain clothes officers who all looked like John Thaw in *The Sweeney*. As the school day progressed, loads of coppers appeared using mirrors to check underneath cars parked in the school grounds.

None of the pupils had any idea Major was coming, so the most common theories centred around drugs.

Before long, the answer to the police presence seemed obvious: 'Darren from year 11 has been caught up in an international drug smuggling ring.' Never underestimate the power of teenage boys to believe a bullshit conspiracy theory. Mostly they eventually grow out of them. Until the internet. The conspiracy theories were finally resolved more convincingly after lunch when a lad called Leo, whose old man worked as a civil servant, let it slip that the current prime minister would be visiting our school to say a few words at Speech Night.

In a way, those two theories summed up the split character of the school pretty well. Rutlish was a grammar school turned comp and class divisions were threaded throughout, such as conspiracy theories about drug rings clashing up agains actual intel from central government. The school had hangovers from a more illustrious past. I'm not sure many comps had a 'Speech Night' for a start. For the big events the senior leadership team would trot out in old capes and gowns over chinos, which made it look like a cross between Hogwarts and a Steiner school.

The school buildings were split between a standard 1950s block of classrooms and a much grander 'Manor House'. The Manor House had ridiculously high ceilings and was decked out in dark oak and burgundy carpets. The only other place I've seen that kind of decor since was at plush hotel Cameron House on Loch Lomond. The head teacher's office seemed to have the same dimensions as the oval office. It all conspired to give the senior leadership a quasi-political elite feel.

It looked old fashioned and Rutlish was similarly brutally old fashioned in its streaming process. You were placed in a class based on the letters of the school. 'R' being the most academic and 'H' being for the more 'vocationally minded'. It soon transpired that there was a level below 'H' so the school, without a thought for the pupil's self-esteem, came up with another new class, 'W', after the founder's name, William Rutlish. It doesn't matter how you dress up streaming, you can never get away from its fundamental principle. Kids aren't stupid. Well, some of them are but that's the point, they're street savvy enough to be conscious of it. When they look around their classmates and see someone getting spammed with a ruler and another trying to light farts off a Bunsen burner, they've got a fair clue which end of the academic spectrum they fit in.

Rutlish's grammar-school past also meant it had facilities other schools didn't, like an old boy's club for one, 'The Old Rutlishians' just a half mile away. It was a unique experience to drink a pint of cider with a teacher on the justification we'd just played cricket together. If you think I'm making it up, ask anyone who went there during this time. Students and teachers drinking together can only lead to a blurring of lines. I'm not knocking it. For me, mixing on an adult level at such an early age gave me confidence to deal with older people of a higher status. On reflection, ending a blazing row with my teacher by saying, 'Fuck off, Tim,' probably wasn't my finest moment. However, if Tim wanted to get me in trouble, his opening gambit to the headteacher would have to start, 'While drinking on a Sunday with one of my year 11s . . .'

The staff at Rutlish, like at most teaching faculties, were overwhelmingly left wing. Coming off the back of the Thatcher years, they were quite open in their contempt for the Tories. And yet, on the night Major came, it's fair to say he surprised everybody by charming their leftie pants right off of them. 'What an honest man,' they eulogised. It was also noticeable that he had a particular effect on the ladies. Before his affair with his Edwina Currie became public knowledge, the last thing you'd have had Major down as would've been a 'playa', but the female staff were disturbed by how charismatic they found him. Power is always an aphrodisiac but it turned out to be more than his status they liked. We all believed *Spitting Image* when they suggested Major to be this small, timid, grey man. It turned out he was nothing of the sort. As my mate Michael put it, having met him, 'The bloke's a fucking unit. He's got shoulders like a cupboard.'

John was, to use modern parlance, pretty 'hench'.

However, Major's address to the school on Speech Night must've disappointed the headteacher because it seemed to centre around the fact he didn't enjoy his time at Rutlish and got crap O-levels. Way to piss on the parade,

John. A message that mediocrity can end up holding high office is not exactly one you want to punt to teenage lads on the crucial C/D borderline who've just discovered cannabis. Despite his lukewarm memories of the school, Major's appeal with women was borne out nationally by his performance at the 1992 general election. It was, after all, the era of the 'new man' and this softly spoken guy who looked like his handshake wouldn't crack a quail's egg clearly struck a chord.

Major's involvement with the school drew outside interest to our 1992 mini-election. The sitting prime minister's party losing at his old school in the run-up to the national ballot would have made a neat final story for local news. My mum, ever one to spy a PR opportunity, reached out to LWT news to inform them. 'MAJOR'S OLD SCHOOL GOES LIB DEM' would've been an irrelevant but titillating story for his opponents. An early forerunner for the trivial political moments Twitter thinks will shape an election. Looking back, I can see that I was a pawn in Mum's political game. She had no love for the Tories and, like a prototype Alastair Campbell, had thrust her man into the fray while leaning on the press.

As our mini-election drew to its conclusion we had a live debate during assembly, which is where you found me at the beginning of this chapter, my throat drier than a peanut shell.

The deputy head, Mr Palding, seemed to savour his

role as a diet Dimbleby and helped steer the debate. I started out by saying all the great things I thought the Liberal Democrats could do by putting £2 on income tax. 'Just £2 out of every 100,' I said casually. I started OK and spoke with passion and sincerity but was aware that I hadn't really grabbed the room.

The Labour candidate had his go and, in time-honoured Labour fashion, lost the room the moment he went too heavy on the social-justice angle. Then my opposite number Imran stood up and ripped into me: 'Do you realise when you talk about raising tax that you are taking other people's money?'

Truthfully, I hadn't actually thought of that.

'You talk about greed but why isn't it greedy to want more of money *you* haven't earned?'

I tried to respond but Mr Palding waved an unsubtle hand across my face. I sensed he liked the cut of Imran's jib and almost certainly earned in the higher tax bracket being defended. This wasn't right, I thought, all teachers vote Labour.

Imran continued to tear into me. The audience of boys were loving it. Being male involves a love of seeing fights of any kind and I was having my arse handed to me.

Eventually, Mr Palding let me have my reply. I wasn't sure I wanted to any more. I stood up to talk but was still processing a lot of what Imran had said. The walls started closing in a bit and I thought I was going to pass out. After what seemed like an eternity of umming and ahhing, one of the lads in the audience helpfully shouted out, 'Sit down, you muppet!'

So I did.

I learned some fundamental lessons about politics that day. I was also having to compute the reality that I didn't fully disagree with everything Imran had said. I tried to talk to Mr Palding about his politics afterwards but he made his excuses and left.

I managed to pull it round a bit in the closing stages of the campaign and come in a comfortable second to the Tories. The Labour candidate had become jaded and disaffected after the live debate. Anger at his own public humiliation in the debate had led him to become even more militant. Which recent history tells us is no barrier to becoming Labour leader.

As far as the media went, 'Prime minister's old school stays Conservative' isn't much of a story, so LWT didn't show up, though maybe they might have used it as an outlier for the way the national ballot would go, where the Conservatives won a small majority. As is usual in British national elections, it was a fight for the centre ground and the Tories edged it.

I was left with many questions about my own political identity, the ethics of taxation, my mum's campaign management and why the only Conservative teacher at the school didn't seem willing to talk about it.

5

BLUR, TRACEY EMIN, CUBA AND ME

It's 1995. I'm anxious again but this time it's not elections and public speaking, it's caffeine and being outside of my social comfort zone.

I'm sitting with a group of well-spoken, mainly female, students in a canteen in the bastion of left-wing agitation, Goldsmiths College in New Cross. I've just had my first 'seminar', which seemed very grown-up. Afterwards, one of the girls, who we'll call 'Phoebe', suggested 'going for a coffee'.

I had never 'gone' for coffee as a specific social activity. I hadn't heard it used as a verb before. When we got to the café – a bright, pastel-shaded oddity with irregular seating – they'd all seemed to know what kind of coffee to order. At home, on the rare occasions I did have coffee, it was the largely pointless Mellow Birds shit my stepdad favoured. If I was at my Dad's I might step it up to a

Douwe Egberts, so I ask for a 'filter coffee' to impress everyone. The barista looks confused. One of the more empathetic girls, sensing my social anxiety, chips in with, 'I think Geoff would like an Americano.'

I'm both grateful and furious with her – a common feeling when you get help you wish you didn't need.

I take my seat and start drinking. This 'Americano' is a lot stronger than the stuff I get at Dad's. My heart is racing and my senses are unbearably sharp. How is this even legal? The caffeine rush and the sense of being a social impostor are rising seemingly without limit.

For some reason, they've chosen to sit on bean bags. I hate bean bags. How confident do you need to be in yourself to chill out in public like you're flaking out in your own front room? They're the same people who come round your house and sit cross legged on the floor. You're flexible, we get it, now for fuck's sake sit up properly.

So I'm perched on this bean bag like a human erection, with bug eyes and the stench of impostor syndrome emanating from my armpits (once again, fight or flight is woefully counterproductive when faced with social peril). I don't know how to sit – I've now got my arms flat against my sides like I'm pushing my chest together, trying to create man cleavage. All the girls are attractive and have nice skin. Quite a few have bandanas in their hair. They're more confident than the girls I know round my way but notably lacking in sass. There is one other bloke present, a painfully middle-class guy called Phil, but he seems even more awkward than me. Or like he thinks seeming awkward carries with it some kind of social merit.

We're set out in a semi-circle and Phoebe is conducting the chat. 'So, what A-levels did everybody get?'

This immediately strikes me as a bit forward. Mum had always insisted, 'Never ask a man what he earns,' and enquiring over exam grades seems equally over-familiar. Phoebe is very attractive and supremely confident, the breezy kind of individual who has reached this point in life having never been told to wind her neck in.

As we go around the group, it transpires the A-level results average at around two Bs and a C. That might not sound like much to the A-star-star generation but exam grades are like house prices, they generally go up over time and what seems paltry now didn't back then.

I'm on the end of the line so when it comes to me I tell my truth and my heart beats harder still: 'I got three As'

Most of them laugh, then pause as they realise the implications of revealing their unconscious bias in this way. Phoebe tries to break the tension by saying '*Really*?' in as cute a manner as is possible when you're casting aspersions over someone's intellect because they seem like a plumber.

'Yes, really.'

I should be pissed off with them for putting this on me but I'm mainly angry at myself for squirming so visibly and I'm also thinking maybe they're right and three As was a bit excessive for someone like me.

Then bashful Phil suddenly pipes up, 'Which subjects?'

Which subjects.

I've had this sort of thing since. In short, and please tell me if this is just a class-sized chip on my shoulder, but I think Phil was presuming his intellectual superiority over me. Stung by the surprise of my grades, he now wants to quantify my working-class success. He's worried that I'll have excelled in the subjects his parents wanted him to – and probably spent a fair few grand on school fees in the process.

Pricked by the possibility of masculine confrontation I chippily reply, 'English Literature . . .'

Good start.

'. . . Government and Politics . . . '

Decent.

Then I falter a little as I know what's coming next.

'. . . and Theatre Studies.'

'That's really great!' trills Phoebe, as if her official endorsement finally legitimises my 30 UCAS points. Thirty UCAS points which, at the time, would've got me into Oxford or Cambridge.

When I got my surprise grades I could've pulled out of Goldsmiths and reapplied to one of the 'big two'. Luckily, one of my wiser teachers at Rutlish recognised that might be a leap too far for me. He'd suggested I stick with my original plan, thereby recognising the difference between a world-class striker getting a hat trick and a bloke scoring all three off his shin.

As the group disperses, and I finally started to come down off the caffeine high, Phoebe pulls me to one side. This is it, I think, this is the non-stop university *tits and arse* my mates back home have promised me.

'Geoff . . . can you get me any acid?'

I frown. That's a big presumption on her part. Based on how I act and sound, she has assumed I have ready access to hard drugs. I do, but that doesn't stop me being offended and resolving to charge her double.

If I ever seem to have a chip on my shoulder about the liberal middle classes it's possible a good deal of it comes from my time at Goldsmiths College in the mid- to late nineties. Recent alumni had included Damien Hirst, Blur and Tracey Emin. To put it in everyday terms, the place was a bit 'up itself'. Consequently, university became an early outrider for how antagonising I found right-on types.

The corridors were full of toytown revolutionaries trying to save Cuba, whales and rainforests. It wasn't that these weren't noble pursuits but it seemed like a privileged position to have that kind of spare time. A lot of the people I knew back in Mitcham were still busy trying to save themselves and their families.

I didn't fit in, which wasn't helped by the fact I didn't stay in halls of residence. Not because of the campus culture, which I didn't know anything about yet. It was because of an on/off teen romance which should've already run its course and a duty of care to my mum. I had a strong sense of belonging to where I came from and wasn't ready to sever it yet.

Having said that, I could still have done a bit more research into where I was going and why. I imagine families more *au fait* with the university 'experience' would have had long and detailed discussions about said 'experience' and which institution would suit their child best. I knew nothing of the political character of where I'd spend the next three years. I put as much thought into picking Goldsmiths as I would a package holiday to Malta. The real clincher for the place I'd spend three years studying was that I could drive there and back each day. It should have been to do with literature but it partly came down to the fact my dad knew a handy little cut-through from East Dulwich to Peckham.

I arrived at Goldsmiths off the back of a tumultuous period in my own life. In the spring of the year coming up to my A-level exams, my nan died one Saturday and the following day we woke up to find Mum couldn't move her legs. It was obviously a coincidence but, given their matriarchal rivalries, also a top-quality bit of thunder-stealing by Mum.

No one knew why Mum couldn't walk any more, least of all the doctors. They toyed with the idea of multiple sclerosis for a while but eventually ditched that. Her medical history was dotted with mystery and remained unresolved by the time of her death.

As my sister was overseas at the time, I had to pitch in a lot during the early days of Mum's disablement. My stepdad worked long hours so I had to help Mum bathe and learn to function with her disabilities. Teenage boys aren't brilliant at taking care of their own hygiene, so having responsibility for someone else's was a serious escalation. Mum was never going to settle for my approach to personal hygiene: shower for one minute, apply full can of Lynx Africa.

I didn't realise it at the time, but news of my mother's disablement had been shared among my teachers at Rutlish. It turned out the tilted head I got from the female teachers wasn't because they thought I was getting a bit sexy during sixth form.

Like many working-class dads, my old man was suspicious of the whole idea of me applying for university in the first place. 'Studying English Lit at uni' to him sounded suspiciously like 'pissing about reading when you could be working'.

My predicted grades slumped as I tried to balance home and school. As the exams loomed I revised when I could, cared for Mum and no one was expecting much. I had offers from two universities I was weighing up. One was from Goldsmiths at two Bs and a C. Though I was surprised to get an offer at all as I'd almost messed up the interview. At the meeting, a very smart woman in her fifties, who seemed to be 90 per cent pashmina, asked me to read a poem and respond with detailed analysis.

It's hard to read poetry generally, not least when you're sitting in a very quiet office with a woman who looks like she stepped straight out of a Gold Blend advert. The poem was 'Ozymandias' by Shelley. I was struggling to get to grips with its overall meaning. In fairness to her, she was trying to spoonfeed me the answers and eventually simply told me that the message was 'art endures'.

I laughed. She asked why I was laughing.

'That seems like something an artist would think. The First World War was more important than the poems they wrote about it.'

Maybe she was in the mood for some cocky back-chat, but I got the offer.

The other offer was an unconditional one from Kingston College, in south-west London. An unconditional offer is basically an institution saying, 'Look, we're punching above our weight here and we will definitely put out, no matter what you look like.'

As the exams approached and home life remained unsettled, it seemed more and more like I'd be hooking up with Kingston, but then my results took everyone by surprise. The day they came out was one of the oddest of my life. I walked into the Manor House at Rutlish School and the teachers were coming out of their offices to look at me in utter bewilderment. I felt like a freak of nature, like a man who'd survived a massive dose of radiation. Miss Mitchell took me in the office and read out the results one by one.

English Literature . . . A.

Government and Politics . . . A.

Theatre Studies . . . A.

I was confused by this total success so I did what the men in my family usually do when we've over-performed: I went out and got drunk in an attempt to ruin the moment and restore some order.

Just before that, I called Mum. She had decamped to Bognor for the week when the pressure was too much for her. Bognor was her Balmoral. When things got on top of Mum she'd spirit away and hide among the fruit machines and cheap cafes until the storm blew over. She was worried her health issues had affected my study. The truth was they had, but in a good way, as it turned out I did OK under that kind of pressure. If university got tough I might have to ask her to see what else she could come up with. Or whether Dad could hop back on the motorbike and see if he could do something with the other arm.

'My boy's going to university!' Mum screamed on the other end of the phone. This was a first for the entire family and, for a woman who started life with nothing, a very proud moment.

University was the first time I realised I was properly working class. At south London comps there were always people with more and people with less. Here at Goldsmiths there was no doubt that I was bottom of the class food chain.

The economic situation of most the students was unfamiliar but, as a place, New Cross was not. It seemed like the epitome of south-east London. High-rise blocks and industrial units, old-looking buildings made black by the constant belch of the A2. Culturally the area didn't have much to offer. The main local nightclub was, somewhat literally, called 'The Venue'. I didn't go there often as the students didn't seem to enjoy dancing properly. They danced ironically, which I've never understood. I love dancing, it's probably the only time I feel in the moment. But I couldn't get there with these kids around me moving like a cross between Morrissey and Jim Carrey.

During another bean-bag circle jerk, we were discussing what everyone would be doing for recess (I still wanted to call it half term because 'recess' sounded too fancy). A lot of them seemed to have 'Daddys' working abroad.

'I'm going to see Daddy in the States.'

'I'm going to see Daddy in Hong Kong.'

Then one girl said, 'I'm going to see Daddy in Saudi.'

I made the mistake of hearing 'in Saudi' as one word, like 'incognito'.

'Why are you going insaudi?' I asked, hoping that I could deduce a bit more meaning.

'Because that's where he works,' she replied patiently.

'But where does he work?' I countered.

'IN Saudi,' she repeated, now as confused as me.

'Saudi is short for Saudi Arabia,' said Phil, who always seemed to be hanging around for my moment of maximum social awkwardness.

However, Phil was the only one who'd worked out my mistake, so I tried to style it out. I got so focused on trying to seem casual I forgot that this latest circle boast would come around to me.

'Where are you going, Geoff?'

'Nowhere,' I said. 'I'll be working nights at the Post Office.'

Instead of laughing, this time they resorted to embarrassed silence, which was probably worse. I couldn't tell if they felt bad for me or if I'd embarrassed myself yet again.

'It's OK,' said one of the girls eventually. 'I think it's great to earn your own money.'

I did not understand this point at all. She was talking about earning your own money like it was some contrarian hot take, a radical new concept that may catch on given time. I bristled. This was becoming a common problem with my social interactions at Goldsmiths. If they looked down on me I got chippy. If they were supportive I felt patronised. I was sensing the class chip on my shoulder, which would only grow in size (a *proper* chip, mind, none of this triple-cooked sweet-potato bollocks).

You could feel sorry for me, but I got some great stories working those Post Office shifts. The bloke who bought a six-month share in an ice-cream van but got October to

March. The woman who had 'bingo debts'. The old fella who reckoned he owned a racehorse with Frank Zappa. As I've got older, I've realised working-class kids tend to have more interesting stories. Maybe that's the reason middle-class kids travel so much. They get to 18 and realise they need to bank some decent anecdotes, as the story about that time their parents built a conservatory ain't gonna cut it.

At another lame college party, I was standing with yet another group of blokes all trying to win at being beta males. The party wasn't like the kind I knew. It was already 9pm and no one was wasted. The volume of the music was at roughly the level you'd find in a lift. A bloke claimed he had 'hash for the whole party' yet pulled out what looked like half an Oxo cube.

A guy called Ralph was holding court, performatively detailing his sexual frustrations and unrequited passion for a girl on his course. He was short but dressed smartly in mustard chinos and a burgundy shirt. He held his wine glass unnaturally and drank from it less often than seemed normal. He spoke like he was going for the home-run aphorism every time, like someone somewhere was writing this all down and his witticisms would survive him.

I found it odd that he was discussing his sexual failure in this way. With my mates, we'd keep the idea of crashing and burning as quiet as possible but he seemed to want some cachet for the self-deprecation.

He finished another sub-Wildean riff by saying, 'I'm out of options, I guess this will go unconsummated.'

I decided to speak my first words in about 20 minutes. 'Have you ever just *asked* her?'

'What?' he said.

'Asked her . . . if she wants to have sex with you.'

He laughed, a knowing laugh way beyond his years or life experience. 'I'm not sure *that's* the answer.'

The other three lads chuckled.

However, I'd been drinking at a proper pace, so felt more confident than usual. 'Well, everything else you've done has been fuck-all use, so it's got to be worth a go.'

His mates laughed again but this time it was with me rather than at me. They were probably just as tired of hearing about his pretentious romantic failings as I was.

'Oh Geoff,' he said trying to wrestle back some status, 'Never change.'

Never change? Where did this fella get off? Once again, I wasn't looking for his approval, I was giving him sound advice. I wasn't a Lothario by any stretch of the imagination but I got the sense I might have had a few more results than Ralphy-boy. No, I hadn't experienced unrequited love, but I had copped off after a few vodka and oranges at the Blue Orchid nightclub in Croydon. Maybe I didn't 'know Brett from Suede' but I knew Brett from Tooting who could do you a fake ID. I hadn't seen much theatre but I was around at the birth of speed garage and had stood in the DJ booth next to Shanks &

Bigfoot. I didn't know exactly what 'large' was but was pretty sure I'd 'had it'.

I didn't say any of that, but I did assure Ralph that I hoped he'd 'never change'. And by that I meant 'remain a virgin'.

Having said that, as university life wore on, I lost whatever small touch I had with the ladies.

The effort of caring for my mum and getting the good grades took it out of me and I idled for a while. I tried to get to know women but the girls at Goldsmiths were a different breed. Serious and politically motivated, they didn't respond well to the banter which had served me well up until this point. The boozy, sexually forward 'Girl Power' movement had largely bypassed Britain's most stridently liberal arts college. To have any chance of getting off with a girl it seemed you had to have a social conscience, speak out against the patriarchy and social inequality and, preferably, not do nights at the Post Office.

I eventually took the 'women in literature' course as I thought there were bound to plenty of 'birds' there, which illustrates the problem with my mindset: I was a bloke who thought reading *A Vindication of the Rights of Women* is a good way to cop off.

Another problem was that I couldn't supress the dickish element of my character. It seemed that every week, no matter who the female author was, everyone on the course would eulogise about them, partly because they were women and they wanted to pray at the altar of feminist icons (echo chambers aren't as new as we'd like to think). Unfortunately, there were only so many times I could hear the word 'empowering' before I decided to put the cat among the pigeons. I decided to find fault with every single writer, even if I thought they were brilliant, just to make the seminars more interesting. I had some niche takes on some of the great female authors of British literature.

Austen? 'Boring.'

Virginia Woolf? 'Up herself.'

Sylvia Plath? 'Terrible mother.'

I could see the group turning against me but I got off on it. You might think this was by way of a rehearsal for the guy who'd later pick so-called 'contrarian' stances on *The Mash Report* but if I'm being provocative there's usually a point to it: without any dissent the course wasn't literary criticism, it was blowing yet more smoke up the arse of a legend. A TV producer once said to me, 'The last thing anyone wants to see is a room of people agreeing with each other.' This made sense, maybe because I come from a household where vibrant debate was something that happened over breakfast. Creatively, consensus is essentially a stagnant thing; once it's reached there's no forward move. Faced with the challenge of my prickly takes on the course, the rest of the group had to justify their praise rather than just continually say they were 'blown away'. I'm not sure if I'm now proud or embarrassed about my behaviour but it certainly made the seminars more interesting, even if my sex life continued to tread water.

This intellectually boisterous behaviour may have been buoyed up by the 'New Lad' movement of the time. All of a sudden, some intelligent people were defending the idea that being a bloke who liked women and football didn't automatically mean you were a shithead. It's easy to forget now but masculinity and football had an awful image problem in the late eighties and early nineties.

When I started going to watch Wimbledon FC regularly, my nan – ever the one for keeping up standards – said, 'OK, but you don't always need to *tell* people.'

As the decade wore on, however, and with the country showing a rare moment of unity and English patriotism during Euro 96, the perception of football as a hobby was starting to change. The trophy didn't 'come home' but, briefly, the idea of being able to wave the St George cross did. It felt like a moment where English patriotism had been reclaimed but it didn't last long. Waving the flag during football tournaments is tolerated in polite circles as patriotism. Wave it at any other time, however, and it is often construed as something far more sinister.

Old-fashioned masculinity was bolstered further when you then had both Oasis and Blur turning up the geezer points to 11 in the top 40 charts. The Gallagher brothers' machismo seemed authentic, like they'd flush their own heads down the toilet as a hangover cure. However, I found it odd watching someone like Damon Albarn don his flat-cap and head off down the dog track. If he did it now it would probably be called 'working-class blackface' but back then it just struck me as plain inauthentic.

Being 'Common People' was cool according to the dominant Britpop music of the time but I wish someone had told the girls at Goldsmiths. I could've taken them for a real night at the dogs. I even knew a bloke who owned a greyhound. But, as Jarvis Cocker rightly intimated, the desire to take a deep-dive into working-class culture wasn't entirely earnest. If the girl in the song called her dad 'he could stop it all'. If I called mine he'd remind me I could've been an earning a wage by now and in a position to stop it myself.

Nonetheless, it was reassuring to see that being blokey was returning from pariah status. It was ambitious of liberal thinking to imagine you can take the cold, hard realities of testosterone and puberty then somehow spin those into a generation of pastel-shaded beta males. I understand why it happened in the first place. The bawdy seventies and early eighties, replete with sexist humour and unacceptable behaviour in the workplace, had created a moral mandate for the 'new man'. But, as a phrase, 'new man' was doomed from the start. Put bluntly, it made you sound like a bit of a wanker.

One of my mates came back to my house for tea during the back end of sixth form. *Top of the Pops* was on and some scantily clad girl group were gyrating around on stage. My mum – with a curious tendency towards locker room banter – nodded as if to say, 'What do you think of that lads?'

My friend, one of my most middle-class pals at the time, looked a bit uncomfortable then said, 'This is objectification.'

My mum, aggravated by both his tone and message, narrowed her gaze and said, 'Oh, you one of these *new men* are you?'

The way she said 'new man' implied that she didn't think it was a continuation of masculinity in any true sense of the word. In a strange distillation of the post-feminist sexist conundrum she finished, 'Maybe they *want* to dress like slappers.'

Blunt though Mum's language may have been, she was onto a paradox that would continue to dog feminism. In the mid to late nineties, dressing provocatively and being sexually forward was seen by many as an active part of feminism. When Geri Halliwell appeared in that Union Jack dress it felt like her cleavage wasn't just for the male gaze, it was part of her armour to take on the world. By contrast, one criticism of the 'girl power' and subsequent 'ladette' movement was that they simply recreated some of the worst elements of masculinity. Personally speaking, I found women much more intimidating back then, partly because the women I knew *really* were. I socialised with one of group of girls who would each randomly get one boob out in the pub and carry on talking as if nothing different was happening. It was bizarre, like they were in a waiting room for a mammogram. Strange things happen when you get on the front foot with men. You'd think the blokes in the pub would've all stared and tried to get nearer but we all got a bit flustered and averted our eyes coquettishly.

Another issue with the 'new man' or the 'woke man' is that he is rarely the 'ladies man'. I'm sure there are many women who will attest to sensitivity and writing poetry being a big turn-on but in the working-class circles I grew up in, those kind of blokes never seemed to have much success. A lot of women like men who do manly things. It feels odd to even have to say that like it's a challenging viewpoint but such is the power of some liberal orthodoxies that stating the bleeding obvious can seem 'contrarian'.

The appeal of old-fashioned masculinity is apparent in my own marriage. It's clear I'm never going to get true credit from my wife for the heroic act of 'writing comedy'. It doesn't involve strength or obvious personal risk. If civilised society collapsed and we had to rebuild from scratch, no one would be looking for my witty take on having to shit in a hole. However, on the one rare occasion I do some manual work (putting together a simple piece of flat-pack) I can see the difference in how my wife relates to me. I once made a curve-around desk and she laid sandwiches on the floor reverentially, like a tribute to a returning Viking conqueror.

*

A couple of years into university life, I was starting to become a bit more trendy by osmosis. Not a new man exactly but I'd learned that knowing who Suede was was an ice-breaker. As the Britpop wave dominated popular culture, I started going to plenty of gigs. It seemed to be one area I could hold the edge over my middle-class beta-male competition. A lot of them talked about music; I thought I'd actually get out and hear some.

I saw Dodgy, Space, Audioweb and Blur. However much the era has been eulogised, young people today should maintain a healthy suspicion of nineties nostalgia. There was a buoyant indie music scene but that was mainly because we only had a few TV channels and everyone still watched *Top of the Pops*. (I'm sure bands of that calibre exist now but a middle-aged bloke like me doesn't know about them as I've retreated into a cultural cave with the songs of Elbow on a giant dongle.) The charts back then still had a fair sprinkling of shit. Now most of the top 40 at least sounds credible but in the nineties for every Oasis there was a Steps. For every 'Higher State of Consciousness' there was a 'Cotton Eye Joe'.

There was a lot about the nineties that was crap. It was possibly the worst era for alcoholic drinks: vodka and orange, Hooch, Thunderbird, MD 20/20. Even beers had lost confidence in just being good beers. They had to have a widget, or lime, or the word 'ice' in their name.

This, however, did not stop us getting very wasted.

Indeed, it's impossible to form an objective view of the music as Generation X set new records in drug and alcohol consumption. Records that will probably never be broken now. We were the Roger Federers of getting off our tits. Everything sounds better when you're on a pill and maybe if we'd have heard Ed Sheeran back then we'd have realised he was every bit as good as Reel 2 Reel feat. the Mad Stuntman.

The high watermark of that cultural era was Oasis at Knebworth, which I managed to blag a ticket for.

To call it a gig was an understatement, it was a festival. But like all huge live events it suffered under the weight of its own expectation. The era we were living through was thirsting for its own Woodstock moment. However, Woodstock became iconic on reflection. In the post-modern 1990s, Knebworth was being sold as iconic from the get-go – which was a lot of pressure on a single weekend. Everyone arriving seemed to be aware of the potential import of the day. One in twenty British adults had applied for tickets, so being there at all made you feel anointed. You could see it in the swagger of all the young men arriving on site, unconvincingly trying to mimic the cocksure gait of the Gallagher brothers.

I was never fully onside with the attitude or fashion trends of the time. The swagger seemed forced and the fisherman hats made the blokes look like dickheads. In fact, nineties menswear was a shitshow from start to finish. None of the clothes looked vaguely masculine.

Blokes' suits were deliberately over-sized and jeans had different-coloured pockets. Women wore dungarees and massive sports jumpers. A modern observer might think 'how androgynous' but that would be giving us more credit of forethought that we deserved. We weren't making any kind of statement. You just needed to be comfortable when you were in a semi-permanent state of comedown.

The weather on the day of Knebworth was good but the vibe was all off. There's something painful about your late teens and early twenties. Kids are naïve, teenagers are self-conscious but the late teens and early twenties is a strange hinterland before adulthood. At liberty to do anything but at ease with nothing. Particularly the boys. The girls seemed to be basking in the power of sexual attraction. The boys were burdened by the pursuit of it.

Even for Oasis at Knebworth I presumed I should be 'on the pull'. Being a young man involves huge acts of self-delusion. No matter what your strike rate had been in reality you have to step out into very complex situations and kid yourself that you'll be walking out of there with a lady on your arm. It's no wonder young men make the best frontline soldiers.

The day started with The Chemical Brothers, one of the big dance acts breaking into the mainstream. I liked their stuff, not least because it didn't have any clichéd words to sing along to. The Manic Street Preachers were next, their powerful brand of anthemic indie music was experiencing a big revival. Then Ocean Colour Scene, the kind of stodgy, backwards-looking Britpop that gave a clue as to how the scene would dry up. People described them as 'great music to get stoned to', which isn't much of a compliment. Doritos tasted good when you were stoned, that didn't make them good crisps. It was already confident of Noel and Liam to think they could follow all those acts, then it transpired the band on directly before them was the insane theatrical rave monsters The Prodigy. Knowing what I now know about live performance, this was madness. Like booking Michael McIntyre as your tour support. They obliterated the gig and even debuted a new track 'Breathe' which sounded like an instant classic. Their music made a lot more sense to me. A lot of the Britpop seemed to be a protracted tribute to the past but these lads sounded like they were on a day-trip from the future.

By the time Oasis came on and plodded their way through stodgy numbers like 'Colombia' they felt like a cheese board rather than the main course. I sang along like everyone else but couldn't identify with the lyrics. I didn't really know what a 'champagne supernova' was, I don't think many of us did. Even if we identified with it, we couldn't afford to experience one. I didn't get the constant obsession with 'sliding away' either, or what a 'wonderwall' comprised of. I really wanted to like the music, I was going with the crowd. It felt like 'something' was happening and I needed to be a part of it. But it didn't fully connect with me.

The iconic day ended like many iconic days, stuck in a massive traffic jam trying to leave the venue, the moment having well and truly passed.

This kind of musical bandwagon hopping had also started to happen to me politically. I was swept up with the impatience to have the heir apparent Tony Blair installed as prime minister.

It was a weird time, having a leader of the opposition so obviously destined for the top job. It was particularly odd because the country seemed to be booming, culturally and economically, but no one associated the rise of Britpop, Euro 96 or the money in their pockets with the seedy, exhausted Tory government. The Tories had got mired in sleaze and for every percentage point growth in GDP there was an MP having his toes sucked.

Politics over the last 30 years has become all about the 'brand'. During this time, the Tories' was dodgy-looking blokes in suits hanging out with a dominatrix. It turned out the country could broadly deal with the pits closing and VAT on domestic fuel but having to picture David Mellor getting it on in his full Chelsea kit was the straw that made the camel violently sick.

I'd decided, like my father, that I was a 'Labour man' and was looking forward to exercising my democratic right for the first time at the polls in May 1997. It felt good to say 'I'm Labour' but I couldn't explain why.

Despite the country's optimism and impatience for

change, my mum, ever the shrewd reader of politics had her doubts over Tony Blair: 'He's an oily bastard that one. Mark my words, when they seem too good to be true they usually are.'

I never knew if she was talking about Blair specifically or her general experience with men.

'Look at him,' my mum snorted derisively, as yet another news clip aired of the PM-in-waiting, 'swanning around like the fucking Pope.'

Despite my desire to believe in the new messiah, I got her point. He was way too earnest and we weren't used to political leaders being that young or presentable. Like a moderately attractive teacher, it was impossible to work out whether he was 'real life' good looking or 'good looking for a politician'. He was tall, had a full head of hair and threw in the odd bit of estuary English. Not only that, he'd sometimes roll up his cuffs and drink a mug of tea on a walkabout, though we never found out if the tea was proper or herbal.

Now used to life in a wheelchair, Mum had developed a pretty dark sense of humour around her disability. Her nickname among the local faces in Mitcham was 'Jan the Pram' or 'The Iron Lady'. Not because of her political leanings but because her wheelchair looked as sturdy as she did.

There had been rumours in the build-up to the 1997 election that Tony Blair might be visiting our constituency, Mitcham. His walkabouts had become akin to a rockstar meeting their adoring fans. Mum felt Blair had cultivated a messiah complex which needed to be pricked so her plan was to play up to it. Like many wheelchair-bound people, she wasn't completely without movement in her legs, so her plan was that she would use her disabled status to get to the front of whatever crowd had assembled, get his attention, grab his hand and put it on her hand, then slowly stand up, take a few uncertain steps and proclaim herself 'healed'.

She never got the chance unfortunately – like most sensible people, Blair gave Mitcham a swerve – but I'd have loved to have seen Blair's slick PR team's reaction to such an odd moment. Although an arguably bigger spanner in the works was the possibility Mum would lose her motability allowance if anyone saw her on telly standing up. A sobering consideration, which consigned her to calling him 'Tony Hair' and other various other pot-shots during the *Six o'clock News*.

By the time election night came around, it felt more like a coronation than a public vote. It wasn't *if* Labour would win but how quickly and by how much. John Major tried to reprise his little soap-box trick but what had seemed endearing in 1992 felt embarrassing during the heyday of 'Cool Britannia'. Blair looked like he might play bass guitar while Major looked like he still played with trains.

Early in the day on 1 May 1997, I savoured my first ever vote in a general election. My mum set up it up as a big day.

Ever since I could remember, she'd seethed over poor turnouts and lament that 'In other countries people die for the right to vote.' I got the impression she thought people in Britain should be shot for passing up that opportunity. Mum believed in democracy, despite running a matriarchy in her own home. We all had to vote in the general election but no one else had a say as to whether we were allowed to watch telly on Christmas Day.

The polling booth that day represented a rare thing in life: an entirely new place. As you grow up, you are aware that there are certain buildings which are, by definition, adult: pubs, bookies, sex shops. Places you wait outside while the grown-up goes in (apart from sex shops, unless you had a very bad childhood). Every time you cross the threshold of one of these sacred shrines of adulthood feels like a milestone but you still cross with trepidation. One thing that struck me was just how quiet the polling station was. I don't know what I'd been anticipating but it felt like a cross between a library and a chapel of rest.

I hadn't really cultivated a sensible expectaion of what a 'voting booth' would look like, partly because I hadn't encountered 'booths' of any kind. When I finally saw it – merely a squared-off area with a small curtain – I realised I had subconsciously been expecting something that looked like the Tardis.

But I still remember the unique feeling of being in the voting booth for the first time. It's unusual to have any space in public entirely to yourself. I like the voting booth for the same reason I like toilets. A toilet is a rare place with a lock; no one else can just barge in (how many parents utilise that facility now, when a 40-minute poo is actually them playing with their smartphone, or crying). There are very few places where we have guaranteed solitude, yet here I was in a scout hut in Mitcham and no one dared encroach on my space.

I looked at the candidates and marked an 'X' next to Labour.

I felt like I was doing something in line with my heritage but, despite my old man being a union rep, things were less clear cut for working-class people in the south-east compared to the north. Not all working-class people necessarily voted Labour. For example, I was never entirely sure how my grandparents voted. They were the generation of people who answered every phone call with suspicion so there was no way they'd ever tell me for certain. Though my grandad was part of the generation who voted in Atlee straight after the war and he did seem to use the phrase 'working man' a fair bit. And my nan's roast dinners came in the kind of modest portions you'd expect under socialism.

I strode out of the polling station confidently. It was probably the first and last time I ever felt total conviction about the political party I'd voted for. It felt morally good to have voted for the Labour Party. I enjoyed telling people. It felt like code for 'I'm a good person.'

That kind of certainty is a preserve of the young. As you get older, you realise British democracy is usually a choice between the least shit of two options. You're going to get waterboarded but you get a choice between sparkling or still. Indeed, if someone strides confidently into a polling station it suggests they haven't really thought it through.

As the night's results played out, I sensed something wasn't entirely 'right' with my reaction. As wave after wave of blue turned red, I shouldn't have just been pleased, I should've been ecstatic, rejoicing, adding to the whoops and cheers I could hear out of the windows in the otherwise still spring night. However, even at that age, my vote was primarily a pragmatic one.

I didn't feel the joy many felt at Michael Portillo being unseated in Enfield Southgate. I guess my political alarm bells should've been ringing there and then. The archetypal Tory toff getting his arse handed to him in his own backyard; I was the son of a trade-union man, of two disabled parents living in council property, and all I could feel was a bit sorry for the bloke. It can't be nice losing your job in public, let alone when the country responds with a conga. Maybe that's been my problem all along. Even then I struggled to think of Tories as baddies. They may have been pompous, prats, privileged or downright pricks but I couldn't credit that more than a tiny percentage of them were moustache-twiddling baddies intent on making people's lives worse.

Nevertheless, it still *was* exciting. Even if I wasn't getting swept up in the same manner as everyone else at Goldsmiths. The result was momentous, particularly for people around my age who hadn't known anything other than Tory rule. Blair was young, progressive and seemed like a nice bloke. How could any politician who drank tea and took off his tie ever get detached from the people? His top three priorities were education. Maybe we should've asked him his fourth. It might have been something to do with regime change.

'Things can only get better' was a nice idea but, more importantly, Labour seemed like a much more competent option for government at that time. If they'd focused on competence over the last ten years rather than the moral high ground, the Left today might not have spent so much time in opposition.

While Britain was motoring under new leadership, my time at university had been a two-year intellectual recession. Having discovered clubbing and all that went with it, my academic commitment had slumped.

The experience of Knebworth got me more interested in dance music. London at the time was in the midst of a clubbing boom, centred around establishments like Bagleys, Fabric and Turnmills. I found something about the experience a bit more honest. Rather than trying to find ways to make song lyrics relevant, it centred around a feeling. You stood on the dancefloor like a surfer waiting for a decent wave. There was the odd vocal but mostly it was a primitive reaction to sound, something far more in keeping with what I imagined to be music's early origins. OK, so I can't claim I was thinking about all of that when I was off my face at 3am, but it was something along those lines.

My poor attitude hit a nadir when I spilt tea on an essay I'd written. Instead of re-writing it, I tried to get away with trimming the edges on either side. I handed in something which my tutor concluded looked 'suspiciously like used toilet roll'. The content of the essay did nothing to dissuade him otherwise.

Also around this time, I moved out of home to rent a flat in Wimbledon with my pal Mick from Pitt Cresecent and a colleague of my sister's. Away from the watchful eyes of my mother, I'm afraid to tell you that I let my standards slip. My attendance at university slumped as well. As I'd discovered weed, the 90-minute morning commute to south-east London seemed less and less appealing. My capacity for sleep lurched all the way back to infancy.

One day my mum rang at about 3.30pm. 'Where have you been?'

'University,' I lied reflexively.

'Well, I believe you because I've been ringing all day.'

The truth was it had been her fifteenth phone call of that day which finally got me out of bed. I'd managed a staggering 17 hours in bed, like John Lennon without a cause. Or sexual partner. In the short nine months I had that flat in Wimbledon, I spent spectacular amounts of money on doing precisely fuck all.

I was lucky enough to be one of the last generation of students to get a maintenance grant. Because of my family's financial position, I got the full whack. I also took out a student loan and had a job at Blockbusters (having experienced the magic of that first store in Mitcham, I wanted to be at the heart of the VHS revolution).

Having that money did nothing to help focus my mind.

My own fecklessness during my degree course informed my later attitude to tuition fees. Especially since I'd spent my three years in various states of intoxication. I practically hibernated one month and routinely showed up for about four of the punishing eight hours' tuition I had each week. At the time, way more middle-class kids went to university. It didn't seem right that an 18-year-old already working as a welder should be paying tax for someone called Hugo to study the classics. So maybe it's no bad thing for students to have their own financial skin in the game. (And maybe my son should never read this book.)

Eventually, our landlord sensed he might've rented his place to the wrong lads when he parked opposite the flat and saw approximately 30 dodgy-looking geezers come and go in one night. Besides, I'd run out of my cash. Just like Mum, I didn't know what to do with lump sums so I sprayed my student loan around like it was cursed. So, in an attempt to get my final year of university back on track, I moved in with my old man. Even Mum agreed I should live with him for a while so it must have been serious. However, being a Norcott, 'moving' involved going a matter of 700 yards down the road.

My family have never been the world's greatest migrants. You would not have to zoom very far out on Google Maps to cover pretty much the whole area in which we existed around that time. When it comes to moving about, recent debate has focused on the concept of 'somewheres' and 'anywheres'. For some people, where you come from, the community and culture in which you spent your formative years matters. They would be the 'somewheres'. The 'anywheres' on the other hand are a growing bunch. They don't really care where they live, so long as it has close travel links to a metropolitan epicentre. And an Itsu.

You don't have to talk to people long before you can work out if they are a 'somewhere' or an 'anywhere'. If they say things like 'I hear Margate's really coming up,' they're an anywhere. They're also anywheres if, when you told them of an offer of a three-year job placement in Singapore, they'd say, 'Wow, you must do it, what a fantastic opportunity!' without considering the fact your family and friends would soon know you only as a small image on a screen.

It's hard to overstate the impact of this aspirational mobility in Western society. Mobility offers opportunities but a hell of a lot of us now live a long way from our ageing relatives. It's very hard to take care of your parents when it involves a five-hour commute, only for someone to berate you for never visiting.

My dad and I were very much 'somewheres'. He only lived outside Wimbledon for one year of his life, during a brief and mysterious spell down in Brighton. My sister, on the other hand, is a classic anywhere, though not quite so fixated on Japanese food. Joanna is very worldly, having lived in Dublin, Norway, Calgary and Houston. Jo has probably travelled further to boarding gates than I have ever in my whole life.

Even when I moved to be with my wife in Bedfordshire I got nosebleeds driving that far north. On my third day living with her I cried because I'd walked back from the shop and seen a cow, which made me think I was too far from home.

I needed to pull out of the academic tailspin I was in. Or as Dad put it: 'What kind of prick gets three As at A-level but ends up with a third?'

Despite him being left-wing, living with Dad was immediately a far more conservative experience than I'd been used to. For one thing, he liked to get up early. He got up so early he'd concocted a whole new eating schedule for the day. He was the first person I ever heard routinely use the phrase 'second breakfast'. His second breakfast tended to come before my first, as Dad typically rose around 4.30am. I was often woken within a few short hours of going to bed with him blaring the radio and the heavy smell of his Douwe Egberts filter coffee snaking its way upstairs, merged with the dense, sweet smoke of his favoured Golden Virginia. There was no way I was going to be missing university under his roof. He literally dragged me out of bed to drink coffee and talk politics with him until sitting in traffic en route to being preached at about Cuba seemed like a better bet.

He had some incredibly sergeant-major views on work ethic. His quote on punctuality still haunts me to this day: 'Early is punctual, on time is late.' I'll say that again because it takes a couple of goes: 'Early is punctual, on time is late.'

He literally redefined the meaning of two words to underpin his own obsession with being on time. He didn't even bother with a definition of being late – for him that was like describing dark matter. Maybe he was right. To this day, I have never missed a gig because of tardiness (though I have arrived far too early in a lot of shit towns).

Whatever my frustrations, life with Dad pushed me kicking and screaming into an improved performance at university.

I never stopped finding my Dad a mystery. I remember the night Princess Diana died I'd been having a smoke around a mate's house. The news broke that she'd been involved in a car crash; Dodi was dead but Princess Diana had suffered 'minor injuries and broken ribs'. I don't know if it was down to how stoned we were but there seemed more to this, so me and my mate Simon resolved to stay up to see what was really going on. A sombre stoned vigil for the princess of hearts.

When they eventually announced her death early the following morning, I got prickles on my skin as Martyn Lewis said, 'This is the BBC from London.' They never said stuff like that when they were doing a story on joyriders. And why did he say 'from London'? There was no need, however it added to the sense of drama.

'Diana, Princess of Wales has died after a car crash in Paris.'

Me and Simon looked at each other with the kind of wide-eyed reaction you get from two stoners who didn't want to be proved right about their conspiracy theories.

I drove back to Dad's in the early morning sunlight. I felt important, trusted with big news. For once he was still in bed and I woke him saying, 'Dad, Princess Diana is dead.'

He seemed to be standing up before I'd concluded the sentence.

'Fuck me, get the coffee on.'

He hadn't realised I'd been out all night and I didn't want to disappoint him, so I sat there in a curious stoned coffee haze discussing the 'deep state' until he went out for a swim.

The reaction of the British public to Diana's death was a watershed. It was the first time I felt like I was experiencing something the whole nation was involved in. There had been tragedies – Zeebrugge, Hillsborough, the *Marchioness* – but nothing had united the country like this. At the time, I found it odd seeing people on morning telly crying their eyes out for someone they never knew. I was onside with Noel Gallagher's point that most of them queuing to sign the condolences book probably hadn't been to see their grandparents in a while.

Naturally, Tony Blair was all over it and Mum couldn't hide her seething contempt. 'Look at him, he's loving it. It's not Hollywood, you prick!'

I couldn't, however, ignore the other side of Britain I'd briefly seen. We talk about the London bubble like it's a new thing but it's been that way for a while. There are things you don't see in London as much as you do elsewhere, like VE Day celebrations, a fondness for the Royal Family and the St George's flag (unless there's either football or a march on). Every city is likely to be more liberal than the areas outside it but England, with its lack of a proper second city (sorry, Birmingham), suffers more acutely than most.

As far as I was aware, the members of the Royal Family were just mild sources of embarrassment to the country at that time. The nineties hadn't been their decade. From tampons to toe-sucking, they seemed to have become an expensive and disappointing luxury. I see it very differently now. A fondness for the Royal Family is one of those things you learn to understand as you get older. Like enjoying strong Cheddar or the value of a nap. I know they're not better people than me, I know their lives are those of sensational privilege, but equally I'm aware this country lacks a cohesive brand without them. How keen would Japanese tourists be to visit London if the main attraction was the M&M store in Leicester Square?

The first shift in my relationship with the Royal Family came in the early noughties. A mate and I were walking through Soho when, from a tight side-road, a black car appeared. The Queen was staring out of it straight at us. I made full eye contact with her. I thought about a wave but felt it unfair to bother her while she was off-duty. As the car moved on through Soho's narrow vehicular nooks and crannies, me and my pal were left scratching our heads.

'That was the Queen!' I said enthusiastically.

He nodded as politely as you can when someone has just stated the bleeding obvious.

'Didn't she look miserable?' he said.

And she did. Bored, but not just normal-person bored. Not the middle of a four-hour train journey bored or waiting for a delayed flight bored. This was a lifetime of boredom. This was the kind of boredom you were contractually obliged to endure. This was 'I've been this bored since Suez' bored. Seeing her felt both magical but depressing. She had a shine around her, like a princess who'd been cursed by a terrible spell. Anyway, I'm aware

I'm reading a lot into it. I doubt our encounter made her diary, 'Day 18,500 of my imprisonment. Yet another gormless twat stared at me.'

Such small-c conservative sympathies were still some way off while I lived at Dad's. For now, I was desperately trying to pull myself up and conclude my degree respectably. With my dad imposing some structure, and having me up drinking coffee before the breakfast news, progress was being made. The manner in which I turned it around in the final year felt like one of those awfully manufactured *Time Team* shows where once again it goes down to the wire of the last ten minutes. I knew that a lot of the degree was weighted towards the final year (something like 90 per cent, which was a red rag to a lazy shit like me).

During the third year of the degree, I finally started reading books which appealed to me. I studied post-modernism and savoured becoming one of those wankers who could throw the word into conversation. Though I had to pick my company wisely. If anyone from Pitt Crescent caught old 'Long Word Alert' calling something 'post-modern' I could have been lobbed into the River Wandle.

Everything was a race towards the end. My final dissertation almost went completely tits up as my dad's PC shat itself on the very last day. Fair play to the old man, he stepped up that day. I rang him and he rushed home from his new employment, having finally found work as an environmental officer for Merton Council. He hadn't spent a year dragging me out of bed for this to go pear-shaped at the final hurdle.

He shouted at the computer, kicked it and – like all good fathers – accused me of 'doing something to it'. Eventually he went for the last resort: 'I'm going to call my IT guy, Kevin.'

That should've probably been the first resort but that's not the way men's minds work in a crisis. We like to believe we can overcome Java and binary script through willpower and rage. His dodgy mate Kevin came over, we recovered the documents and the old man drove me across to New Cross to hand in the dissertation.

'You drive all the way here?' asked my dad, taking in the grimmer aesthetics of south-east London, suggesting he'd upgraded his view of my endeavours. The dissertation in, all I had to do was wait for my grade.

The day I went to Goldsmiths to find out my result was a nervous one. It was a long drive to get there and it struck me how odd it was to do something as mundane as 'commute' to a fancy liberal arts college. Trawling through Norbury, up into Streatham, through East Dulwich, into Peckham, Nunhead and finally New Cross had hardly put me in the right headspace for the metaphysical poetry of John Donne.

I pulled up on the last day like almost every other day, reluctantly. For someone who was all about roots and belonging, I'd been studying somewhere for three years and not formed any sort of bond with the place. There were a few kids and their families scouting out the institution with a view to next year. They all looked significantly better suited to Goldsmiths than me. They looked like they'd already saved a couple of whales and had one of those picture of Che Guevara, probably signed.

In an unusual method of posting the results, they were displayed in one corridor of the main building, printed on those vast dot matrix sheets still used for mass data in the mid-nineties. I had to scour hundreds of eight-figure codes to see whether I'd scored a first (nope), two-one (hmm), two-two (I'd bite your hand off) or third (most likely).

I finally got to my eight-digit code. It seemed to be under the collection of students who'd achieved a two-one, an honours degree. I read it time and time again to be certain.

A two-one?

How had I blagged this?

There were no college staff around to verify the result with. It was a remarkably flaky way to share the result of something students had been working towards for three years.

I checked a fourth, fifth, sixth, seventh time. It was definitely real. I had scored a two-one. It didn't have the box-office appeal of the three As at A-level. It felt like a test match where I'd been 46–7 and had somehow escaped with a draw.

The graduation ceremony was a tense affair. Mum and Dad still weren't brilliant together in social situations but had learned to grin and bear it. Students were only allowed two places for the ceremony but Mum had given the unwitting Goldsmiths staff the same treatment she'd once given Merton Council. They were mainly used to middle-class parents making polite enquiries, not Mum bellowing down the phone: 'I need my daughter there to hold me up! I will not have that bloody man pushing my chair . . . He can't push it anyway! He's only got one arm. I'd be going round in circles.'

Everyone else dressed casually for the day but, like a plank, I followed my mum's advice and got dressed up in strides and a collar. As I came off stage, I noticed her struggling to hold back the waterworks so I broke protocol and went over to give her a cuddle. It was performative but I knew what I was doing. When she told the story all around Mitcham for the next 20 years, it wouldn't be the degree she'd boast about (the first in our family) or the fact she'd got her son to that point from humble beginnings. It was the fact her son said up yours to convention and gave his dear old mum a cuddle.

So I left the most notoriously leftie liberal arts college in the country as a Labour voter who felt distinctly uncomfortable around the Left.

6

WHO THE HELL DRINKS 'SOYA' MILK?

My eventual Conservatism is so unlikely it makes me wonder if someone got at me young, like Peter Parker getting bitten by a right-wing radioactive spider. That could've happened during my teenage years when I did an unlikely work experience placement at the *Daily Mail*. I was only 14 at the time. The placement was another bizarre piece of over-reach by my mother who'd got on to the *Mail*'s HR department and given them the hairdryer treatment for several months as to why 'her boy' should be allowed to spend the day with a national newspaper.

So I took the tube into central London and checked in with my boss for the day. He was a nice, jolly bloke who quickly informed me, 'No one starts work until ten. Lunch is from twelve.'

In the morning, I took in the sight of many ashen-faced middle-aged men sat moving cursors around a screen. At midday the place came to life as they all started discussing what they'd be doing for 'lunch' (drinking, mainly; many of them seemed to be functioning alcoholics). My guy, whose surname was Macdonald, was asking his colleagues about the whereabouts of an evidently sexy PA.

'She's gone out for a Big Mac,' said one of the hacks.

'And you're just a little Mac,' chipped in another.

My boss for the day was quite short. It was a good joke but one which nerves prompted me to laugh way too hard at.

The period after lunch was a lot more productive. At one point, a graphics guy with a very early version of Photoshop asked me what football team I supported.

I said, 'Wimbledon.'

He gave the usual surprised response to this news. Five minutes later, he called me back to his desk to show me he'd put John Fashanu's head on the body of a white guy. He looked at me is if to say, 'Cool, huh?'

I wasn't very wordly but even at that age I got the sense he'd lost his love for the job. The day then finished as it started, with a load of increasingly crotchety blokes once again eyeing the clock for when they could next have a drink.

Despite that weirdness, I still harboured a loose idea that I was good with words and could use them to be a journalist. It's also possible I liked the idea of dicking around, drinking and getting paid for it. I thought it would make sense to start with a local publication. However, during a subsequent placement at the *Wimbledon News*, a journalist there warned me to 'Either work for the big boys or nothing at all.'

His name was Ken and he looked defeated. He elaborated, 'My life revolves around tea with old women who can't remember why they called.'

Having graduated, I'd heard you were supposed to apply for hundreds of jobs. I saw one which appealed to me: assistant press officer for Carlton TV. It paid £15,000 a year and looked like an excellent entry-level role. It also had the word 'TV' in it.

I didn't hear anything back from them so, crushed that my Herculean efforts of applying for one whole job had come to nothing, I forgot any idea of being a journalist and fluked my way into working for the first company who would take me. A job in 'broadcast compliance' for a company called Laser, one of the main sales houses for ITV advertising. It was the kind of nondescript decently paid job you could fall into back then. Now you'd probably need a PhD in marine biology.

Advertising is a decent barometer for the economic health of the nation so it was good to enter during boom-time. The noisy sales floor seemed like everything university had promised but failed to deliver on: a strong drinking culture and meaningless sex, plus it was pleasingly devoid of twats like Phil from Goldsmiths. It was the end of the nineties and following hot on the heels of the new man revolution the ladette scene was in full swing. If you could stand your ground in the face of the odd exposed boob in a pub, you stood a chance.

Unlike Goldsmiths, the company contained a healthy mix of classes. There were middle-class people who'd under-performed and people from more humble backgrounds whose patter made them ideal for sales. The working environment at ITV felt like a diet version of a city trading floor. It was noticeable the degree to which, even in an environment like that, assortative elements of friendship affected who you bonded with and why. I made a group of friends who had similar backgrounds to me. Humble beginnings, good families, just trying to get on and screw a few quid in the process. Our 'group' felt similar to people I'd grown up with. These lads would've all lived on an estate like me but they'd also have been the only ones with a phone.

The hard-drinking and sexually febrile environment of working on an open-plan floor of 200 or so early twenties types was aided and abetted by the sense of the country flourishing. We were in the midst of the dot.com boom. Remember that? When simple websites were being valued higher than national utilities. When your mate thought buying a domain name was going to allow him to retire before he hit 40.

My mate Jason had heard about this particular gravy

train, that if you bought a domain name that a large company would one day need they'd have to buy you out for big money. I asked him what domain he'd bought.

'Iwantabeer.com,' he replied.

'OK,' I paused. 'Is there a company called I want a beer?'

'No, but I bet loads of people type that into Ask Jeeves.'

'Do they? I'd think if you wanted a beer you'd just go out to the pub. Or a supermarket and buy some.'

If *Dragon's Den* had existed back then Duncan Bannatyne would've drop-kicked him out of the window.

He wasn't the only one hopping on the cyber goldrush. Lastminute.com shares rose from 380p to 510p. The whole company was valued at £768 million, mainly, it seemed, because the website sounded cool. Their business model reflected the slacker mentality of the boom: hoping that you could do something half-arsed at the very last moment and still get rich. Businesses were seeing their share prices rise simply because their website had a '.com' or better still an 'e' in front of their brand. The value of the UK tech sector started to find a more rational point in early 2000 but, alongside a growing GDP, it underwrote a lot of the economic confidence that turbo-boosted the start of the Blair years.

It didn't matter that a lot of the money was theoretical. In a way, that tech boom was like the onset of the millennium itself – a concept more than a reality. As the year 2000 had come into view it sounded futuristic so we made plans to treat is as such. The government built a dome to honour the event, with exhibits like 'Body', 'Mind' and 'Faith'. The whole thing looked like the mad imaginings of an RE teacher who'd won the lottery. We planned events big and small to honour something everyone assured us was significant but couldn't explain why.

The Y2K bug had furthered the idea of nebulous concepts most people were at a loss to understand. History suggests bold early action by companies and governments spared us the worst effects but you couldn't dodge the feeling at the time that IT consultants were like dodgy mechanics standing around doing their best 'this'll cost' grimaces. Planes did not fall out of the sky at midnight, and when they did the following year it was nothing to do with Gavin from IT.

I was at a house party on Millennium Eve. Many people ended up settling for this, having initially entertained the idea of going into London, then baulking at paying £45 on the door at their local and instead praying someone would be foolish enough to have a do at theirs. It was the first year of London's now ubiquitous mental fireworks, which we watched on telly. But this was before the flat-screen revolution, when the only people who had huge TVs were footballers and international drug traffickers so we crowded around something not much bigger than an iPad.

New Year's Eve always promises much and delivers little but the stark reality of the hype of Millennium night was never sharper than the following day when I ventured out to my local Esso garage hungover to buy a steak slice and a Fanta. This didn't feel very futuristic. I blame Prince; he'd spent years promising us we'd party like it was 1999. What he failed to mentioned was that partying 'like it was 1999' still involved beige snacks and Asti Spumante.

So much energy goes into determining how effective or skilful governments are but a lot of it comes down to economic factors outside their control. How much of New Labour's spending was facilitated by the tech explosion and the low inflation legacy of their predecessors? How much of the Tory 'jobs boom' was driven by a gig economy that would've happened with or without them? Governments are like football managers. They can make a few signings but mostly they start life with an inherited squad. If the squad is a bunch of ageing cloggers there's only so much they can do. When New Labour took charge, the economy had already been growing for five years and inflation was finally under control.

It was odd that the late nineties and early noughties had a distinct feel of Loadsamoney but happened under a Labour government, which somehow made the pursuit of wealth seem less conspicuous. Blair had pulled off the trick of leading a left-wing party that seemed onside with aspiration. However, they'd done it by simply being more right-wing than previous versions of Labour. When the minimum wage did eventually come in, it was much lower in real terms than was originally hoped for by the trade unions. Blair was terrified of seeming unfriendly to business. Maybe he over-corrected. The first time that I could remember the country having a serious discussion about the tax-avoiding giants like Starbucks and Google was during the early years of the coalition.

As with all economic growth in this country, that era was accompanied by harder drinking. 'Thursday is the new Friday' became 'Wednesday is the new Thursday'. All of this was a way of saying 'I want to drink every day.' The sandwich shops around the ITN building on Grays Inn Road were typically packed every Thursday and Friday morning, dealing with the effects of midweek drinking. People were lining up for bacon baps like they'd one day queue for bog roll in a pandemic.

Despite the sense of economic prosperity, not many of us working in ITV airtime sales had much money. When I started there, I was briefly living back with Mum. I then moved into a flatshare in Mitcham. Rent was comparatively low back then but transport and general subsistence weren't. There was a lot of cheap money around in the form of loans but I'd hit the threshold where I'd started paying off my student debt and had come to the sobering conclusion there was no such thing as free money. If there is a tick-list of things to cross off on the way to being right-wing, that is a big one.

The intensely social scene in advertising meant that my biggest overhead was 'lunch'. There were good things about a 90-minute lunch (sorry, millennials, it really did happen) but you also had to find things to do during that time. I was spending more on lunch every month then I was on rent. It wasn't uncommon to spend £9 on a curry, two pints at £6 and then a fiver playing pool.

I'm sure my middle-class colleagues weren't spunking their cash in this feckless manner, I'm sure they were all squirrelling money away to get property in up-and-coming Dalston, but there's something about being working class that compels you to live in the moment.

Some of the lads I worked with had a 'five-year plan'. That kind of long game seemed alien. Socialising with middle-class people, I frequently came across these kinds of unusual concepts. I remember the first time I heard the word 'sabbatical' (another excruciating moment at Goldsmiths). I asked a girl what her dad did for a living. She said he was 'on sabbatical'. I wasn't going to get tricked again into thinking it was one word.

'Right,' I said, 'And what's he doing for . . . that?'

'He's travelling. Gone to India for a year.'

'Right,' I said knowledgeably. 'Doing his work in India. Nice.'

'No,' she corrected me, 'he's not working. His company gave him a year to go and explore.'

This blew me away. You could get so good at your job they'd pay you to piss about for a year? No wonder middle-class people lived longer.

*

My jobs in advertising were always hard to explain to the family. Dad and Grandad had always made or designed things. To them, my job sounded every bit as flimsy as millennial tension and the Y2K bug.

'But what do you *do*?' asked my grandad again and again.

It's a decent rule of thumb that if you can't quickly describe what your job is, your chosen profession might not have legs. Or you might be Chandler from *Friends*. In short, I had to make sure adverts were allowed in their allocated spot. A lot of it was pretty basic common sense: no alcohol advertised during kids' show *SMTV*. No airline ads in *The World's Greatest Airline Crashes*. However, some of the protocols were less clear cut, which led to mistakes and a lackey like me costing ITV a lot money.

My worst spilt-milk moment was, ironically, to do with milk. One particular commercial break was throwing up a clash between two products: 'Unigate doorstep deliveries' (whose dated business model was still hanging in there) and a new brand called 'So Good Soy'. I didn't understand how these things could possibly relate. As far as I was concerned, soya was something middle-class pricks ate when they should've been eating meat. So, without phoning the creative company to check the actual content, I overrode the clash and the spot went out.

I came in the next morning and my manager Mark, possibly the nicest guy I've ever worked with, was furious. There's something awful when nice guys get the hump. One, you're gutted to be the person who caused them to finally lose it, like getting a dry slap off the Dalai Lama. Two, they're not used to this level of rage. They don't deal with it well. He was pacing, stuttering and sweating profusely. I'd always prefer to be told off by someone who was constantly angry. At least they know what they're doing.

'Geoff, can you explain why you overrode the clash between doorstep deliveries and So Good Soy? Which, incidentally, went out last night and was seen by an audience of 14 million people?'

'Yes,' I ventured confidently, as there's always that point where you've dropped a bollock at work but momentarily convince yourself you can wriggle out of it. 'Milk and soy aren't the same thing.'

Mark scratched his chin intensely, 'Right . . . only in this case they *are*. Are you aware that some people in Britain drink soy milk?'

And truthfully, no, I was not aware of this fact. I was not even aware that soy could *be* milk.

It turned out that this was So Good Soy's big-money launch campaign. Their spot on *Corrie* was the high-profile first slot. Their message to your average British consumer that soy milk wasn't some faddy option for people who survive on mung beans but a workable milk alternative. But because of my error, straight afterwards came the advert for Unigate doorstep deliveries. It was like saying, 'Modern hippy muck? Don't bother with that shit, stick with what you know.'

You might think I'm an idiot, and I was, but this was the late nineties, long before people were routinely drinking pea milk or eating wasp mozzarella. Back then, even semi-skimmed was viewed with suspicion in working-class communities. Most of our parents drank milk that had the consistency of Greek yoghurt.

Mark mentioned the cost of the spot and that ITV might have to refund it. I was acutely aware that if I worked for the channel for seven years I'd have barely paid off half of that sum, so I became desperate.

'Why don't they call it soy 'milk'? I asked, as though no one else in the country would associate the two things. 'And who the hell even drinks soy milk?' I added.

Mark gave me a bewildered look, which I've had many times since. He couldn't tell if I was thick or taking the piss. I've since learned that even back then plenty of people *were* actually drinking milk substitutes, especially in the hot house of faddy food that is central London. I just didn't know. Not for the last time, I was lagging behind metropolitan tastes and predilections. I didn't eat an olive until I was in my late twenties. I only found out what chateaubriand is while a television camera was pointed at me. Sometimes I'm defiantly anti-foodie. Sometimes I simply don't know about stuff. This was one of those times.

I topped it off by then trying to blame the IT system for my failing. That was the last straw. Mark was a decent man but he was also an IT man at heart. Never question 'the system'. Before asking me to leave his office, he pointed out that with my bluster and casual eye for details, I might be perfect for a job in sales.

Life in sales started off OK. I was working on the LWT – London Weekend Television – region, which, as it broadcast on weekends, meant I literally did nothing until Wednesday afternoons. At first, I was into the job and enjoyed the macho posturing that came with selling high-value airtime. It was around the time the cultural influence of *Lock, Stock and Two Smoking Barrels* and various 'geezer' films were still resonating, so those of us who had any geezer credentials were amplifying them and those with none were trying to conjure them out of thin air. Lads were walking around the sales floor in long coats that looked like they'd been nicked off their dads. If the Gallagher brothers had given Britain swagger, Guy Ritchie made us all act like we knew someone with a 'shooter'. All of which seemed a bit incongruous when our role was basically junior sales.

We were administrating the terms of the deals so, despite the company we worked for having a good profile, we spent our days largely haggling over smallprint. It could, however, be over access to well-known programmes of the time, like *Who Wants to Be a Millionaire?* Or, equally, it could be over poorly rated daytime spots. One of my lowest ever moments in the high-powered world of advertising sales came when I was standing up shouting down the phone to a buyer over a spot in a kid's cartoon. There was an awful macho cliché in the industry at that time that you'd 'get a black cab round there' to 'discuss it in person'. It was code for 'I will fight you over this disagreement'. Imagine it, two blokes in their early twenties rolling around in their dads' coats over a 30-second cleaning product ad in *Scooby Doo*.

I did OK in the role but felt they were slow to promote me to exec level. I got headhunted by the only major rival for ITV sales, Carlton. They asked me to come in for a chat. I loved the clandestine nature of it all. There was some rivalry between the two ITV media sales houses: Granada (the name Laser had now rebranded to) and Carlton. It felt like playing for Celtic but having a meeting with Rangers. The 'chat' went well and they offered me a promotion and to take my salary up to £21,000 a year. This felt significant. Though I'd done well academically, my family were starting to worry that it was all a waste of time, as, despite having plenty of lunchtime drinking stories, I was always skint. To further focus the spotlight on my inertia, Joanna, my sister, who had left school with barely a GCSE to her name, was coining it in as an accountant.

I took my typical male hubris to visit her at work one day. I noticed she was the only person with their own parking space. I then noticed she had her own corner office. I also clocked that the people who came in to see her spoke reverentially. 'Joanna?' I said. 'Are you a big deal?'

'Yes, Geoffrey,' she said, with the perennial patience of an underestimated woman.

How had this happened? I was the bright one. I was supposed to be making the big bucks. So crossing the £20,000 a year threshold would be a belated but welcome milestone. I've never been jealous of my sister's success, I was delighted she was a big deal, but it was a kick-up-the arse reminder to at least be a medium-sized deal.

Oddly, despite having working-class impostor syndrome, I've never had any problems standing my ground when it comes to negotiations. I don't feel self-worth as a matter of course but the moment anyone questions that by trying to low-ball me, I take it as a diabolical liberty. So I went back to the bosses at Granada and told them about the offer. They said I was valued, that they had 'great plans' for me. However, it became clear they weren't going to offer me anything more than praise, so I informed them I was handing in my notice. They seemed surprised and started to make all sorts of bizarre noises about Carlton being like a slave-driven Nordic long boat – another reason I'm not always taken in by 'Project Fear'. Their final threat was the weirdest: 'OK, Geoff, but it won't be pleasant, we'll have to put you on immediate gardening leave.'

Just like 'sabbaticals', I hadn't heard of 'gardening leave' either. However, even without any flesh on the bone it didn't sound bad.

'OK,' I said, trying to imply I knew what the fuck they were on about.

'You'll have to be escorted out of the building. In case you take . . .' – the head of HR floundered, realising that a lowly exec hardly represented a threat to the future of the ITV corporation – '. . . in case you take secret things.'

So I left the meeting and went straight to my desk. I got my personal items together before any of security could be arsed to get upstairs. My colleague, Kev, thought it was hilarious and quickly got a piece of card on which he wrote 'SECRET THINGS'. I milked the moment as I left, like Jerry Maguire with his goldfish, except, unlike Jerry, money was the sole reason I was leaving. It may sound crass, but with my background and student debts I couldn't be arsing about with five-year plans. I wasn't operating under the knowledge that my family would one day settle all of this for me and lob me a deposit for a house. Someone was offering me money right now, so I took it. Plus it was the beginning of December. The busiest month of the media year for parties and free booze. In effect, gardening leave was them paying me to get pissed for a month without having to set the alarm for the following morning.

The job at Carlton was good fun. I worked on the small and developing businesses for a guy called Carl (not his real name). Carl was the ultimate spiv made good. He seemed like the kind of guy Lord Sugar bought cars from. Carl loved wheeling and dealing. At that time, we were working with new businesses who were trying to become national brands. One such newer company trying to go stratospheric was a now well-known energy drink. They had a bit of cash but Carl was always open to doing a contra deal. In fact, given his humble beginnings, I think *quid pro quo* excited him more than actual money.

At Carlton I heard rumours of two deals that went down in media-sales folklore. One was for a spot on ITV late night, which was purported to have been paid for by six printers, actual printers, which must've proved a headache for ITV's accountants. The other mythical deal suggested Carl had once taken payment for airtime in the form of hundreds of pairs of designer jeans. They were great office legends but I will say this, we rarely had to replace ink-jets and everyone looked the bollocks on dress-down Friday.

Carl had that sharp working-class wit and intelligence. During the awful events of September 11, we were standing at our desks watching the horror play out on the big tellies (more evidence that adults standing up watching TV is a sure sign everything's gone tits up). The general feeling was that the world as we knew it had come to an end, forever. Understandably, all advertising was pulled that day.

I had a chat with Carl. He said, 'The world ain't ended, Geoffrey, but I tell you one thing: every Tom, Dick and Harry with a shit campaign will be trying to get their airtime pulled off the back of this.'

Over the next few days, advertising was gradually reintroduced to the ITV schedule. Sure enough, there were campaigns with totally valid reasons to remain off air: airlines, tourism, the Al-Qaeda recruitment drive . . . but there were also brands chancing their arm. I heard my colleague Glen have one particularly animated chat with a media buyer which ended with him saying, 'But Ed, what the fuck have nappies got to do with terrorism?'

Fortunately, the UK general election that year had happened long before such a moment of international upheaval. On reflection, it almost seems like a prelapsarian moment of predictability.

The 2001 election was the most apolitical I've ever known. In the early years, pre-Iraq, no one could land a punch on Blair. Then-Tory leader William Hague was excellent at the dispatch box but if you compared it to an era of tennis, Hague was Stefan Edberg while Blair was Pete Sampras.

The campaign was such a formality it provided little in the way of memorable moments. Labour's win was so hotly anticipated that some bookies paid out early on them being returned to power. The only time the Tories got within touching distance was the previous autumn when public anger over petrol shortages saw the Conservatives briefly open up a small lead. This was a different Britain where the main things that could get the people to march on Parliament were fuel and foxes. It felt like a national inconvenience to have to rubber-stamp the continuity we were all anticipating. Despite the collapse of the dot.com bubble (the least menacing sounding of all the financial crashes), the economy remained in a state of permanent growth.

Turnout was Labour's only fear and this produced the one memorable poster of the campaign: a photo of Hague's face with Thatcher's hair photoshopped onto him. I'm not sure it worked. Anyone living near one was more likely to stay in rather than be confronted with something that looked so much like an image from a left-wing fever dream. The eventual turnout reflected the apathy: 59 per cent, probably the lowest I'll ever know in my lifetime. God forbid my mother had ever got her hands on the electoral register and the details of that 41 per cent. She'd have given them one almighty democratic handbagging.

The Tories, following five years in opposition, had only produced a gain of one poxy seat. Even that gain amazed me. I was 23 by then and still didn't know any openly Conservative voters. I saw them on telly, I knew they existed, and by recent numbers nearly a third of the country had voted for them, but they remained largely anonymous in real life. Living in London in the early noughties, Labour felt like the natural party of government.

But looking back, the numbers offer a foreshadowing of what was to come. Only 40 per cent of the country voted Labour that year, a time still seen as part of the New Labour heyday. That's less than voted for May in the 'disastrous' election campaign of 2017. Less than voted for Major in 1992. A long way off Boris's 'stonking' 43.6 per cent in 2019. However, perception is everything and in London we assumed our mood was shared around the country. I felt, like most people around me, that 'everyone is Labour these days'. But they weren't. Indeed, that was the last election where Labour won the popular vote in England. However, for now, the Labour Party did the better job of epitomising continuity and stability. Maybe they had their own pervy MPs with light fingers but they were keeping their hands in full public view . . . for now.

I, however, was not in the mood for continuity. I'd started to have those terrible Sunday nights familiar to anyone who's realised they're wasting themselves in the wrong job. It first manifests as a call to get drunk shortly after *Antiques Roadshow*. You start developing an argument whereby Sunday beers are 'arguably the best beers of the week'. Then you realise the reason you want to spend Sunday night in an alcoholic fug is to drown the dread of what happens on Monday morning.

I'd also met the love of my life around that time, Emma. I should stress that my wife is a private woman who doesn't really want details about her life splashed over the pages of a book. It's part of what I love about her. When one of you is a tummy-baring pussycat it helps if the other doesn't need the validation of limelight. But suffice to say, she struck me immediately as beautiful outside and in (or inside and out, to try and make me seem less shallow). Someone who'd faced down serious life traumas and not been beaten by them. Maybe in that respect she reminded me a bit of my mum. Emma was also charismatic. It's a word that mainly gets applied to blokes but I've always warmed to women who have that kind of spark. Bias isn't just political, it also informs the very people we want to spend the rest of our lives with.

Meeting someone better than you who loves you is a great catalyst for a man to sort himself out. Maybe she did really love me for me but I couldn't ignore the risk that one day she'd wake up from this spell and make a more sober assessment of our relative merits.

I explored various things I could do using my decent level of qualification. Army? Yes, the bloke who wouldn't move to New Cross because it was too far would somehow get on his bike around the world. Plus, with Blair and Bush starting to face off against the whole Muslim world, this didn't seem like the best idea. So I decided I was going to be a lawyer. I talked to my dad and calmly explained how I was going to be one of those 'hundred grand a year blokes' he had always spoken about with disgust and reverence. Dad listened to my plans. I closed by telling him all I'd need was the small matter of a loan of 25 grand and I'd be well on my way to becoming a millionaire barrister.

He laughed. Actually laughed. In my face. At the time I felt burned by the experience but, looking back, he was right to laugh. Arguably, given my variable work ethic at the time, he didn't go far enough. He should've strapped me to the top of his car and driven me around Wimbledon with a loudhailer going, 'Everybody! This lazy prick thinks he has what it takes to become a lawyer!'

So I did what anyone of good qualifications and low-to-medium motivation does during such a personal crisis. I decided to become a teacher.

7

MR NORCOTT

I take a dramatic pause. Like an English teacher in a film, I'm about to blow these kids' minds. I'm going to read out the words of a well-known rap song like it's poetry. I know, pretty out there, right? The song is 'Lose Yourself' by Eminem. I start with the familiar opening bars, speaking of a single shot and opportunity. They lend themselves to my idea that I too am taking a risk. I'm speaking with a much more pronounced RP English accent than usual, just to throw them fully off the scent that it's a rap song.

I seem to have the class's attention but I'm not sure for how long. It suddenly strikes me that reading out the lyrics of a rap track is one of the most awfully clichéd things a teacher could do. It's up there with going, 'Hey, kids, did you ever think like how Shakespeare was *also kind of a rapper*?' The kids aren't giving much away. They're staring at me with a post-lunch blankness that could be inspiration or a post-prandial dip caused by eating two chicken burgers.

I continue with Eminem's iconic song despite my reservations.

Thankfully this is a top set. Even if they did think this was shit, most of them would be too scared to let me know. So far, I've even held the attention of the naughtiest kid, who'd briefly stopped twanging his ruler. But I can see his finger starting to twitch, so I speed up. For some reason, my accent is starting to go full Brian Blessed. It's weird. Ruler lad is on the verge of a full and disruptive comedy twang so I drop the RSC intonations and switch to a committed impression of Eminem. It's decent. The kids laugh.

Yes, I've deployed a fairly cheap gimmick, but teaching is like comedy. You do what you can to get an idea over the line. You can make a point about the connections between poetry and rap until you're blue in the face, but what people really enjoy is misdirection and a silly voice.

I particularly enjoyed teaching during my training year. I started off at St-Martin-in-the-Fields, a girl's school in Brixton. There's something about teaching in a deprived inner-city area that makes it feel like the job in its purest form, missionaries in corduroy.

Just like the kids on Pitt Crescent, the pupils at St-Martin-in-the-Fields had finely tuned bullshit radars. If I'd tried to rap here there would've been less applause and more eye rolling. Whenever I mention that I taught in Brixton, people instinctively presume the school was rough. It wasn't. A lot of the kids had African and West Indian heritage so God was a bigger part of their lives than for many of their white contemporaries in south London. As a teacher, it's always useful to have a higher power to refer to; God is way more useful than an exhausted-looking head of year.

My next placement in Watford didn't carry with it the same sense of urban urgency. However, the English department had some impressive characters. The head of department was married to one of the other senior English teachers. They were both funny and experienced. She was called Eileen and came from Belfast. I've always been drawn to people with the Northern Irish accent. It manages to bridge a unique line between humour, threat and clarity – ideal for teaching. She was a funny, charismatic woman with a unique sarcastic method of dealing with the griping and bitching from her underlings. One of the younger teachers in the department was a bit liberal with the truth. Eileen was getting fed up with her far-fetched stories as to why she'd had yet another sick day so stopped the morning meeting to say, 'You know what, Claire? Why don't you teach your students about Walter Mitty. He was also fond of making shit up.'

The modern sensitivities of the British workplace aren't set up to deal with blunt reality checks like that but it got the job done.

Eileen had presence, which meant people were a bit scared of her – no bad thing when the forward-facing element of your job involves getting teenagers under control. Modern teaching philosophy has moved towards more collegiate practice between staff and students but you can't get away from the fact 13 is still very young. They might complain just like adults but it's still best if some decisions are made for them. Some schools were letting students sit in on job interviews, which is like letting your toddler do the weekly shopping. They're at an awkward age, prone to rebel, launching themselves daily at the wall of adult power to see if it will come down. The mistake is to think they actually want the wall to come down. They might even think they do want it to crumble but really they're checking it is a solid wall.

Time and again in teaching, I came across teachers with a genuine love for the subject but no ability to command a room. Maybe I'm being overly simplistic but it felt like there were a number of basic things you could do which would make any lesson more manageable. One was to make the kids wait outside before entering a classroom. You wouldn't let punters into a nightclub without checking they were in a fit state of mind to be there, so why pupils? Watching them file in was always a good opportunity to tell which kids already had a strop on and who'd been injecting Red Bull.

Also, it helped to insist they talk to you respectfully at all times. How many times have you seen a snotty kid in a supermarket talk to their parents like they're staff? It's the same in a classroom, you have to deploy a zero-tolerance approach to disrespect (apart from this one kid whose father I knew was in an organised crime syndicate; there's consistency and there's common sense).

Most importantly, teachers need to look presentable. Teenagers are pretty shallow creatures; if you look shambolic they may well conclude you are a shambles. Think back on the best teachers at your school. How many of them rocked up looking like they'd done a trolley dash through a Sue Ryder? It may be unfair on men but suits should be mandatory. As far as female staff go, it's a tricky time to tell women what to wear. The furthest advice I'd feel confident going with on this is that female staff should ensure their clothes are ironed.

You also have to be consistent with imposing and carrying through sanctions. It was all too easy to kid yourself that letting a pupil off a detention is a favour to them. But that's no preparation for life after school. As Eileen said, 'You're letting them down by letting them off.' The amount of times I'd tell a class I was keeping them back and they'd respond by asking if they could earn the time back for good behaviour. Absolutely not. A footballer who's been sent off doesn't get allowed back on the pitch because he didn't punch a fan on his way down the tunnel.

In short, despite going into teaching thinking I'd be a 'Hey, guys! Call me Geoff' teacher it quickly transpired I was a 'Oi! Call me SIR' sort of guy. It wasn't a conscious choice, just an instinctive response to standing in front of a class of teenagers and working out the main thing they needed from me. You had to have status and consistency, especially with the boys. Teenage lads' need for a strong male role model is palpable. The 'sir' thing was mainly for them. I never let it go. Not during sixth form, not outside school, never. I saw an old student recently. I haven't taught him for the best part of 25 years. He'd seen me do a bit of telly and confidently asked if he could now call me 'Geoff''. I said no.

I passed my trainee teacher year with distinction. I got a one on my course, the highest mark available. I was assessed by an Ofsted inspector on my final day. She reminded me of the woman who'd interviewed me for a university place at Goldsmiths: very middle-class, middle-aged, but willing to let me off with a couple of fairly basic mistakes. In the lesson, she observed me teaching a close reading of a chapter from the novel *Holes* by Louis Sachar.

I focused in on the use of the word 'lean'. Unfortunately, I thought 'lean' meant 'fat'. No idea why, I guess must have been carrying out my boycott of Southfields the week they taught us that word. And sabbaticals. So much for 'Mr grade one distinction'. Idiot. So I spent a good ten minutes asking the class why the author wanted us to think of this character as overweight. Luckily for me, the class was as dense as I was and none of the kids questioned it.

During her assessment, after commending me on all the good stuff, the Ofsted lady politely asked, 'If I said I thought I was lean, what would you think that meant?'

I was now concerned. I forgot that I'd focused on the word during the lesson and thought this powerful woman was suddenly having an attack of body consciousness. She must've made it sound like a loaded question for her own amusement, or realised the ambiguity, because she quickly interjected, 'It means very little fat on it. During the lesson you implied that it meant overweight. It's worth being secure in meaning as an English teacher.'

'Right,' I nodded. 'Do you still want an answer to the . . .'

'Absolutely not.'

I proposed to Emma after just six months of dating. It might seem hasty, but I'm strong on gut instinct. I'm also strong on knowing when you're punching several divisions above your weight. Around the time I qualified as a teacher, we moved in together.

We decided to live in her flat in Bedfordshire. It made sense for both of us and I couldn't afford anywhere decent in London any more. That logic didn't stop me having anxieties about moving 'up north' as my dad called anywhere north of Willesden. What with the Norcotts being *somewheres* rather than *anywheres*, chained to our roots in south London, me moving to distant Bedfordshire raised eyebrows in the family.

Driving up the A1 with my pathetically modest belongings comfortably fitting in the boot of my Fiat Panda, I felt like a pioneer. As the motorway section of the A1 faded into a simple A road and the scenery moved from buildings to fields, I wondered how I'd fit in with what I saw to be 'country life' – forgetting that the town I was moving to had a population of 15,000 and five trains an hour into King's Cross.

In a very early rude awakening, I got proper hayfever for the first time in my life. I had no idea what was happening. My eyes swelled up like a battered Rocky Balboa. I was trying to fit in but even my London body seemed to be rejecting the fields and country air. I've still never totally fitted in round these parts. I work in London regularly and whenever I get off the train I always take in a big lungful of that dense, humid air, like Frodo Baggins going back to a polluted Shire.

I needed to be earning fast to finish paying off the new debts accrued during teacher training. I'd been paid a salary to train but, typically, still managed to over-spend. A job came up near where I lived at the Samuel Whitbread Community College so I took it. In the same way I'd once applied to Goldsmiths, I did so without really wondering about how the culture of the school would suit me. It was a big place but I got a word of warning early on from one of the more savvy deputy heads: 'This will be different from what you've experienced in London. The biggest danger these kids face is apathy.'

And so it proved. Despite having 1,500 pupils, there was something sleepy about the school. It was so dozy I sometimes wondered if they were drugging the giant iced-buns with Mogadon.

Like all teaching faculties in a middle-of-the-road school, most of the staff had no idea how good they had it, so would moan about problem classes like they were being asked to reintegrate former child soldiers. Having taught but also gone to school in London, there was no comparison between the supposedly bad kids at Samuel Whitbread and the wrong 'uns I'd grown up with. Their definition of 'nightmare year 11s' was nothing when I'd been to a school where kids lit joints off the Bunsen burners.

I got on with all my colleagues individually but the English department was all female and I found it difficult being the only bloke. The department office was small and it was hard to get on with work because they . . . talked a lot. OK! Shoot me down for saying it but yes, eight middle-aged women in a confined space did talk more than would be usual if there was an equal gender split.

The constant chatter made it hard to get on with the work they were all moaning about having to do. I got on particularly well with two teachers from the media department who informed me there was a large spare cupboard if I wanted it. So I fashioned a makeshift office there. I cleared it of old textbooks and managed to get a small table and chair. When I shut the door I could lean against it with my back. It had one light dangling from the cobwebby ceiling. It looked like the kind of place a poet might've hidden from the Nazis.

I didn't tell any of my colleagues in the English department; they just saw a lot less of me. Eventually one came looking and was clearly offended by where I'd chosen to work. I was a bit naïve to think they wouldn't take it to heart. One of their colleagues had literally shut himself in a cupboard with no window rather than sit with them. Like a prisoner requesting solitary confinement just for the peace and quiet.

The close-knit nature of the English department also made it hard for senior staff to speak to the faculty. It was – as one of the female deputy heads explained to me – a 'petticoat hierarchy'. The head teacher, Roger, would often struggle with their collective pushback. One day he came to our department staff room to try to lay down the law over the completion of end of year reports. As he waddled into the small amount of floor space available, one staff member bustled in with her books. She looked Roger up and down and said, 'Ah, Mohammed had to come to the mountain.'

The rest of the staff burst out laughing. He looked crestfallen. Never underestimate the power of a group of women working in unison to take down a powerful man. From that point on, he conducted all staff meetings one by one in his office. As he confided in me, 'I'm a gentle man. I never thought teaching would be a job where I'd have to divide and conquer.'

I also started to take exception to the school's increasing penchant for pupil power, the low point of which was when students were allowed to sit in on interviews for new staff – up there with letting drink drivers set the legal limits. You also had to 'work them through the levels' when issuing a punishment, letting them know at each stage why they were in more trouble – presumably so they understood exactly why calling you a 'fat prick' was unacceptable.

It seemed most of these were acts of indulgence, something the students seemed to be getting plenty of from their doe-eyed parents at home. One of my weekly responsibilities was to sit with a student from my tutor group for half an hour and basically counsel them. In my opinion, most of these kids were in a better financial position than me. It was a bit galling to hear them describe petty gripes about the size of their bedrooms while I was an adult living in a shoe box.

One student started a session with the crushing news that she'd 'have to share a room with her sister'. As she continued gabbing on about how unfair it all was, I thought about my mate Mick crammed in there with so many brothers, desperately trying to learn. I thought about my mum at the convent, going to sleep in a cold dormitory of people she didn't know. I started a daydream where I led her to the window to administer a much needed reality check.

'Look, Freya, look out there. What do you see? That's right, the school field. And what beyond that? Correct, a fence . . . Well, beyond that fence is approximately seven billion people who don't give a fuck about your petty problems. And that includes me. I know I seem like I give a shit now but that's contractually obliged.'

As I came to, Freya was on to detailing how her brother kept using her cereal bowl. I'm not saying comfort precludes anxiety and depression but maybe I was the wrong guy to be hearing about it.

However, unpaid therapy aside, teaching isn't that hard. It really isn't. If you're organised, if you get in an hour before school starts and leave an hour after it finishes and use a sensible portion of the 12 weeks' holidays marking and doing prep, you can enjoy the job. The hardest element wasn't snotty kids but moaning colleagues. I don't like moaning. Moaning is one of the biggest drains on the lamentably poor productivity of the UK economy. It's one of the main reasons almost every single meeting overruns. The main business is usually concluded in good time but the AOB becomes a counselling session for the professionally needy. School morning briefings always went long because teachers wanted to file their latest complaint monologue. Every industry has these people. They start their contribution with 'If I could just have a little moan.'

If I'd stayed in teaching and reached senior management I would've caused mutinies in the rank and file staff by my reactions to that kind of employee. If anyone started a contribution to a group meeting with, 'If I could just have a little moan', I'd have cut them off with, 'No, you can't just have a *little* moan, Janet. 'Cos it's never *little*, is it? It goes on and on, is usually wildly parochial, of little consequence to the wider faculty and, let's be honest, rarely about the issue in hand and more a code for the fact you've been mildly depressed for 20 years but find it more convenient to pretend that *pigeon-hole protocol* is the real reason for your unhappiness.'

I'm sure you'll agree that me leaving teaching was probably for the best.

Shortly before moving out of London, I'd started earning the odd bit of money here and there from stand-up. Unlike today, when many people identify comedy as a career early on and study it exhaustively online, I'd fallen into it. My best (only) mate at university, Neil, and I had – for reasons I can't remember – formed a double act called 'The Boobka Brothers'. The premise being we were Soviet dissidents in hiding and had chosen to make our way on the London open-mic circuit. We did OK early on. Neil was by far the funniest and most watchable of our double act. We made our debut at the Comedy Café having done only two gigs and won their prestigious open mic night. We shared the 'run before you can walk' gene and decided that the next logical step should be a two-night residency in the studio room at Wimbledon Theatre.

Unfortunately, Neil got unwell, so, with the kind of naïvety that I'd never have had a career without, I thought, 'How hard could it be?' and decided to host a night of straight stand-up, which I'd compere. A contact from advertising knew a few good acts on the London circuit so they came down and helped me out. I have no idea what I said on that night but I'm fairly sure the jokes weren't great. The main thing that got me through wasn't comic ability but the goodwill of family and friends.

The feeling after that gig was a hard one to explain. This was, after all, my first time onstage alone (if you discount winning a crappest cowboy competition). I should be loading in the superlatives about how it felt for me. How I floated home on an uncut dose of pure adrenaline. How I was dreaming of emulating my comedy idols. But if comedy was a drug then I wasn't hooked straight away. Stand-up felt less like a calling and more like a whispering. Besides, my paranoia about money meant my first buzz after that debut gig wasn't to do with the performance, it was because I'd covered the guarantee to the theatre manager. Many comics describe themselves as walking long distances after their first gig and not really taking in time or detail. It was different for me, the feeling I got was much more subtle, like a number of little fires in my head had been put out. Presuming I'd solved a lifelong mental health problem within the space of 20 minutes, I had no intention of taking it any further. Except I got up the following day and the fires had started again. With the benefit of counselling and hindsight, I can see there was something in me that had formed a bridge in time between comedy now and that brief childhood moment on the Isle of Wight, when me making everyone laugh made everything seem momentarily OK. Knowing that didn't change anything.

It's one of the poxy things about therapy: self-awareness doesn't stop you trawling through the exact same shit again in a couple of weeks.

Maybe that's what I should've said to Freya.

Unlike most comics, who move to London to do the open-mic circuit, I left London just as I was getting OK at comedy. The only gigs I could now contemplate were paid ones. It was an unusual way to do the apprenticeship. The open-mic scene was a bit insular, whereas I was immediately working with paid professionals. The scene also seemed to have some of the same cultural snobbery I'd encountered at Goldsmiths.

'You *haven't* heard of Bill Hicks?' one comic asked me.

No, I had not.

'George Carlin?'

'Nope.'

'Patton Oswaldt?'

'No.'

'Who are your *influences* then?' he asked incredulously.

I didn't know we had to have *influences*. It was another moment where I knew that telling the truth would make me seem like an idiot but, on the other hand, I've always chosen honesty over credibility.

'Russ Abbot, Dave Allen and Eddie Murphy.'

He laughed derisively (though I'd argue that you'd struggle to top the mixture of Abbot's gooning, Dave Allen's everyman qualities and the swagger of a young Eddie Murphy).

Not that my act betrayed any of those influences at the time. I honestly have no idea what I was trying to do onstage back then. I had a few observations but it was like my teaching – a modest amount of prep and an over-reliance on stupid voices. I was just occupying the stage like a tummy-bearing pussycat who hadn't worked out why he wanted to be stroked.

For most comics, in the first couple of years, stand-up is a cross between hobby and obsession. For me, it quickly became a financial necessity. Despite my wife and I both working, interest rates were much higher in the early noughties. We bought a house together shortly before our wedding in the summer of 2004. Underwritten by cheap credit, the housing market was in the throes of a long boom. We hadn't found anything in the town we lived in so looked at another, larger town 20 miles up the A1. We found a row of six old cottages being more or less rebuilt from within. Just as I was trying to think how I'd play this negotiation, my wife said to the estate agent, 'How much is it?'

He told her.

She replied, 'We'll take it!'

I looked at the estate agent who seemed confused. He then did something I'm not sure any estate agent has done before or since and added, 'You might want to take at least a couple of grand off the asking price.'

You know you've dropped your drawers when an estate agent is telling you to trim your offer. It's like a black cab driver saying it'd be quicker to walk.

Being on the housing ladder does something to a person. People often wonder why men lose the ability to cry as adults. It might be to do with getting that big debt under your belt. You think, 'Right, time to bury some feelings.'

Under Labour, my bills seemed to be going up each month. The one that hit the hardest was the huge rises in council tax. They argued that it was to improve the community but the scale of the upgrade never seemed to be in line with the rise. The average council tax bill in 1997–8 was £564. By the time they left office, it was £1,439, a rise of 109 per cent. Even when you adjust for inflation, people in the lower band D were paying just under 70 per cent more. How could the Labour party have overseen such a tax rise which had hit people on lower incomes harder? They were supposed to be about progressive tax. I saw some improvements in public services during that time but for that kind of hike I'd be expecting the country to smell of Febreze and find a mint on my pillow every night.

I sat down with Emma one night to look at the numbers. Between both our salaries, with a small two-up two-down, we were somehow behind every month. Yes, house prices were lower but interest rates were much higher, peaking at 5.75 per cent just before the crash. The threshold of income tax earnings was much lower too. By the time Labour left office, you could earn £6,475 before taxation. More recently it's risen to nearly double that at just over 12 grand. Gordon Brown, keen to continue his claim that he hadn't put up income tax, did put up National Insurance, a snidey sleight of hand that rankled. It felt like Labour had created an economy where people on my level were playing a constant game of catch-up. The promised land felt in sight but it was exhausting trying to get there. Consequently, the people around me living a good lifestyle seemed to be underwritten by cheap credit, something I didn't want to get into. There was something about the word '125 per cent mortgage' that sounded wrong, like 'enjoyable family holiday'.

For the first time in my adult life, the bit of my brain associated with economic risk lit up, plus now I had a wife so the stakes felt much higher. I had to do something as the idea of simply getting poorer each month caused me sleepless nights. It was like going back to pushing a car up a hill, except this time my hands never came off the bumper but it was still rolling backwards.

So the comedy was, initially, a necessity, to avoid borrowing against the house. What a terrible story for a so-called artist to share as his original motivation.

'How did you get into comedy, Geoff?'

'Well, I'd say a love of performance and satire, but it was mainly because I owed NatWest.'

Teaching and comedy started to overlap. As I was being offered decent money for midweek gigs, I started to travel further and further, yet still had the responsibility of teaching the following day. It was unprofessional and also dangerous to drive that much while tired. I once drank so much Red Bull I could hear the blood in my ears. The low point of my attempts to balance both jobs came when I took a midweek gig in Truro. Pre-smartphone and satnav, all I knew was it was 'in the West Country' so I said yes. I finished teaching at half past three and drove the six and a half hours to get to Cornwall. I did two shows in the same venue and then set off home at half past eleven. I got home at about half past six in the morning, having nearly fallen asleep several times at the wheel. As I slapped my face repeatedly to stay awake, it occurred to me that if I had died, the last words I'd have said to another human were 'I've been Geoff Norcott, goodnight.'

I laid down next to my still sleeping wife and put the £200 on the side. It felt like a lot of hassle for that much money, even if my tiny car did achieve more miles to the gallon than your average lawn mower. As a stand-up colleague at the time once put it to me, 'If someone told you there was £200 on the bar of a pub in Truro, would you drive all the way to get there?' It was a rhetorical question and his inference was reasonable enough but, honestly, with my fear of debt, I may well have still taken that drive. If you'd put another £50 behind a bar in Penzance I might've done that too.

Lying on the bed, I stared at the ceiling for 30 minutes until my alarm went off. I sat bolt upright in bed like a bad Dracula and headed into work. Schools can be surreal, anxiety-inducing places at the best of times and are more so when you've driven 700 miles on no sleep. It felt like the bit in the film *1917* when the two lads continue through the tunnels, their ears ringing after another explosion.

I sat down to teach the first lesson. The next thing I knew, I was opening my eyes with a class of year nine children staring at me. I felt strange, a little refreshed, but acutely aware that there was an odd vibe in the room.

'What just happened?' is the question no grown-up should ever ask a group of children, but I did.

'You were asleep for about 20 minutes,' said one of the girls sitting nearest to me.

'OK, and what did you do while I was asleep?' I questioned, totally at their mercy.

'Nothing,' she said, 'We just sat here.'

This was the benefit of teaching a good class. If I'd have been teaching a rough one, or any class from my own experience of comprehensive education, they'd have taken liberties. Probably shaved an eyebrow and drawn a cock on my head if I was lucky.

'Wait here,' I told them, still trying to assert some sense of moral authority. I went to the staff room and confided in one of the PE teachers. With surprising confidence he said, 'My advice is have a very large glass of cold water and see if you can manage a shit.'

It wasn't the advice I'd been expecting but I took it. I felt better and, as a PE teacher, he had finally done something useful with his day.

*

Gigging with increasing regularity, I eventually got an offer from a comedy agent called Geoff Whiting. We did a show together in Farnham and he said something simple, but persuasive: 'You do know you could make a living from this?'

He detailed his offer of representation but what was really turning over in my mind was the very idea I could make a living from telling jokes. It seemed far-fetched and something I'd have to work hard pitching to my dad, who thought an English degree was an expensive version of book club.

I accepted Geoff's offer of representation. Stand-up might have seemed like a perilous income but, as things stood at that time, I was getting poorer each month. That felt risky too. If I gigged four times a week and did supply teaching I'd be earning more (and be knackered, and probably stink of motorway Ginsters). However, I stressed to my new agent that I wanted to work out my contract at the school until December as I didn't think it morally or professionally right to abandon the kids mid-term. This attempt to do the right thing was tested fully when, out of nowhere, I was offered a TV job on a prank show. The problem was I'd have to be available for recording before I was free from my contractual teaching responsibilities so I turned it down. My new agent was keen for me to reconsider but I stood my ground.

The TV heat went away and I had to tell my tutor group that I was leaving. They seemed disappointed but not quite the abject desolation I'd been hoping for. I grandly explained that I'd been offered a TV job and could've gone sooner but wanted to do the right thing. The class fell silent and I imagined they were feeling overwhelmed at the duty of care I'd shown them against my better interests.

It was nothing of the sort. They all felt I was an idiot to have turned down the TV show. Furthermore, some of them implied it was an act of moral vanity: 'You were going to blow us out in the long run, why not straight away?'

I told them I would miss their honesty, which was dishonest, because in this instance I'd have preferred a reassuring lie.

And so I started life as a 'full-time' comedian.

I was usually only busy Thursday to Sunday, which left the early week open for me to top up my earnings with supply teaching. I learned more about education in the first year of doing supply than I had in the previous three. There's something about going from school to school, seeing different approaches to pastoral care and discipline that makes you realise certain things about the education system. Mainly that the strict ones are better.

I had less than fashionable approaches to resolving issues between students. I was doing regular supply at one school when I found out one of the nicest lads in the class had been suspended for three days for fighting. I asked around to find out what had happened. The first story was that it was a vicious, unprovoked assault on one of the more vulnerable kids in the school. Though it should be said that this account was from one of the more militant drama teachers, who once told me off for reading *The Times* (if you think comedy seems left-leaning, try being anything right of a Liberal Democrat in the staff room). So, sensing her account might not be entirely reliable, I dug deeper and found out the true story.

Lee had been playing football and Joshua, one of the more vocal kids in the class, had been spraying Ribena at him. Lee warned him to stop. The kid continued. Lee warned him a second time and said that if he continued he would punch him in the face. The kid did it again, so Lee punched him in the face. As I was being told this by a deputy head, I did my best to hide my 'that seems entirely reasonable' face.

When pressed on the harshness of the punishment, the school proudly trumpeted a 'zero-tolerance' approach to violence. It's hard to argue with that without appearing to endorse playgrounds looking like a ninja academy. However, when I found out Joshua had faced no punishment at all for repeatedly spraying Ribena in Lee's face, I blew my top. I spoke to the head of year, a guy called Chris, whose eyes suggested he'd tapped out of caring many years ago and mainly communicated through spreadsheets. I asked him what kind of lesson Lee would be learning from this episode. He just kept parroting the school mantra, 'We have a zero-tolerance approach to violence . . .'

This is one of the problems with groupthink. An idea takes root and it becomes a quasi-religious distillation of something far more complicated. I shared my ideas with him.

In turn, he shared his idea that I was a supply teacher, and therefore very easy for him to fire.

At that same time, a similar groupthink issue was happening around further education. Following Blair's slogan 'Education, education, education', the idea seemed to be that more or less every kid needed to have a degree. Labour wanted to be the party of higher education even though they'd recently become the first to demand people pay for it. With the threshold for repayment of student loans at the time being less generous than now, the decision to attend university was different for someone from a working-class background but teachers everywhere toed Blair's line that the only route out of poverty was a drama degree from De Montfort.

I've since realised not everyone *should* go to university. It's no coincidence that many of my wealthiest friends have their name on the side of a van. Having a manual trade creates a noble, steady and lucrative career. I don't know why we lost sight of this. Loads of blokes I know working as project managers or as 'creatives' don't make a fraction of what my pal the carpenter does. The coronavirus shone a blinding critical light on that idea and the inherent value of different professions. Plumbers will always work. You could drop an atom bomb on

London and there would still be a chirpy bloke bustling around in a van fixing leaks. My view of the value of university has changed dramatically. I now actively want my son to get a trade rather than engage in formal study. In the space of one generation, it's gone from Mum crying at me holding a diploma to me misting up at the idea of my boy knowing his way around a combi-boiler.

Over the next few years, I was earning more from comedy but kept up the supply teaching. Despite being a general optimist about the human condition, for the first time in my life I had to concede that the kids' behaviour did indeed seem to be getting worse. This wasn't just a consequence of being a whipping-boy supply teacher. Given my experience on stage, I was good at getting a room under control. I spoke to staff in every school I went to and they were becoming increasingly exasperated.

It seemed that hand in hand with economic growth had come a rise in anti-social behaviour. I'd seen it first-hand in schools. I also started to see that there had been a change in the kids who had behaviour problems. In the past, difficult students mainly came from difficult families but now *laissez-faire* middle-class parenting meant a lot of the kids most likely to throw a dart at your head also had a pool table at home. And a pool. This put an intolerable stress on schools as parents were effectively outsourcing their child's moral code so they could continue being their best pal. The way they sat there during parents' evening batting back any implied criticism of the spoiled little shits made them seem less like parents and more like football agents.

One girl who epitomised this trend of over-indulgence was a pupil at the school in Watford, Jessica. I dared to call her attitude a 'disgrace'.

The air went out of the room as the rest of the class – more used to her acute sensitivity to criticism – braced themselves for what was to come. Her head moved from side to side, like a lethal predator extending its jaw muscles so that the victory may be quick but painful. She then let rip with a full-stop free tirade about how dare I question her attitude, about how her brother was in the army and her nan was an *amazing* woman . . . I decided not to back down and got her dad up to the school. The moment I saw him I knew he was a big part of the problem. Passive, hunched and painfully timid, he tried to justify his daughter's actions, no matter what I told him.

I told him she'd once held up the class for 20 minutes because she wanted to talk about a book she hadn't even bothered to read for homework. He looked at her, simpering, and said, 'Bless Jess, she just likes expressing herself.'

That was the problem. Expressing yourself is one thing, but you need to have something of merit or consequence to say. The trendy teaching of the early noughties put too much power with the pupils and coincided with the early swathe of narcissistic ITV talent shows. Every week we saw various 'Jessicas' have their dreams blown away because of deluded dads like this guy, who didn't have the balls to tell his kid to shut the fuck up.

In 2019, the spike in youth knife crime was linked to Conservatives cutting the police force but the last such spike in 2007 happened during a period of record police numbers and public investment. A lot of the ASBOs that Blair had championed were going to young people. Young people with whom teachers had to sit in rooms for the best part of a week. There has never been a scientific study of why it happened during the economic prosperity from 1997 to 2008 but we were also seeing a growth in the number of children who'd grown up in a house where they'd never seen a parent work. Possibly because, despite the prosperity, unemployment had remained stubbornly high. Having already seen how a life on benefits could be a life half-lived, I could see how it could lead to people going to seed on welfare during the boom years. Public spending had risen more than four times under Labour than the previous Conservative government but the net effect didn't always match up. I was worried that their desire to seem 'nice' might result in a whole generation of youngsters tempted by the lure of wearing dressing gowns until midday.

While I wasn't politically Conservative yet, my dial was moving all the time. These and other reservations about the New Labour project were already taking root in the run-up to the 2005 election. Despite all the grievances lefties had following the invasion of Iraq, many still seemed primed to vote for Blair again. I wasn't going to. Despite them being called 'boom years' I wasn't exactly booming, like the boyband member no one fancied. I weighed up my other options. The Tories under Michael Howard seemed to be exactly the sort of malevolent presence people had always claimed them to be. Their slogan 'Are you thinking what we're thinking?' didn't work for me. Looking at Michael Howard, I imagined he could be 'thinking' about anything, from lowering crime to the reintroduction of bear baiting.

My dad sensed where my head was moving and, after another intense discussion about politics, he said, 'You're not going to vote for those Tory bastards are you, son?'

I said no. I wasn't.

Instead, I did what anyone does who can't make up their minds politically.

I voted for the Liberal Democrats.

8

WHAT THE HELL IS A LEHMAN BROTHER?

The credit crunch was arguably my favourite financial crisis of all time.

Let me explain.

Often, we only find out about important institutions when they're already in trouble. Lehman Brothers collapsed on 15 September 2008. I was on a beach in Crete with my stand-up colleague and friend Ian Stone.

'Fuck me,' Ian said, looking at his phone, and no doubt incurring some hefty pre-data-roaming era charges, 'Lehman Brothers has gone down.'

I was blissfully unaware of what a Lehman brother was. At a guess, I'd have said wrestling tag-team or jazz quartet.

'Fuck,' I said, still relaxing and squinting into the sun, having learned by now that when you're intellectually out of your depth the best thing to do is mirror the behaviour of whoever seems better informed.

Ian, knowing me well enough, pursued the matter. 'This is a big deal, Geoff. Global banks don't just *collapse*. This is uncharted territory.'

Now, I didn't know much about banks but I had to accept he made a good point about the frequency of global ones collapsing. He also used the word 'uncharted', which usually meant some kind of shit was hurtling towards a fan. But as is usual with bad news delivered on a sunny day, I found it hard to credit that the world was teetering on the brink of ruin. How could it be? The sun was shining heedlessly and my toes were nestling into the cool, coarse sand. (One thing I've since learned about the sun is it has a design fault. Great at sustaining life on earth but sometimes has a habit of popping out when you need a bit of gravitas, like a practical joke in very poor taste.)

Once I'd returned to the UK, I had more credit-crunch-appropriate weather throwing milky-grey light on the unfolding financial crisis. I became increasingly alarmed about what was happening. I was in Manchester a week after returning from Crete, performing at the Comedy Store. I celebrated my thirtieth birthday while on stage, opening the second half of the late show. Late shows are notorious for heavy drinking and rowdy behaviour and, as I stepped out on stage at five past midnight, newly minted as a 30-year-old, I was greeted by a woman two rows back throwing up. If you're into omens, a woman vomiting you into a new decade isn't an especially good one.

The following day, I decided to venture out to investigate this thing called 'footfall', which was apparently down. As I walked around the Trafford shopping centre, I got a sinking feeling in my stomach. The thing I was trying to pretend wasn't happening was there right in front of me. Practically no one was out spending money. Footfall wasn't just down, it was non-existent. It was peak shopping time, just after lunch on a Saturday afternoon, but it seemed more like the last minutes before closing. Even the shoppers who were there seemed apologetic and uncertain. Women in clothes shops seemed to be scrutinising purchases that bit harder. A sparkly halterneck is always a big shout, particularly if it costs £50 and you work in the 'vulnerable service sector'.

Financial crises can be exacerbated by people losing their financial bottle. In most recessions, the overwhelming majority of people stay in employment. The highest national unemployment rate in my lifetime was still just over one in ten. However, a heightened sense of personal jeopardy – in other words, the *fear* of unemployment – is a major factor when it comes to how people behave and spend their money. People will often postpone the big-ticket purchases like cars even if their financial circumstances have not changed. All it takes to make you question that new patio is hearing about your mate Dave who got laid off. Poor bastard, two kids already and another one on the way. In recessions everyone knows a 'Dave'.

I didn't have children during the credit crunch but I'd turned thirty and had a wife and mortgage. This was the point where I was supposed to 'get on'. I was earning reasonably well through comedy but the circuit is an empire built on sand – a few permanent venues surrounded by hundreds of transient pop-up comedy clubs. Like all self-employed people, my optimism could swing wildly to pessimism. My head was permanently like the floor of a stock exchange. Rumours of a well-paid corporate gig could have my blue-coated traders bullishly talking the whole game up. Equally, one venue in Weston-super-Mare pulling a weekend's work could trigger the bears, making me think my dad was right and I should go back to teaching. I always nursed this concern but the credit crunch caused the economic-risk node in my brain to flash up like an oil light on a dashboard. I started to become obsessed with the recession, constantly updating market data on the BBC news in the same way I'd one day look at 'curves' during the coronavirus.

Like everyone, I was becoming aware of new words, like 'sub-prime'. One curious side-effect of any global clusterfuck is the acquisition of a whole new glossary of terms. The disputed presidential election of 2002 gave us 'dimpled chads'. The war on terror produced 'extraordinary rendition', while Brexit would give us 'backstops' and coronavirus would have us all talking about 'flattening the curve'. It's incredible how quickly we seem well versed in new ideas, these curious little phrases which suddenly emerge. Without much more than thumbnail knowledge you'll quickly find groups – mainly blokes – duking it out online over their understanding of such things.

'YOU IDIOT, THEY SHOULD BE DEPLOYING KEYNSIAN ECONOMICS.'

'THERE'S NO SUCH THING AS HERD IMMUNITY.'

'WE *HAD* SOVEREIGNTY, YOU DICK!'

In these arguments, the combatants rarely know a great deal about the subject in hand and yet the crisis gives them a new way to feel superior to others, a brand new conker to play with. A conker that, no matter how many times it gets battered, remains, in their eyes, pristine and unconquerable. A concrete conker, undefeated in perpetuity, the kind Thanos would've played with at school.

Now, I was no stranger to partially informed polemic but it was always underscored by the knowledge I didn't have any *actual* knowledge. Like anyone, I had a set of hunches and was on the lookout for things which dropped into my slot and allowed to me to parade those hunches as conviction. So, Geoff Norcott's reading of the global financial crash of 2007–8 was this: every country suffered but the fact Britain went into it with a deficit accrued during the good years meant we were hit harder than most. The right-wing press hadn't manipulated me into thinking that Labour had actually caused the financial crash, just that they were at the wheel when the coach ran out of gas and had ignored several service stations.

In a way, it was all a bit rough on Gordon Brown. He'd waited so long to be prime minister but within just over a year he had to navigate his way through a financial shitstorm. If Blair inherited a strong, young economic squad, Gordon had taken over a team where every player had developed arthritis. I didn't doubt that when things got truly dicey Gordon Brown did eventually 'save the global economy' but that didn't change the fact he'd been flashing the credit card during the run-in. Gordon's problem was that his heroism wasn't the stopping-a-speeding-bullet kind. The bailouts he helped orchestrate were incredibly complex and, frankly, boring. His success was like almost everything he did well: complicated, well-intentioned but hard to unpack. He was a hero, but if he'd been a Marvel Avenger I doubt there'd have been much appetite for 'Global Bailout Man'.

It also felt like the Labour government employed far too many people. When you looked through the job vacancies pages, so many seemed to be in the public sector. Not only that, a lot of them seemed to be new job titles, which, at the time, might've sounded frivolous outside the liberal bubble, such as 'diversity officer' and 'director of life enrichment'. Cynically viewed, such high levels of state employment were an effort to ferment a patrician-style loyalty from the nation. You'd be cautious to vote out the people who'd created a cushy public sector job for you. Tax credits also felt like performative state intervention where you have to pay the government before they give you anything back: like a parent holding back the pocket money until you've paid them rent.

It's since been argued that it's natural for Western democracies to run deficits in the good times but it felt like Labour had been playing the same game as much of the population had with their houses. Between 1997 and 2007, the ONS found that Britain had the second largest increase in public spending out of 28 major industrial nations. Their additional borrowing against the idea of perpetual growth was every bit as deluded as the people borrowing beyond the value of their own home. It didn't help that Labour had shown so much hubris about it. Who in their right mind proudly declares time and time again that they've 'ended the era of boom and bust'? Like finally getting a baby off to sleep, then proclaiming the 'end of sleepless nights'.

The populist narrative around the financial crisis was that it was all the bankers' fault. Indeed 'banker' became a byword for 'evil bastard'. I noticed at comedy clubs that stand-ups were routinely deploying that word as a placeholder where a joke should've been. The word operated in the space once occupied by 'Tories' or 'estate agents'. The lack of a clear-cut baddie had been a problem for political stand-ups throughout the noughties. They had a pop at Blair but going at the Labour Party ran the risk of indirectly identifying them as Tories, so the bankers were an excellent substitute.

I found the reaction to those jokes odd. Stand-up is

often said to be at its best when it's 'punching up', taking the difficult shot at the people in charge, a daring sortie on the powerful. Having a go at bankers felt comedically risk-free. Who was going to angrily respond, 'Now hang on, mate, that's a bit below the belt. Some of my best friends are hedge fund managers'?

When the alternative scene had climbed into Margaret Thatcher they were doing something new in British comedy. Hitting the bankers, however, felt like the satirical version of air guitar.

In the absence of big ideas to rub up against, stand-ups in the noughties had sometimes gone for religion. Despite Britain having a largely temperate version of Christianity, many comics tried to portray it like the hardline bible-belt of the US. When a comic's routine portrayed British Christians like the demented nutters of the American Westboro Baptist Church it became hard to square. The vast majority of people I'd met at church liked free biscuits and something to do on a Sunday morning.

The narrative around bankers also prompted one of my first stirrings of contrarian thought. Sure, there were reckless bankers but there were reckless people too. On news report after news report, I saw 'stricken' couples telling their hard-luck stories. The reporter would nod sympathetically while they told how mortgage brokers 'allowed' them to forge their income in order to get a deal. It felt like a drug user putting full blame on the pusher, but things are never that simple.

To me, the credit crunch represented a three-way failure: failure of the state for excessive deregulation; failure in the banking sector which acted recklessly and failure at an individual level, with people leveraging themselves way beyond the realms of logic. As I struggled to make the payments on my own house, a 125 per cent mortgage felt like the kind of offer which should set the alarm bells ringing. Like seeing an advert for 'entertaining poetry'.

Despite initial fears, my own financial circumstances began to buck the trend and even improve. My biggest overheads at the time were my mortgage and petrol bill, the two things whose values plummeted quickest in the first phase of the crisis. I stayed busy and my outgoings were slashed, which is why it really was my favourite financial crisis of all time.

As the crisis wore on, the more the press raised the level of hyperbole, the more I instinctively felt it wouldn't be quite as bad as their most dystopian prophecies. The press gets let off very lightly for their worst predictions in a crisis. Yet they claim credit every time they turn out to be proved correct, despite the law of averages. If your entire business model is based on suggesting everything will go tits up, you'll end up being right at some point.

The press in a crisis often sound like my mum's notorious catastrophising. 'You'll fall off that and break your head . . .' 'You'll slip . . .' 'If you don't do stretches, one day you'll have problems with your knees . . .'

OK, so she was right about the last one, but on

the whole Mum just played the law of averages; if she predicted enough exceptions she could eventually make one of them the rule. Smokers will often use a reverse of that logic to validate their own habit. 'You know old Edith? Smoked 40 a day well into her nineties.'

Well, for every Edith there a lot more Jans.

Another reason why my mind eventually drifted from the global financial crisis was that, in late 2008, my mum, Jan, was diagnosed with incurable lung cancer.

I don't want to get too maudlin about it because this is not that sort of book and I'm not that sort of person. Indeed, one of the negatives of having a conservative character is an inability to accept or seek pity. I respond to pity as a challenge to my beloved idea of personal responsibility and the almost infinite hope that you can always turn things around by working a bit harder. Unfortunately, cancer doesn't care how often you pull your socks up or 'get back on your bike'.

Gritty matriarchs like Mum are excellent at throwing you off the scent when it comes to just how bad their illness has got. Mum did it by carrying on as normal. She also did it through humour. People often keep their sense of humour during illness but Mum upped her game considerably. Among many moments of gallows humour, she'd sometimes discuss chemo like she was going to to the pub: 'Just a quick half for me today, love, I'm driving.'

Looking back at the photos of her during this time, it's clear how ill she was but she always put on a good show and we always left her company convinced she was looking 'surprisingly well'. Charisma is a remarkable thing. Too remarkable in my mum's case because when she entered palliative care the family struggled to accept we'd reached her endgame. This powerhouse of a woman, who was still trundling into Mitcham town centre on her mobility scooter and shouting the odds at policemen for driving too fast, was suddenly being placed in end-of-life care.

When I went to visit Mum on her final admission to hospital, she could see her daft son was struggling to grasp what was going to happen next, so she asked a consultant to sit down and be blunt with me.

'Don't mince your words, mate, this one's like a tit in a trance.'

After he finished telling me Mum was going to die soon, I looked at her and she gave the most incredible, phlegmatic shrug, as if to say, 'Well, that's that then.' This woman who'd had a hard early life, who'd stayed in a difficult marriage for 14 years, who'd become wheelchair bound, who should've been around to reap the harvest of grandchildren, had been dealt yet another shitty card.

In the last four days of her life, my sister and I and our partners were with her more or less continually. She carried on making us laugh. When a local south London gospel choir came around the ward singing 'Amazing Grace' she shouted 'Not yet!', as if they were undertakers who'd arrived too early.

On the Friday night she had all of us by her bedside.

I can still see her now, propped up in bed, enjoying the audience, holding court. As my sister and I went to steal a few hours' sleep at the nearby family home she called us back one last time.

She did what had once been her trademark mime, which neither my sister nor I had seen her do since we were children. First she threaded an imaginary needle. Then she pierced a pretend hole in her top lip and mock winced as she inserted a few imaginary stitches. Then she stopped and looked around, like something important was about to happen. However, all she did was pull the imaginary thread and raise her lip up and down in time, like the thread really was connected.

We laughed.

Thinking about the pain she was in and the medication she was on, her mime was pulled off with astonishing clarity, a reminder when I'm tired and waiting to do a tour show that I should belt up and stop whining.

I sometimes doubt that recollection (time adds selective edits to those kind of memories) but that really was the last thing I saw her do. She'd taken humour back to its most basic and important function. A smile in the face of danger. A left turn before oblivion. Something unexpected.

Mum passed away on the evening of 4 July 2009. That year had been an awful one weather-wise, but it was a glorious day. Twenty-seven degrees with a light breeze. As is always the case, it's very hard to get your head around something terrible which happens on a beautiful day.

9

BEHIND ENEMY LINES

'So, Grandad Geoff. What was the most danger you've ever been in? Was it gigging to stags and hens in Newcastle?'

'No, though that was terrifying.'

'Your first appearance on *Question Time*?'

'Not quite, though I was cacking my pants.'

'Then what was it?'

'Well, my boy, it has to be the time I was doing a show in a warzone in Afghanistan and we were on the verge of causing a global diplomatic incident.'

'Did they not like your jokes, Grandad Geoff?'

In early 2010, having been thrown back to an almost childlike state by my mother's death, I was a nervous hypochondriac on the verge of digging out my childhood comfort blanket. I needed to get a bit of pride back. So I started doing gigs for the British Armed Forces. I had little understanding of military terms like 'regiments' and 'ranks' and so enjoyed a new challenge and discovering this world within a world. I was fascinated by army people.

At that time, the reputation of the British army in comedic circles wasn't good. Post-Iraq, some of my stand-up colleagues would describe the forces in deeply cynical terms. In one green room, a comic described them as 'baby murderers'. No one else said anything but I bridled at the idea. The simplicity of reducing people into simple goodies and baddies was too seductive for some. Instinctively, I didn't believe soldiers were murderous psychopaths any more than I believed Tories were malicious Bond villains.

The military personnel I met were a different breed but in a good way. I reckon I could still pick out a person who's done active service from a line-up of civvies. There will always be something a bit different behind the eyes when you've spent a good chunk of your adult life being told off by other adults.

The crew for the gigs often comprised a band (usually excellent, with a strong repertoire of covers) and professional dancers (who'd do anything from West End shows to well-paid PR work and gigs for the forces). We did a Royal Navy gig out in Jakarta and were chatting in the mess when one of the lads got the hairdryer treatment from an officer who charged angrily into the room. The officer was a barrel-chested guy with bright ginger hair and a beard. Not only that, he was wearing skimpy white shorts. How can you keep a straight face when an extra from *Popeye* is acting like your dad?

The guy even used parental language. 'You know what it is, Martin? It's selfishness, that's what it is.'

I half-expected a female officer to run in shouting, 'Let him be a child, Ken, for God's sake!'

As I worked my way around the army gigs, both at home and abroad, I became aware comics were doing shows in Afghanistan. Emma didn't like the idea but I was curious about going. When eventually asked, I signed up quickly and explained to her that Camp Bastion was statistically safer than Leeds. She countered that, in that case, she didn't want me gigging in Leeds either.

When the departure day came, I drove to RAF Brize Norton in a strange state of mind. The preparation for going away had the feel of a holiday. I felt like I'd be sitting by the pool but in reality would be shitting in a bag. The plane taking off was an odd feeling. If you've ever done something which involved going beyond a point of no return – the safety bar coming down on a rollercoaster; exchanging contracts on a house you can't afford; saying 'I do' – this was an exaggerated, physical version. I had no idea how that moment felt for actual soldiers heading out to do foot patrol in Helmand Province, given my main jeopardy was usually whether or not my knob gags would land.

Our flight landed and I disembarked into a heady mix of truly foreign sights and smells: the dusty humidity of the Kandahar night air, the heavy diesel of the military vehicles and curious sight of American infantry in their large fatigues, which looked like sleeping bags for giant toddlers. The first night's sleep, in one of the 'upmarket' living quarters (a customised portacabin, which looked like a prison for serial killers), was bad. I didn't sleep well but, as is often the case, ending a failed night's sleep sometimes brings with it a certain relief. Not being bombed in my bed also felt like a win. I had a walkabout and discovered that the base wasn't without its creature comforts. They had a genuinely pleasant coffee shop, a KFC and, weirdest of all, a steakhouse you had to book. I don't know why that was such an odd detail but 'booking ahead' seemed far too fancy for a warzone, like wearing a tie to the football.

Of all the places we gigged on that first tour, Kabul was the most intriguing. It was the only time when we were 'outside of the wire', which sounds like a Netflix spin-off but simply meant we were beyond the perimeter of a main base. Having said that, we weren't outside it for long. The 'outside the wire' element was a short one-kilometre convoy ride from Kabul airport to Camp Souter.

We arrived at night, which made the whole thing seem even more ominous. Not to all of us, mind; many of the dancers had been several times before, to the point where one of the girls took the short, slow ride through enemy badlands as an opportunity for a post-flight nap.

It was 1am. The long road, a bustling market street by day, was completely empty. All you could see was the white light of the trucks magnified and redirected by the asphalt stones beneath. We were all completely silent, save for the sound of a snoring dancer. No more than 200 yards from the entrance to the camp a small boy on a bicycle appeared as if from nowhere. It was nothing but we all shat ourselves. Most of us shat ourselves. In fact, I've never checked exactly who shat themselves but I may have let out more than just a noise.

The next morning, I was astonished to find I could have a coffee right at the top of the main camp building in full view of the surrounding houses and wider conurbation. I asked how this was possible and the garrison sergeant major explained exactly how they had built up a high level of trust within the local community in Kabul They did all the things wider British culture imagines itself capable of. For them, 'Keep calm and carry on' was more than a cliché on the front of a cushion.

We headed on to a base at Lashkar Gah. It was more impressive than the other bases, which earned it the nickname 'Lash Vegas' (though for reference, in military terms everything is relative. 'Luxury' can just mean that the bags you shit in come with a wet-wipe).

Like Camp Souter in Kabul, 'Lash' was in the heart of the city. Relations with the locals had been good but in light of a Koran-burning incident at Bagram air base the need to be careful around religious sensitivities was impressed upon us on arrival. It was a functional necessity they needn't have bothered with in my case. I got it, in the same way I didn't do my 'Cromwell, what a guy' routine when gigging in Dublin.

The show started OK but the atmosphere was a bit muted as we'd begun at 5pm to a crowd who weren't drinking (my industry's reliance on alcohol comes closely behind kebabs and morning after pills). I was hosting, which was a big responsibility, but also meant I could chat with the punters and try and drum up a bit of camaraderie.

The dancing girls went down well (they always did) but I had to issue the audience a reminder to applaud and cheer as they performed. One of the challenges with an audience of young, sober males who hadn't seen a woman in a sexy outfit or make-up for some time is that they tend to go pretty quiet when they do see a glamorous girl. I had to break it to them: 'Lads, if you're worried about seeming pervy, you do realise it's much worse to stare in total silence?'

In the second half, the singer went out to do a half-hour set. The gig was particularly tough going on this occasion and became even more so when the guitarist had to re-tune his guitar mid-set. It coincided with the call to prayer. That unique, exotic sound of the muezzin's voice started to drift over the base. The singer, unsure what to do, started strumming along with it gently.

It could've felt awkward but somehow didn't – a unique and welcome cultural collision I and a hundred-strong crowd of soldiers silently took in.

Then, out of nowhere, the singer said in his broad Australian accent, 'Right, shut up mate, I'm ready to play "Wonderwall".'

There was a brief laugh followed by astonishment. In comedy, it's become very easy to be drawn into debates about the power of words but here they really were dangerous – they had potential to do actual harm, and not just to feelings.

I was standing, dumbfounded by the side of the stage. I realised that, as host, and wearing the symbol of the Ents group who ran the show, I was the most visible person involved with the performance. I was quickly surrounded by a group of interpreters – all locals working on the base. They were irate. The stakes felt high. This wasn't like someone accosting you after a weekend Jongleurs gig for taking the piss out of their shirt as they staggered to the toilet.

I tried my best to make conciliatory gestures but they were talking all at once and the anger seemed to be snowballing and threatening to erupt. The singer on stage was becoming vaguely aware of a disturbance in the edge of his vision, so the music became disjointed and out of key, which added to the sense of disarray. Luckily, one of the higher-ranking officers present noticed and came to mediate. I don't want to be a 'boot licker' but there is something reassuring about a posh bloke in a crisis. He also spoke a bit of Pashtun, a reminder that the posh lads didn't spend all their time at Sandhurst eating veal and thinking about their inheritance. First, he offered for me to go onstage and make a formal and unreserved apology on behalf of the entertainment team, which began the process of mollifying the interpreters. He then asked me if I'd consider avoiding profanity for the rest of the show. I said yes. It left me with only four minutes of useable material but I was willing to take one for the team.

I then offered, 'And we were due to have the dancing girls back on after the interval but we can cancel that too.'

There was a brief pause as the most senior interpreter smiled and relayed my apparently indecipherable south Londonese to the other 'terps'. The senior interpreter gave his answer to the officer who laughed. They all went back to their seats.

'What did he say about the dancing girls not going back on?' I asked.

'He said, "Let's not overreact."'

Camp Bastion felt like the safest place we'd been during the whole tour. In the middle of the desert with excellent sight-lines all around, it had earned its name. We did three shows there. The set was quite a sight. Made up of freight containers, camo awning and a primitive lighting rig, it was a fitting setting for guerrilla comedy.

On the third night, all of the cast and crew were encouraged to crowd surf. I'd never done it before so backed away at the first time of asking. One of the roadies rebuked me, 'When else will you get a chance to crowd-surf in a warzone?'

It was a fair shout. Up until this point in my life, crowd surfing opportunities had admittedly been at a premium. I've had gigs go well but a tour show at a corn exchange rarely ends with the punters passing you over their heads to the foyer. So I ran and jumped. It remains one of the best moments of my life and the most ironic. There I was being passed around like a hero by people who did actual hero stuff.

When I got back to RAF Brize Norton after two weeks and an epic three-leg, 22-hour flight, I felt different. Not only had I rediscovered a bit of pride, I'd also had corroboration for my suspicion that the army weren't just a bunch of thugs gleefully attacking the Middle East. I'd heard soldiers called baby killers but in reality I'd seen them clearing towns of landmines so a school could re-open. I'm not saying they were all saints but, once again, ideas that were common in my line of work were easily disproved by real life. I often found myself more at home among soldiers than I did with teachers or even comedians. This was unusual. For a long time, the only comics who expressed an affinity with the army also expressed an affinity with golf and racism.

It seemed that everywhere I looked, my political and cultural instincts were being turned on their head. A head which, for a variety of reasons, I seemed to have permanently up, on the lookout for new things.

*

I'd had that same open mind a year earlier in 2010 walking across Waterloo Bridge on my way to the South Bank for a gig. That walk over the water is often a bit fresher than the prevailing London air and there was every reason to take in the bright spring day around me.

Some movement below the bridge caught my attention. As I leaned over and looked down, I saw a cabal of journalists and photographers moving like a singular animal both stalking its prey and in fear of being eaten. In the middle was David Cameron, striding confidently. I know politics is supposed to be rational and philosophical but straight away I liked the cut of his jib. (Even using a phrase like 'cut of his jib' should've been a clue I was already leaning to the right.)

Cameron was tall, which is never a bad thing in the leader of a party, but he also seemed to be walking like he knew where he was going. It must be awful for the great political thinkers to know people like me can be swayed in this way and I'm not saying David Cameron's easy glide along the South Bank was the only thing that turned me, but it didn't do any harm.

Maybe it's an overhang of leadership criteria from simpler times: 'Elect the big bloke.'

I was aware that an election was looming in May. I already knew there was no way I was voting Labour. Gordon Brown looked particularly exhausted, which isn't saying much as he generally looked like a person who'd lived his entire life in the midst of a sleep-deprivation experiment.

My brief flirtation with the Lib Dems had ended. The likeable Charles Kennedy had quit because of his drinking problem. Ming Campbell did a caretaker-manager role before Nick Clegg got the job fulltime. With both Labour and the Tories already talking about the need to reduce the deficit, the Lib Dems were running on an anti-austerity line, which seemed less like a policy and more like 'Where can we fit in?' I never really considered myself a Liberal Democrat, it was just a phase on a political journey, a rebound party. Everyone needs to experiment, don't they? I never really inhaled Lib Dem and they knew it.

The mid-to-late noughties had been distinctly anti-politics. Throughout my life, I'd heard the phrase 'They're all the same' about politicians. However, one scandal broke on 8 May 2009 which suggested that might be true. I remember first reading the headline 'MPs' expenses scandal'. It seemed like the least surprising thing in the world. I, like most people, presumed this would be a procession of dodgy Tories who'd been on the take. As the *Telegraph* exhaustively published the details day after day, a depressing picture emerged.

It wasn't that the Tories hadn't taken any liberties (you kind of expected Lord Hinchley of Toryton would've used public money to resurface his wife). The shock was that Labour had also got their beaks wet. Numerous cabinet and backbencher resignations followed, high-profile figures like Geoff Hoon and Hazel Blears. It's a dangerous move in business, politics or entertainment to go against your brand. The Labour Party had historically elevated themselves to a moral pedestal as the 'caring ones' and here they were holding forged receipts while their husbands masturbated with the aid of public money. All five MPs eventually jailed over the expenses scandal were Labour.

Under the cloud of the financial crisis, this story couldn't have broken at a worse time. As the general public were bracing themselves for the chill winds of austerity to blow in, it transpired that there was a difference between the two main parties after all. In this instance, Labour had been worse. I'd been pulling at the thread for a while, but this story was a jarring final challenge to the presumption that the Tories were alone in venality and greed.

Meanwhile, as the election campaign developed, it wasn't just public money Labour were developing a cynical attitude to, the notorious exchange between Gordon Brown and Gillian Duffy suggested they weren't that fond of the general public itself. As Brown had been on a walkabout in Rochdale (presumably to let the public feel his rockstar charisma up close) Mrs Duffy had asked him about a number of issues, including uncontrolled migration from Eastern Europe. Brown had flashed his trademark rictus grin, got in his car and was then caught on a 'hot mic' calling her 'some bigoted woman' who 'used to be Labour'. Calling a woman you've never met before 'bigoted' for asking one reasonable question about immigration, which had spiked dramatically since the mid-noughties, turned out to be a big mistake.

However, as I watched this infamous moment play out on the news, I wasn't just seeing the ambassador for the political class display lazy contempt for the white working class, I was seeing myself. I'd had a similar exchange with my own mother just a few years earlier.

After I left Mitcham, it had become the default area for Merton council to house asylum seekers and refugees from Rwanda and Sierra Leone. As the older, post-war generation of Mitcham had died off in a short time-frame, the town changed rapidly and council properties became available. The London Borough of Merton was never going to direct immigrants to the favoured first-born area of Wimbledon, so Mitcham took most of the new arrivals.

Many people who had lived in Mitcham for a long time felt unsafe and linked the new arrivals to a rise in criminal activity. You can debate the veracity of the link but when things change rapidly the very least you can do is listen to people's concerns. I didn't.

Mum volunteered at a charity shop in Mitcham town centre and complained that Eastern European women would enter the shop in groups and steal. I instinctively rejected the idea. I had no facts to face her down with but her claims represented an inconvenient challenge to the uncomplicated idea of multiculturalism I harboured back then. It was easier to intimate my own mother was lying.

Mum didn't help matters by coming up with a pejorative phrase for the women she thought were stealing, and I'm still unsure whether it was racist or not.

'Those bloody *long-skirts* come in here . . .'

'Mum, you can't call them that.'

'Why not? I came up with that because they all wear long skirts, to hide the clothes under. You tell me how that's racist.'

I couldn't specifically but it didn't feel *not* racist either.

Believe it or not, I trotted out the clichéd, liberal-left platitude that immigration made London 'brilliantly diverse' and she should actually be pleased at how 'vibrant' the area had become.

She gave that characteristic short shrift. 'Great, there's different kinds of food.'

Mum kept repeating the same line, which I and people like Gordon Brown would've done well to listen to: 'It's not change I don't like, it's the pace of change.'

If Gordon and I had listened, who knows how different the next decade could've been?

By the time the PM was casually dismissing the exact people Labour should've been representing Mum had already passed away but in his exchange with Gillian Duffy, I saw a hint of how Brown might have spoken to her if she was still around. I got the sense people like Gordon Brown would not like people like my mum. Maybe it was emotional and sentimental but it was keenly felt and I wasn't alone.

So frustrations over stealth taxes, questions over the Left's relationship with the working classes, concerns about the national debt and a weird subconscious duty to my dead mother had put me in the ideal place to break the seal and vote Tory for the first time in the 2010 election.

I'd love to tell you the first time I voted Conservative was a dramatic moment, once again in the sacred privacy of that polling booth, but it wasn't. We would be on holiday in Egypt on polling day so I voted postally. Nevertheless, there was something very odd about putting the cross by a Tory candidate for the very first time. I didn't feel the visceral pull of my ancestors, like someone in the Labour heartlands drowning out the sound of dead miners, it just *looked* odd to see it on the page – like I'd spelled my own name incorrectly. This was something my parents, my teachers, colleagues and most people from a similar background had told me was taboo.

I sealed the envelope and popped it into a post box. It's easy to forget now but the Tory brand wasn't quite so toxic back then. Yes, they'd always be associated with Thatcher but Labour were exhausted and mired in Iraq and expenses. If there was a nasty party at the time, Labour could easily be seen as the one who'd illegally invaded another country and paid off their second homes with public money.

The Tories looked posh – don't they always? – but Labour had also received flack for packing north-London intellectuals into safe northern seats. As much as the Miliband brothers achieved in politics, it's worth remembering they both started life being parachuted into northern constituencies Labour felt certain they could win, Ed in South Shields and David in Doncaster North. I don't know about you, but when I look at the Miliband brothers there's very little about them that screams out 'Doncaster'. They gave the impression of the kind of people who'd only spend any time in the town if their train to the Edinburgh Festival was delayed. And even then, they'd mosey a few hundred yards outside of the station before hurriedly returning to the familiarity of the concourse Upper Crust.

It must have been an odd experience doing constituency surgeries, needing a local phrasebook on hand to work out whether the old dears coming along were in rent arrears or needed a new boiler. Then finding out that the usual range of coffees wasn't available and the local word for 'latte' was still 'milky coffee'. This was an era when the England football and cricket teams had foreign managers, so the idea of going for the 'best talent' wasn't entirely unfamiliar, but nevertheless, it did feel like the left-wing equivalent of jobs for the boys. It was at the very least complacent but worse still suggested that the Labour Party were struggling to find local northern people who wanted to represent them. As the current complexion of the parliamentary Labour Party is still painfully lacking in working-class voices, it's worth remembering that it all started under New

Labour, with well-meaning PPE graduates jumping out of planes all over the north like a Fabian parachute regiment.

As the 2010 campaign hit the home straight it seemed like Cameron was faltering at the finish line. He was uncharacteristically timid in the live debates.

'Come on, Dave,' I thought. 'You're over six foot!' Where was the *brio* I noticed that day on the South Bank? Maybe it would've been better if he could do all live debates on the move, striding purposefully like Simon Cowell at the beginning of *Britain's Got Talent*.

I followed the election and subsequent fallout from a hotel room in Egypt. There's something odd about British men on holiday; we never follow the news more closely than when overseas. Furthermore, a lot of us can't relax abroad until we find a reliable vendor of British newspapers. If we aren't kept in touch with the ups and downs of our gossipy little island there's a very real danger we might relax and enjoy ourselves.

I wasn't surprised when the Tories failed to win a full majority. I knew from personal experience that the move from left to right was a complicated one and many would've blinked at the final minute or when they heard big Dave say words with long vowel sounds. Still, I was pleased Labour weren't the largest party any more. ('See, Gordon, that's what happens when you call my mum a bigot . . . or someone who reminds me of my mum . . . you know what I mean.')

Despite having the second highest number of seats, Labour exercised their constitutional right and tried to broker a 'rainbow coalition'. It seemed desperate and surreal. It would've involved Gordon Brown getting every single opposition seat onside and all for a working majority of one. It was never going to work and felt futile, like the UK trying to curry favour at Eurovision.

The Tories had their chat with the Lib Dems and things moved pretty quickly from there. In some ways, I was relieved it would be a coalition. This being my first dalliance with the right, I didn't mind a dash of bland centrism.

My dad, usually so prudent with money, said sod it to the cost and phoned me in Egypt to talk about the unfolding political drama. He was animated about what was happening but extremely pessimistic about the Tories being in power.

'How did you vote, son?' he asked at the end of another rant about Eton bastards.

Oddly, I hadn't anticipated him asking me this. Looking around for a get-out, I told one of those diversionary lies that wasn't exactly a lie: 'Dad . . . I'm abroad.'

Luckily his faith in my general uselessness deterred him from thinking I'd have had the wherewithal to set up a postal vote.

'Right, well, it's good your mother isn't around. You know what she was like about not voting. She'd have had your guts for garters.'

He was right, she would. But it wouldn't be for not voting, it would be for what I'd done with my vote. As for my dad, 'coming out' was something I'd have to leave for another day. He'd rather think of his son as disorganised than one of these 'bloody Tories'.

After travelling the world doing gigs for the Armed Forces, I got the sense I'd fallen into a creative rut. The army gigs were great but, like the weekend stag and hen circuit, they weren't the greatest environment for taking risks. I had something else to say, though I didn't quite know what it was yet.

Things changed in early 2013 after a conversation with Emma. It was a Sunday morning and I was feeling bruised by yet another rowdy set of weekend gigs where I'd jettisoned the new stuff just to keep control of a lairy room full of inflatable penises and a stag do who'd hired an actual dwarf dressed as a Smurf for the day.

Being grizzled noughties stand-ups, that night we had ignored the ethics of the venture and had become desperate to find out what money the Smurf was on. One of the more brazen performers on the bill exited the green room, bought the guy a beer and straight out asked him. He came back to the green room to relay his findings.

'£250,' he said triumphantly.

Most of us pissed ourselves laughing at the modest sum versus the labour and degradation (however woke comics may *seem*, *no one* is nice in a green room). That is, until one of the more experienced comics calmly pointed out, 'You're about to do 20 minutes of knob gags at Jongleurs Portsmouth.'

It was a fair shout; in this situation it wasn't entirely clear who was the most desperate.

So, among the indentured dwarfs and sea of inflatable penises, I was a bit jaded with the circuit and wondering aloud with my wife about what else I could talk about. Annoyingly, Emma has a habit of being right about everything.

'Geoff,' she said, 'you voted Tory at the last election. That's a bit weird for a comic, isn't it? They're all lefties aren't they? Talk about that.'

She was right. It was novel but more importantly it was *funny* and could be interesting. Comedy was always supposed to 'punch up' but equally it was supposed to provide misdirections. What could be more of a left turn than an alternative comic who voted Conservative and admitted it? It's statistically likely but unexpected, like seeing a vicar smoking. But the context for me 'coming out' would need to be the right one. I couldn't just blurt it out in the middle of a club gig in Leeds.

I had an hour's new material gig booked in for the Leicester Comedy Festival in February. Overall, the show was about admitting I'd sold out in the past; done things for the money rather than because I believed in them (it was called *Geoff Norcott Occasionally Sells Out*, which was both a creative admission and an accurate reflection of my ability to sell tickets).

When it came to compromising my principles in this way, one particular gig stood out. I was doing a few shows for the Butlin 'adult weekenders'. Given my background, if I wasn't doing comedy I might well have been there socially. The snootier alternative comics might scoff at these kind of shows but I never had a problem with Butlins gigs because they give you an idea of what regular people laugh at. However – and this is a big however – some of those Butlins shows could get properly out of hand. I did one in Skegness which still gives me shivers. I donned a shiny silver suit for the gig, the kind worn by old mainstream performers back in the day, believing that visibility in a big room full of drunk people would be an advantage. The theory was OK but in reality I just looked like a shiny-suited prick.

The room was one of the big, wide venues favoured by mainstream performers in days gone by. We had a thousand people in which meant that the gig was so big that the character of the crowd at the front was very different from the one at the back of the room. At the front there were mainly women and the back was comprised of blokes who'd rolled out of bed and were starting their day with a bacon roll and a Jagerbomb. It created a highly distracted atmosphere.

About 15 minutes in, one woman from a group of about 25 older ladies from Sunderland put her hand up. 'Excuse me,' she said, 'You remind me of my son-in-law.'

I replied, 'Why, do I look like him?'

She said, 'No, he's not funny either.'

Against a wall of contempt and indifference, I somehow got close to my contractually obliged 30 minutes. I can't describe how it feels to have worn something you hated to get approval but still died on your arse. I'm all for bending over and taking one for the team if I get carried out shoulder high. When you drop your drawers and there are no takers, the shame is intense. It's like wearing smart clothes to try and get upgraded on a flight but then having to be the only bell-end in economy wearing a blazer.

Ever the contrarian, I decided to stick around. All Butlins sites have a covered boulevard which houses food, bars and events and amplifies heat and noise. I became aware of cheering and a good time being had over in the corner (everything my gig wasn't). When I got there, I saw a crowd of about 300 people with a huge skipping rope being held at each end. In the middle was a ginger bloke, stark bollock naked and skipping with gay abandon. What made his confidence even more impressive was that he possessed one of the tiniest cocks I – or I presume anyone in the assembled throng – had ever witnessed. It sounds odd, but we all found something uplifting about this bloke owning his physical limitations in this way. It was liberating; here he was being himself, oblivious to any criticism. He was defiant and stark bollock naked, while I was wearing a shiny suit – a needy peacock with shit feathers.

I knew there and then I had to make some changes. Once I'd had my chat with Emma, I knew it would mean swimming against the tide and I'd cop some flak, but that sort of appealed to me – I hate being told what to do, a trait I'd inherited from my dad. Though he was probably worse, in fairness.

In the early nineties, during his redundancy, I came back from school to my house in Mitcham. I clocked my dad painting the nearby fire station. This was odd for two reasons. One, my dad was not a painter by trade (not the most obvious choice for a bloke with one arm). Two, he lived a few miles away in Wimbledon and had no reason to be here. I walked over and he was surprised to see me.

'What you doing, Dad?'

He looked at the wall he was painting and appeared to be forming a blag in his head. At that moment a bloke turned up with a lanyard and a high-vis jacket and said, 'OK, Norcott, you're done for the day.'

It turned out my dad had been in the process of doing 40 hours' community service. How it happened is what makes the story another Norcott family heirloom.

After being made redundant, he was doing a bit of minicabbing just to make a few quid. A couple of young coppers pulled him over and took great joy in asking him why he wasn't wearing his seatbelt. This was the early nineties and there were still a lot of men who didn't even think the state should be able to insist on such things, let alone take such great joy in patronising him about it. Dad just about bit his lip and they drove on. But, still smarting from being told off, Dad noticed that they were not wearing their seatbelts either.

So what would any normal person do in that situation?

That's right, he sped off after them and pulled *them* over.

As he was taking great pleasure reciting their own words back to them, 'simply reminding them of the Highway Code', the copper in the passenger seat clocked the aerial on top of Dad's Ford Granada.

'You doing a bit of minicabbing, mate?'

'Yes.'

'You declaring that revenue?'

Dad tried to wrap things up quickly by just giving them a 'verbal warning on this occasion'. But by then it was already too late.

My 'coming out' Leicester show came around fast. I had managed to pull a crowd of about 35 people and for the first time in a long time was going to try something a bit different. OK, it wasn't a huge crowd, but decent enough for a work-in-progress show. The audience had no idea that I was going to 'do' politics. You have to supply your blurb long before the festival itself, so everything I'd sent in had been pretty generic.

I'd become pretty comfortable as a circuit headliner and had forgotten what it felt like to turn up for a show feeling nervous. At club gigs, I'd often be sitting on my phone or talking to the other acts right up until I sauntered on stage. But that night felt different. I hadn't felt proper nerves for so long that I arrived at the venue not really knowing what was up. I felt a bit dizzy. I couldn't talk to the promoter because I was frantically scanning the punters, trying to work out what their political persuasion was. They were mainly middle-aged (good). But a few of them had beanie hats (very bad). Emma had come with me (as it was her idea, I thought the least she could do was watch it succeed or go down in flames). I also saw the main reviewer from industry website Chortle, well known for being fairly left-wing.

On stage, the stuff about not wanting to sell out went OK but I was distracted. I had something I wanted to say but had to get through the other stuff first. Just like a social interaction where that's the case, sometimes it's good to just cut to the chase. . .

I took a deep breath and told my first ever right-wing joke: 'I vote Conservative, but I'm not a Tory. I'm a cunt, but with a small c.'

Now, the right wingers among you may detect a bit of ingratiating with the lefties there. It's true that in those early shows I was way too apologetic when I dealt with my political views but this approach was untried and untested, so I felt I had to tread lightly at first. It might not feel so radical now but then it had been more than 20 years since comedians had openly spoken about voting Conservative and certainly never on the alternative scene.

I continued and talked about the fact I didn't buy that David Cameron was evil, 'He's a well-meaning prat, every stag do has one.'

I had one walk-out from an older left-wing couple who said, 'We didn't come here to be preached at.' Which seemed to give little consideration to any Tory voters who'd been to an alternative comedy night over the years and been blind-sided by the comic calling them evil, heartless bastards.

Overall it went well. I felt liberated – not just because I'd got the tricky bit done but I'd also said something of consequence on stage and there were still people sitting there. The couple walking out actually helped as it gave me the sense of the endeavour being a lot more daring than it really was. I'm not going to equate the experience of admitting being right-wing with 'coming out' as a gay man but I did feel like a load had been lifted. I didn't really know what to do with the experience once it was done. I just went home and carried on gigging. I was prepared to put it down as a one-off, like a weird busman's holiday.

A couple of weeks later, I got an email from the Leicester Festival telling me *Geoff Norcott Occasionally Sells Out* had been nominated for best new show. I'd never come close to this kind of acclaim from the luvvies before. Then a few weeks after that, the head comedy commissioner for Radio 4 wrote an article asking where all the right-wing comics were. She had a good point, maybe that's why what I'd done in Leicester felt so thrilling. The more I thought about it the more, the more I felt that being honest with people about who I was and how I saw the world felt right. Like voting Conservative itself, this wasn't a radical act but somehow seemed so because of the political persuasion of the arts world.

Other acts said, 'You're brave.' (Which may not have actually been a compliment.) Either way, it was a creative risk not a real risk. Maybe gigging for the army had changed my perception of the word 'brave'. Especially when I'd done a show at a forward operating base at 9am. Immediately after which, half the audience had donned their rifles and body armour and congregated at the entrance to go on foot patrol in one of the most hostile areas of Helmand Province. An area I latterly found out was so hostile the whole base was pulled out less than a week later.

My first intention on stage had always been risk-free, to be liked. Yet here I was embarking on an angle which, at the time, seemed like the best way to lose the room. And yet, I'd kept the room onside.

A bigger challenge would be if I could do the same with my dad.

10

ECHO CHAMBERS AND BACON SARNIES

On the day of the 2015 general election, I was once again out of the country. Maybe I'd figured out that being publicly Conservative and in Britain on election night wasn't always the smartest move. Or maybe Emma deliberately took me somewhere where tweeting would cost £6 per megabyte.

The rhetoric leading into this particular election had been much more divisive than in 2010. The liberal bubble had little self-awareness back then. The smack on the backside Brexit would deliver hadn't happened yet, so moral and political certainty ran almost unchecked. In the circles I moved in, it seemed it had been universally decided that no one agreed with austerity and unconvincing head of sixth form Ed Miliband would surely become leader of the world's fifth largest economy.

I wasn't so sure.

Since 2013, I'd been copping flack on a personal level for my support for the Tories in the tight-knit stand-up world. I mainly found myself fighting a lonely and ill-advised battle on social media with my comedy-circuit colleagues. It was mostly civil but some of them still thought I was making the whole thing up, that any expression of Conservative sympathies was me 'building my comedy brand' (though I'm not sure how much brand you build duking it out on a 500-comment-long thread tucked away on your personal Facebook page).

I also started to get accusations of being a 'class traitor', as though your politics was determined by how many Pot Noodles you'd eaten as a child or whether your main family tradition is doing 'Oops Upside Your Head' at weddings.

A presumption during the election campaign had been that all working-class people were opposed to the recent cuts to welfare. That the attack on 'scroungers' would've been deeply offensive to anyone on modest incomes who would then duly launch the nasty Tories from power at the first opportunity. What they ignored was that the welfare cuts, in particular the 'benefits cap', had played out pretty well among working-class people in polling and focus groups. If you came from that background, the stories of people taking liberties with benefits arguably made more sense, as you could think of examples first-hand. When you saw the tabloid front page of 'Janet, 41, 68 kids by 75 fathers' you kind of knew a Janet on your estate. When you saw some feckless bloke on Jeremy

Kyle who wasn't 'stepping up' to his responsibilities, you remembered you'd played football with a guy who had tattoos of all his kids' names, mainly so he could remember them.

The liberal middle classes would often push back on the idea of benefit fraud with the statistic that only 0.7 per cent of benefit fraud was found to be illegally claimed, which would always draw a wry smile if you'd ever actually lived on a council estate. To this, I'd draw a parallel with the police standing proudly next to a haul of seized cocaine with their arms on it, like hunters standing over a lion. It may look impressive but anyone with sense looks at the size of the stash and wonders how much else must've got through. I knew how the system could be worked because I'd been involved in doing it.

While we were living at Pitt Crescent, I did something monumentally stupid which ended up with us working the council for a brand new kitchen. I was 11 and had been left on my own and was watching *Superman II* (message to my son: if you're reading this, please jump ahead 500 words). In the film, a car catches fire as it goes down a hole. Like all young boys, I had an inexplicable fascination with fire so got a lighter and set fire to one of my toy cars. Inside the house.

I watched it burn for a while, but the smoke coming out of the back started to get thicker, so I moved the burning wreck to the kitchen sink (where we working class play out most of our best dramas). My plan was to use the taps to put it out, but the flames were too hot and I couldn't get around the back. I looked up at the ceiling and the dense black smoke was already circling around the Artex paint. I thought about how useful a fire extinguisher would be but we didn't have one. To my left was a can of Glade air freshener. It looked sort of like a fire extinguisher – that is to say, if you pressed it stuff came out – so I grabbed it and discharged it on to the burning car. As you'd expect, the moment I let loose those Mountain Glade CFCs the flames roared back at me. At this point, one of my neighbours stopped by and looked in through the window.

'Jesus Christ, Geoffrey!' said Lynn. 'I'll go get a tea towel.'

She returned and threw me the towel. It was dry. I imagine she expected me to go and wet it in another room but I threw it on the fire and it swelled the flames further still.

Eventually the flames abated just long enough for me to get my arm around the back of the sink and finally put out the blaze using the tap.

At this point the fire service knocked on the door.

'Everything OK, lad?' they asked.

'Absolutely fine,' I replied, smoke now snaking out of the front door above my head, my face blackened like a tiny chimney sweep.

Remembering how well I'd handled the whole thing with the police, I offered my hand for them to shake.

I was petrified as to what Mum would say on her return, but she was less angry than I expected.

'We needed a new kitchen, boy. You go out and play, I just need to do something before I call the council.'

I heard her banging away in there. It's safe to say the fire damage got a lot worse after the fire went out, both with the council and the insurance company. And how those flames in the kitchen melted jewellery in the bedroom I'll never know. I don't judge Mum for that but from an early age I knew there were lots of ways to work the system if you were smart enough.

It wasn't just my crafty mother who gave me a suspicion of the scale of provision of the welfare state, it was some oddities within the system itself.

In the late nineties, when Mum became wheelchair bound, she was accepted on the Motability scheme. Through it, you could either have a couple of hundred quid a month to help you get about or a brand new car, fully insured, MOT'd and serviced. My mum – like a contestant on welfare *Bullseye* – understandably went for the car. It seemed like a pretty good deal and no doubt helped the car industry in the UK to get new vehicles out on the road.

I benefitted from it too. Despite coming from a council house in Mitcham with a disabled mother and a stepdad earning modestly as a removal man, I was able to punch above my weight and drive a brand new motor. Not only had Mum's disablement got me three As at

A-level, it also had me bowling about in a spanking new L-reg Vauxhall Astra.

The desire to help disabled people get about wasn't the thing that jarred with me. It was the capacity for excess within the system that stood out. In one of the brochures we were sent, the available range included sports cars. One of the cars being offered in the brochure was a Vauxhall Tigra, small and nippy, but sadly not enough boot space for a wheelchair.

As Mum put it, 'I could drive wherever I want, though I wouldn't be able to get out at the other end.' Which would been fine if we only drove to Croydon.

I'd also seen some of the flaws in the benefits system when I did a summer working at Brixton DSS. The Brixton of today has become well and truly gentrified but back then it was a seriously impoverished area. It had high crime rates, violent crime in particular. The main risk in Brixton these days is being run over by a middle-class mum with a Bugaboo. During my time working for Lambeth social services, I saw the effects of poverty. I saw genuine hard-luck stories and people treading water until they could get back on their feet. I also saw a life on benefits as a mindset you could easily get sucked into.

At that time, the government offered community care grants, which were supposed to help people live independently. Legitimate reasons for being awarded a grant included decorating, bringing heating systems up to spec, anything to make a dwelling functional. One of my jobs was to filter out the most frivolous applications. I had to throw out applications for the following: 'mobile phone' (far from standard issue in 1995), 'Suzuki Vitara' and 'trip to Australia'.

I'm not saying these represented anything like the majority of applications but there were enough there to leave me astonished that anyone would think the state was responsible for jeeps and holidays (quick test here – if your response to this list was to think 'maybe they needed to visit sick parents in Australia', I think I can guess how you vote).

However, I was 18 and paying taxes for the first time. I can't deny the experience was formative. Who knows, maybe I saw the only people ever to try to play the system in that way but the point is, when you've lived in that world and one day the public finances become tight and a political party comes along and says that no one on benefits should be able to earn more than someone in work, it does strike a chord.

The Tories had also made an issue of households where successive generations had never worked. Believing in cuts around benefits wasn't a case of wishing to punish the poor, I was also conscious of people living unfulfilling lives. The moment my mum became disabled there was no sense that the state had any meaningful desire to get her back to work. The money she got through the DLA and Motability meant she'd have been a fool to even consider it, even if workplaces had been properly adapted for wheelchairs. Whatever benefits people were on, letting their talents go to waste didn't seem caring, it seemed like hush money.

The Labour Party in 2015 was stuck in a bind between having to acknowledge the high-spending mistakes of their past but offering some kind of vision for the future. All of which left the choice between the Tories' austerity and Labour's diet austerity kind of like picking between two meat-free salads.

There weren't many successes early on in the Miliband years. The main things that stuck out were the 'Granny Tax' and 'Pasty Tax' – which amounted to little more than putting the word 'tax' after things people were fond of. Miliband was reduced to leading his election campaign on the 'cost of living crisis'. I don't deny that rising grocery and energy bills represented significant challenges to the average household. The increased cost of living was a genuine problem, but not a sexy one.

The public had also got quite used to the idea things might be a bit tight after a global credit crunch, which we were all told was the biggest financial calamity since the Great Depression. Left-wing commentators seemed to forget that when they were telling us the 'effects of this crash could be with us for generations' a lot of us had listened.

From the get-go, Miliband never seemed prime ministerial, a big oversight when you're pitching to lead the country. The idea the public had of Miliband as being a bit of a numpty was subsequently put down to the photo of him performing bad cunnilingus on a bacon sandwich. But for me, the defining moment was during his interview with Jeremy Paxman in the run-in to the election. Paxman pointedly asked him 'Are you tough enough?'

Miliband fumbled his reply. 'Of course I'm toffee nuts . . . tough enough.'

It reminded me of a conversation I'd had with my then agent six months previously. I – just like every comic in the country at that time – was outraged that I hadn't yet been on *Live at the Apollo*.

My agent had countered, 'But do you think you're *ready* for *Live at the Apollo*?'

I said 'Yeah!' but my voice went up several octaves, like an aunty had just asked me if I liked the two-bob jumper she'd got me for Christmas. Sometimes you think you're ready for something when everyone else can see that you're not.

Moments like the one with Paxman are relatively microscopic but they matter. Miliband's supporters often used to say, 'Ed is great if you get in a room with him.' Which is like me saying, 'I'm hilarious when I tell jokes in my front room.' Ultimately, Ed Miliband seemed a bit unconvincing and the fact that his next move was into podcasting while his number two, Ed Balls, went on *Strictly* hasn't convinced me that we missed out on one of the great prime minister/chancellor combinations.

But, despite the obvious flaws in the Labour campaign, the liberal bubble was getting increasingly confident they would win. The turning point seemed to be when Russell Brand, who'd previously been apolitical, came out in support of Labour, like a hipster version of Obama finally declaring his hand for Joe Biden. I was in a comedy writing room that day and couldn't comprehend the reaction to the weird interview between Brand and Miliband in the comedian's flat. It looked like Will from *The Inbetweeners* being granted an audience with the school bully. Neither man came out of it well. Brand sacrificed his status as a political outsider and Miliband looked like he was going through the rigmarole of trying a cigarette just to appease the cool kids.

Did wider Britain give a flying fuck what Russell Brand thought of the Labour leader? We were still coming to terms with the scope of social media and it hadn't yet occurred to anyone that the vast majority of the country weren't on Twitter and, further still, the ones who were could hardly be seen as an accurate focus group for the nation. The scale of Twitter's detachment from Britain can hardly be overstated. Cameron's quote 'Twitter is not Britain' was one of the most prescient things he ever said. That and 'Samantha, I think we've left the kids in the pub.'

As the campaign approached polling day, I found myself getting more and more confrontational with family and friends. The more emotive they got about politics, the more I shut off to it. The more they thought my intention to vote Conservative again made me a bad person, the more I was happy to let them think that. But it wasn't just politics that made me more belligerent, life had changed me a bit too.

This book isn't just about the political views we have, it's about why we have them, the life experiences that shape us in the background, the true engine room of our worldview. So why was I able to handle my friends and colleagues calling me out as heartless or selfish? Why had I flipped so definitively to small state-ism, individual responsibility and the idea of tough love? Why had I gone a bit tone-deaf to emotive appeals?

I'd have preferred not to talk about the events of my personal life leading up to that election but in writing this book, it's become clear to me that telling a story about forming my political identity without mentioning them would not be giving you the whole picture. So, because of my difficulty talking about feelings with strangers, I'll blurt it all out first in a dispassionate way then fill in some blanks.

In July 2014, my wife and I lost our daughter at 34 weeks of pregnancy. A 'stillbirth', as they're called.

Six weeks after that, my best friend, Mick (remember him sitting there trying to get some homework done while his numerous brothers performed knee-drops from the top bunk), died after having Hodgkin's lymphoma then getting pneumonia during the subsequent stem-cell replacement therapy.

Then my dad got pancreatic cancer in the autumn of 2015 and died after a short illness. Not long after that, my stepdad, Roe, also passed away.

That's a lot of information. If you want to skip to the next chapter, I wouldn't blame you.

Emma and I realised we were pregnant again on New Year's Eve 2013. We'd had a miscarriage in the autumn so it felt like a blessed way to end the year. However, we had a sense of bad omens early in the pregnancy and went for a lot of scans. It wasn't just paranoia because of the miscarriage, it was something deeper, a foreboding reported by many people whose pregnancy doesn't eventually go to term. But despite our fears, the pregnancy progressed serenely and – despite it once seeming impossible to us – we were now closing in on becoming parents.

On 12 July I came downstairs to find my wife already up on what was an impossibly bright summer morning (the sun once again getting its cameo all wrong). She looked white with fear, and not just anxiety that she hadn't felt the baby move, but the glow, the look, the extra life that surrounds pregnant women had gone. It might sound like being wise after the event but my gut instincts weren't good, despite the fact we'd been for an antenatal check-up just two days previously.

We rushed to the hospital and the medical staff searched increasingly frantically for a heartbeat but it was eventually concluded that Connie's (the name we'd already chosen for her) heart had stopped beating. We were given some time to gather ourselves and then informed that we would have to return to the hospital to 'deliver' the baby two days later.

I'll spare you the details about that period of time but suffice to say that the experience of the following days, months and years were every bit as sad as you'd imagine. Not without some light and a bit of unexpected spirituality, but a huge gouge in both of our lives which neither of us will ever fully shake off.

There has been a lot written on toxic masculinity of late, of the problems with men bottling up their feelings. It's been hard for me to read some of that because, in the instance of losing a baby, emotional retentiveness was something I felt was both right and useful to my wife. On top of everything else, she had gone through the emotional trauma of labour. One of us needed to be functional and put a cork in their feelings for a while.

The problem is when you pack feelings away like that, when the coast does eventually become clear to grieve, it's sometimes hard to remember where you put them.

The stiff upper lip was still in place just six weeks later when my pal Mick went into stem-cell replacement, having finally achieved some success in shrinking his cancer only to become unwell again. In a transient state without an immune system, he started going downhill and died a couple of weeks after going into hospital.

His family asked me to give his eulogy at the funeral, a genuine honour, but so shortly after delivering one for Connie I had to once again get myself together to stand talking about a second devastating event.

It was such a cruel short passage of time, like flying through an emotional asteroid field. I sometimes wonder if it might have permanently changed the space I had for the suffering of others. I started to find I was only able to truly empathise with people who'd suffered unimaginable loss. The traffic of friends and colleagues arguing over politics started to seem like trivial background noise.

Consequently, when it was leaked that Ed Miliband intended to 'weaponise the NHS' in the election maybe I didn't have the reaction I would have done previously. Not just because I'd become temporarily blind to emotive appeals, or that I felt any party trying to fully privatise the NHS would never govern again, but also because, for whatever reason, my family don't seem to have fared particularly well at the hands of our beloved national health service. So I didn't view it with the same fondness as most people. Once again, depending on your politics, what I could tell you about the failings in care the Norcott family received from the NHS could be accepted or dismissed. It'll either go down as signs of a bloated overly centralised monolithic health service or the consequence of an under-funded band of saints who otherwise would never make mistakes.

When my dad died months after the 2015 general election, on top of the chaotic treatment given to my mum, we had more issues with misdiagnosis. We also encountered a certain flippancy around his end-of-life care, which jarred at the time. But this is where the sadness ends temporarily, because some of those moments were so flippant they were funny. In true Norcott style, they've become family heirlooms.

Emma, my sister Joanna, my stepmother (Dad had remarried, very happily, to a lovely woman in 2011) and I were sitting in an NHS meeting room waiting for Dad's diagnosis. He had become seriously ill in a very short space of time and we were primed for the worst possible news.

The consultant breezed in. You might think 'breezed' is already a verb loading the bases for bias but there's no other way of describing it. She was in her early forties, seemed to be sporting a recent suntan and bore no hallmarks of someone about to deliver the kind of sombre news she was there to impart. As she checked the notes she seemed to remember the context and did a tilted head sad-face which reminded me of Jennifer Saunders in *Absolutely Fabulous* when she feigned melancholy with her daughter Saffie.

She started with a decent level of gravitas, 'So I'm afraid to say it is late-stage pancreatic cancer.'

We all stopped, breathed in and looked at one another.

Then, after a brief pause, the consultant added, 'It's the same cancer Patrick Swayze died of.'

I stared straight at her. It was such a bizarre thing to say. I didn't know what she was getting at, whether she'd said that to shed light on the condition or if she was suggesting we, as a family, should be proud that our dad was going out with a relatively high-profile cancer twin. Meanwhile, Dad was staring so hard at the woman I was convinced he was about to turn the air blue.

'Who the fuck is Patrick Swayze?' he eventually asked, never especially up on pop culture.

I was already shaking my head. Knowing my family, I could see the way this was going.

'He's the one from *Big Trouble in Little China*,' my sister explained.

'No,' I interrupted, 'that's Kurt Russell, he just *looks* like Patrick Swayze.'

And lo, a serious moment became a Norcott argument. We'd managed to turn a cancer diagnosis into a family game of Trivial Pursuit.

Even at the hospice, the unusual care my family so often seemed to receive continued. My sister and I were keeping a vigil by Dad's bedside. Having seen the way end of life had gone with Mum, we wondered if he'd slipped into the coma which often forms the final stage before death. There was a doctor doing her rounds in the hospice who we were able to accost in the corridor and ask into the room to check him over. She moved to the side of his bed. We were expecting her to go through all sorts of official metrics to see whether he was indeed now in a coma. I don't know what exactly but off the top of my head I was thinking maybe a light in the eyes, blood pressure, that sort of thing.

What she did instead was start whispering, 'Geoff . . . Geeeeoffff . . .' into his ear, like a mother trying to rouse a sleepy toddler.

Then she shook his shoulders a bit. When that didn't work she pinched him as hard as she could. That still not having elicited a response she exhaled deeply, as if to say 'Very well.' She came back around the other side of the bed to me and my sister and gravely informed us, 'I'm afraid your father is indeed now in a coma.'

We couldn't wait for her to leave the room so we could laugh at the primitive method of diagnosis. It was odd and wrong, but so funny. We realised we were now making a lot of noise so I made the shush sign to my sister, which only seemed funnier still given what she'd told us.

It's easy to forget the election of 2015, due to all that came after it, but it was the start of a lot of things for me both personally and politically. Maybe all the flak I took that year 'radicalised' me into being more Tory than I might have otherwise been. The personal loss I experienced around that time temporarily tuned me out of the suffering of others. Out of necessity, I had to become more intent that only the individual could pull themselves through difficulty, because that seemed like my only option.

Evidently I wasn't the only one feeling that way. The prototype echo chambers of 2015 had lulled the Left into a false sense of security. When the election returned a surprise majority of 17 for the Conservatives, it floored most of the people I knew and worked with. My timeline was awash with recriminations.

'WHO DID THIS?' they asked, as if it was a game of Cluedo with a single assailant.

'11.3 million people,' I wanted to answer, but was hesitant about throwing sarcasm into an already febrile environment.

For the first time, I saw the now familiar trope of people petulantly saying, 'I'm sorry, but if you voted Conservative I don't see how you can care about people, please unfriend me now.' Many comedians seemed to feel personally betrayed by millions of people voting for the party they wanted in a democratic election.

'Did they not see my brilliant routine about David Cameron, the pig and global capitalism?'

Shutting out alternative thought was beyond an echo chamber, this was actively seeking out a life in a vacuum-sealed greenhouse.

The 'Shy Tory' phenomenon received a lot of media attention but most of it overcomplicated the matter: all that really happened was people had seen the increasingly vengeful moral certainty of the Left in full view since 2010 and had wisely decided to keep schtum. I was not a shy Tory at that time and got into my fair share of heated discussions with friends. It wasn't just that they held me accountable for their election-night party being ruined, they looked at me in wonder, like they were reassessing if they'd previously known me at all. A bit like those neighbours of serial killers you see on the news,

'Well, Geoff always seemed like such a nice bloke. I even saw him give money to charity once. This has all come as a bolt from the blue.'

The righteous anger was so great that the morning after the election people were frantically sharing old news stories about Tory austerity cuts with the message 'And so it begins' as if they'd just happened. They were implying the Conservative party, who'd all stayed up until stupid o'clock, had somehow marched straight into the Commons to lay down heavy-duty legislation. Even if the Tories were evil, I'd have to conclude that any government who is able to pass a bill off the back of 40 minutes' kip clearly wanted it more.

There was a lesson available for the Left at this point which they failed to take. Those stories were meant to guilt-trip the voter, to make them feel repentant. It was a wide-scale demonisation. But when you demonise a voter you risk losing them for ever, a principle that would play out again in the EU referendum of the following year.

One of the big legacies of the 2015 election is to see it as the great crossroads for the country, the moment when we could've pulled back from the brink. It's become fashionable, especially in the turmoil of the Brexit years, to cite David Cameron's famous tweet: 'Do you want stability with the Conservatives or chaos with Ed Miliband?' The suggestion is that Tory voters from 2015 should be perpetually slapping their own foreheads like a political Homer Simpson. I don't think it's quite so clear cut.

The best Labour could've hoped for would've been a coalition with the SNP, who if you don't like referendums, would've certainly leveraged another Scottish independence ballot before the end of the Parliament as the price of their support. The SNP's socialist leanings would've prompted Labour to jettison their pretence at fiscal prudence and spend in a way that would've jeopardised the jobs-led recovery which had already begun. Also, as we know, Nicola Sturgeon – to put it mildly – likes to take a lead on things. If you think the Tory–Lib Dem coalition was a bit one-sided, imagine if you will Ed and Nicola appearing in the rose garden, her speaking over him at every opportunity. It would have been like a five-year version of that dinner-party nightmare: 'Actually, I think what Ed meant to say was . . .'

Then there's the issue of what would've happened with Europe if Labour had won in 2015. One of the main reasons Cameron won a majority was because he was willing to let the British people decide on the country's relationship with the European Union, which had changed drastically since the first referendum on joining the Common Market in the seventies.

Miliband contemplated offering the same but finally elected not to. Who knows what would've happened if he had? Labour could've handled the whole thing very differently. And Miliband was actually a Remainer. Imagine that, Corbyn fans, a Labour leader who actually said out loud what he thought about Europe instead of you having to throw some options at him and hoping he twitches when you say the right one.

What I don't accept is that the public having a say on the vastly different relationship with Europe was something that could've been kicked down the road indefinitely. An act of democratic postponement that would've been further complicated by the second referendum Miliband would have had to grant the SNP. It would've been difficult to deny the British people one referendum on Europe when he'd almost certainly have had to give the Scottish people two.

Fun though it is to speculate on the Miliband years we never had, it doesn't feel like a utopian timeline we were denied.

The real shortcoming of the 2015 election was that Labour failed to offer a positive aspirational message. Brand is so important in politics and if you were working class it felt that in signing up to Labour's you were aligning yourself with the idea of victimhood. That your life was shit and you needed the state to swoop in and come and save you. I, like many people, preferred the narrative whereby you could take responsibility for yourself and screw some decent dough. Noel Gallagher once wisely said that the Tories have no message for the vulnerable while Labour have no message for the aspirational. Under Miliband, not only did they not have an aspirational message but they'd resorted to apologising for the period under Blair when they did.

Experiencing the open contempt and reproach of family and friends to the election result, and the way I voted, was like aversion therapy for me. The big gouges in my personal life meant I no longer gave a shit what people thought of me politically. I was sad on a personal level but also liberated politically. It felt like if I was offered another radical choice at this point, then I might well take it.

Like leaving the European Union, for example.

11

BREXIT 1 A.D.

It's 24 June 2016, the day of the Brexit result. Britain has voted by a massive or tiny majority (depending how you see these things) to leave the EU. I'm sitting at the offices of a TV production company writing for a panel show on Channel 5 and wondering if I might have booby-trapped my own career. Virtually the whole comedy industry voted against this thing and here I am at the heart of it, a cultural splinter cell trying to keep a low profile. The tantrums after 2015 were nothing compared to this. Back then, the liberal Left spat the dummy – now they've set fire to their pram. I hope they don't set fire to mine.

A bit of context. I've been blessed with a gorgeous and brilliant son who is now three months old. If turning 30 focused my mind, having an actual child and being the main breadwinner has made me put on a pair of blinkers and stare at a sign marked 'money'. It's not just that he costs money; I'm acutely aware that, as a boy, he will one day assess me in the way only sons of fathers and daughters of mothers tend to. I need to really *do* something.

As the referendum came into view, I went public with my intention to vote Leave. If my baby boy could've spoken at the time he might've said, 'Do *something*, but maybe not *that* . . .'

This time, my vote was delivered in an actual polling booth. I'd got up early to vote before heading into London. We now live in a small town in Cambridgeshire. You might say 'Cambridgeshire' in invisible quotation marks, just as people once said 'Wimbledon', but where I live is a fairly standard English town. Out here in the sticks, voting Leave didn't seem like a particularly big deal (however, in fairness, neither does fox hunting).

The day of the vote had played out like many prologues to an upsetting defeat for the liberal Left, with the cruel tonic of false hope. As the hours ticked by, a growing certainty had taken hold that Remain would win. That outcome wouldn't have surprised me. I hoped it would at least be reasonably close, to give the EU cause to reflect on its dick-waving faith in its own immutability. It was natural to suspect the incumbents would swing it. Indeed, how *could* Leave win? Remain had the full force of the government. Remain had dropped a leaflet into every home in Britain (though one day we'd be led to believe that was nowhere near as persuasive as a Russian bot shit-posting on Twitter).

Remain had all the celebrities. Remain had David bloody Beckham. A man who, having shown true radical instincts with his hair, was apparently incredibly conservative when it came to continued membership of a supranational economic trading block. Remain had all the experts, apparently. Economists were fêted as oracles even though their recent strike-rate had been nothing to be proud of. As my mate, a broker, said to me of financial institutions, 'Most of the financial sector are like GPs, we can only diagnose things for certain once they've already happened – and even then we're not entirely sure.'

The FTSE had a big rally as expectations of a Remain win swept through the City. The same Tory-hating lefties who'd spent the last six years pouring scorn on those motivated by money were now sharing screen shots of the pound rising against the dollar, like currency markets had suddenly become the nation's sole moral compass. The same artists who were supposed to be led by a maverick spirit were hailing the likely continuity of the neoliberal status quo. Many of the people who declared themselves socialists were loosening the champagne corks for the ongoing membership of a political body with strict rules on state aid.

And here I was, a Conservative – and we're supposed to sacrifice everything to the gods of economic stability – betting the family estate on the feeling that somehow 'Britain would be OK'. Whatever the result was, one thing was clear, the Brexit vote had thrown a hand grenade into the old political certainties.

The first I knew of the result was when I woke around 5am. I'd been staying in a hotel as I had a busy writing job on in town. The TV had been on all night and I became loosely aware of the moist sounds of David Cameron's dribbly voice drifting through the chintzy haze of the hotel room. His face was obscured by a sunbeam which had crept through the curtain and nudged me awake.

I caught something about him thinking it would not be right for him 'to be the captain'. I opened my eyes a bit wider to take in the bar at the bottom of the screen which was variously reading, 'Britain votes to leave the EU . . . Pound crashes . . . everything will be shit now.'

I hopped out of bed. There are a lot of clichés which real life never fully delivers on, but I really did 'hop', like a rabbit who'd had mustard smeared on his arse.

I, like everyone, had gone to bed thinking Remain would win, maybe gotten a little used to the idea. I felt that Britain would be better off outside the EU in the medium to long term but could see too that continuity would also bring benefits. At the very least it would've resolved the question. Either way, this was Britain and I was certain that if it had gone the other way the Remain side would be equally magnanimous.

My first thought upon hearing the result wasn't about the comedy industry or the jeopardy my career might be in (that would come later), it was whether my wife knew about the result. I rang her to see if she was reeling, or hated me, because she had voted Remain. The fact we voted differently often gets a surprised reaction from liberal middle-class types. It's another piece of unconscious bias. They presume a guy like me tells his wife how to vote just after he's informed her what time dinner should be on the table. Thankfully, she has a mind of her own. Though I admit I would prefer more stable mealtimes.

So I wanted to see whether she was angry with me, but having a child is a great means of focusing on the here and now. The fact the prime minister had resigned came a distant second to the fact our son had just rolled onto his tummy. Prime ministers would come and go but there would only be one time our boy developed this particular motor neurone skill.

'It'll be all right, won't it?'

'Of course,' she said, before wisely adding, 'maybe stay off social media today.'

Like most idiotic husbands I said, 'Yes of course,' then immediately checked social media. It was more of a scan than an in-depth evaluation but the initial signs weren't good. Buzz words included 'racists', 'stupid' and 'you stole my child's future'. Still, maybe they were just crabby because they hadn't drunk their first morning coffee. I was sure they'd chill out as the day went on.

I did have a nagging concern. At this point I wasn't aware of any other comedian who'd been quite so open about their intention to vote Leave. Having hauled myself up to a decent living through writing comedy as well as performing in the clubs, I was now wondering if I'd comprehensively shot myself in the foot.

The first thing I see when I enter the office is a producer crying in the kitchen and I don't think it's because we've run out of Nespresso pods. All around, people are standing in hushed corners discussing things in a low voice. The atmosphere is heavy, funereal even. Voting to leave the EU has created a feeling like a relative has just died. In typically middle-class style, it's a relative they didn't talk about much until the last few months. A relative they didn't give much of a shit about until they felt there was a chance they might be written out of the will.

I don't know how many of my immediate colleagues are aware I'm a Leave voter. Most circuit stand-ups would be but in this context I'm very much a writer, a joke monkey. I've written a few articles indicating my intention to vote for Brexit but I doubt if anyone here has read them. So I decide to keep a low profile and just crack on with my work. The show I'm writing is a dating panel show. It feels very odd to go from epoch-shaking news of our times to writing knob gags for Eammon Holmes. However, adversity has sharpened my mind. The first joke I write is, 'An Egyptian guy offered me 20 camels for my wife. I said, "Throw in the lighter and you've got yourself a deal."'

I know, right? In the same way Wilfred Owen found his voice in war, I appear to be hitting new heights as Britain thrashes itself free of continental rule.

Having bashed out a number of gags easily of this gold standard, I log on to Facebook. Most of my feed features fellow comics and industry professionals. I'm hoping to get a sense of the mood, maybe a more level-headed reaction since the very early morning. This is Britain right? Magnanimous in victory . . . magnificent in defeat.

The very first post I read is from a stand-up colleague I once spent a whole week gigging with overseas and it reads, 'So that's it then. Britain is a country of 17.4 million racists.'

My heart races. I look at the likes for this comment, it's already in the high hundreds. Foolishly I decide to read exactly who has liked this comment – that peculiar impulse when something hasn't gone your way to roll the dice again even though the dice are on fire. The likes turn out to be almost exclusively people I know and have worked with. They've concurred with a sentiment which implicitly defines me as a racist. This can't be good for business, not in the comedy game. I wouldn't normally accord social media so much gravitas but this is comedy; Facebook and Twitter represent our watercooler.

I think about my son. It'll be odd explaining to him one day that I lost my job for voting in line with just over half the country. It might seem paranoid but the moment racism becomes synonymous with a political decision you're in trouble. You'd be more likely to keep a job in TV if you'd drunk-driven and actually risked human life than if you used a racist term. Personally, I think it would great if human beings did neither, but if Ant McPartlin had mown down a person of colour when he was driving over the limit, the first thing ITV bosses would've asked is, 'What did he *say* as he was doing it?'

For a long time, 'political correctness gone mad' has been mocked as a phrase, repeated ironically as a stick to beat the populists and reactionaries. It was true that there were absurd mythical stories of people banning Christmas or prohibiting anyone saying 'baa, baa, black sheep' but as the 2010s wore on there were more and more examples of political correctness morphing into something much more unhinged. In Rochdale, the amount of time it took for authorities to believe victims of Asian grooming gangs suggested a hesitancy to get to grips with a potentially explosive issue. In 2004, Colin Cramphorn, the then chief constable of West Yorkshire police, demanded Channel 4 withdraw a documentary on the issue because it could trigger violence in a 'racially tense area'. Journalist Julie Bindel was the first to report nationally on this issue and was, in her words, placed on 'Islamaphobia watch'.The general reluctance of left-wing media to talk about this difficult issue created space for the far right to take full ownership. Political correctness couldn't just go mad, sometimes it could go certifiably insane.

So I had my reasons to be worried. It had become commonplace to make an inextricable link between a Leave vote and racism. Billy Bragg spoke with some nuance but a certainty that jarred with me: 'Not every Leave voter is a racist, but every racist will vote Leave.'

Fair enough, but I'd argue there must have been at least *one* racist Remainer. Perhaps someone who hated people from other countries but also owned properties in France?

I did have a view on immigration and – several years later – it's still not one I've heard articulated much. I accept all the arguments about the positive things immigration has done for Britain. But I also find the 'freedom of movement' idea a bit absolutist – the idea that any citizen of an EU country should be able to live and work without limit in fellow member states. The idea was nice but 'unlimited in perpetuity' seemed extreme to me. Even 'all you can eat' data has fair-play limits.

I didn't understand why nations shouldn't have a mechanism to adjust targets while they trained enough doctors, nurses and police to keep up with the rate of new arrivals. The problem with medics and law enforcement is they take a while to get up to speed. No one wants a 'crash course' for doctors.

The truth is my experience of immigration had been a positive one. When I was growing up in south London, it was around the time of a period of high influx from Asia, Africa and the Caribbean. Unlike many middle-class people throwing the term 'racist' around, I actually had friends in those communities. Not just friends, even; the Asian family who lived upstairs at our first family home in Wimbledon became a surrogate family to me – they still are. It's always tricky to try and establish your non-racist credentials by pointing out the people close to you who aren't the same colour as you. The liberal Left have come up with the derided booby-trap cliché: 'Some of my best friends are black.' Being friends with a black person doesn't entirely exonerate you of racism but it's a decent start. I'd be more worried by someone who mocked that phrase but had a whiter friendship group than Hitler.

The working classes have historically been on the front line of racial integration. Our kids are more likely to go to school with and marry outside of their community. We are statistically more likely to work with Eastern Europeans. We work in industries more likely to be threatened by wage competition, like construction and factory work. What would the middle-class reaction to immigration have been if the influx had been Romanian marketing gurus?

Furthermore, the rhetoric Remainers started to adopt after the vote sounded more and more like the reductive xenophobia they claimed to despise. 'Who is going to pick the strawberries? Who will look after our children or work at Pret?' All of which made the EU sound less like a peacekeeping force for good and more like a production line of economic Oompa Loompas. I lost count of the amount of times supposedly liberal friends would proudly tell me how they've stopped using British builders because 'Eastern European ones have such a great attitude.' The 'attitude' they seemed to be particularly fond of was doing jobs for less money.

It's now lunchtime at the TV production company. I've had my head down writing jokes all morning, stealing nervous glances at the currency markets. We're shortly due to holiday in Disneyland Paris and I'm anxiously looking at the value of the pound. My wife is one of those naturally smart people. A week before the vote she said to me, 'Don't forget to get Euros, Geoff. If the vote goes Leave we'll get stung.'

The rest of the afternoon is pleasantly soporific. Whereas the morning saw adrenaline coursing through people's bodies and everyone you spoke to had their eyes out on stalks, the rest of the day is the exact opposite. It's amazing how much lunch can take the wind out of people's morning anger. On a primitive level, your most basic human fear for the day has been assuaged. Yes, we might crash the economy and housing market but, equally, I have a cheese sandwich in front of me, so I won't die of starvation. A win's a win.

Even some of the more uptight people are now engaging in various shades of gallows humour. One of the assistant producers who'd been giving me evils in the morning notices my sandwich comes from Pret and says, 'Enjoy it, Geoff, you'll be making your own soon.'

I almost bite but realise this is serious progress from earlier when she was looking at me like I was the bastard son of Farage. I suppress the desire to point out that immigration was never going to completely stop because of Brexit; instead I wave the sandwich back at her. I wonder if she notices it's plain cheese and if that confirms her opinion of me as one of the Little Englanders; the kind of guy who pulls up his socks with the same force he pulls up the ladder on economic migrants. These new layers to social awkwardness are only just beginning and I suspect they'll be with us for some time to come.

As I leave the offices in Docklands, there seems to be a lot of people getting drunk in the sterile, soulless bars lining the route back to Canary Wharf. Fair enough, it's been a confusing day and getting shitfaced is a sensibly British method of postponement. I look at a couple of the suits standing in the smoking area outside one bar. I can't tell if they're hammered already or just punch-drunk from a bewildering day. It's a hazy sort of summer evening too, which only adds to the general sense of discombobulation.

I reflect on something a cultural pundit said on Sky News as I was having my lunch. He said that this was an attempt by people to stop the march of globalisation, to 'take the batteries out of the globalist clock'. He also went on to some clichéd bollocks about Little Englanders but I wondered if his first point might have been valid, especially about me. I can't speak for all Leave voters but did part of my vote come from a desire to hit that pause button? As I'd lost so many people and the world carried on heedlessly, maybe a part of me saw Brexit as a chance to slow that forward process. It wasn't *on* my mind when I voted, but it might've been under it.

'Geoff! Geoff!'

Someone appears to be calling my name. Given the atmosphere of reproach and recrimination I shrug it off as the echoes of my own paranoia. It persists and I notice one of the heads of the production company is beckoning me into the bar to join her team for a drink. It's been a long day. I'm on the winning side but success feels exhausting, so I accept the invite.

The bar is heavy with motormouth chat and nervous laughter. The production head is holding court with a pleasant crew of TV minions. She talks brightly, trying to wave away the events of the day and theorising freely about Leave voters as these 'stupid people' who 'believe things written on the side of buses'.

Ah, the advert on the bus. That famous claim printed on the side of Boris's tour bus that suggested we could use the £350 million we give to the EU per week to help fund the NHS. A very 'creative' bit of advertising the likes of me were supposed to have fallen for hook, line and sinker. After one and a half pints, and with no thought for my son's college fund, I decide to engage. 'I voted Leave. I wasn't swayed by the bus.' (I daren't also add that it was clearly a coach.)

She's surprised more than angry. I guess she didn't expect, on this day of all days, to find any Leavers in the metropolitan hotbed of terrestrial TV. The discussion plays out like many more I'll have in this vein. Simmering, sometimes driven by the genuine spirit of enquiry, but mostly underscored by tension. Like complaining to customer services but not going so far that you get cut off.

I can't tell if my argument as to why I voted Leave has placated or wound her up more. I try to lighten the mood by suggesting Remainers have got nothing to lose: 'If we Leave and it turns out all right you can enjoy the prosperity. But if it all goes tits up you can dine out for the rest of your life on being proved right.'

In some ways, that's the most noble death for a *Guardian* reader, getting to die saying 'I told you so'.

This glib comment does not land well. I look at my watch and shake my pint as if to say, 'Well, this one's done, best be on my way.' Except it's very much not done and beer splashes over the edges and forms a horrid urine-coloured pool in the corner of my open bag of crisps.

She says, with genuine good intent, 'Ah Geoff, you're one of the OK ones.'

It occurs to me that the only other time I've heard this phrase is when racists are deciding who is 'all right' and who isn't but this really isn't the time to split linguistic hairs and I'm not sure comparing my unease to the race struggle is wise at this point. Plus, I've still got that three-month-old son I need to provide for.

As I'm fumbling with my things getting ready to go, the colleague who'd flashed me the morning evils says, 'Aren't you going to Disneyland soon? That's gonna cost a bit more.'

I should've countered that point by calling holidays a preoccupation of the liberal elite, that democracy and sovereignty are more important than how many times they get to hit the slopes this year, but at that very moment I remember that I didn't change up those Euros like my wife suggested.

This is turning out to be a very challenging day.

12

DID YOU SERVE IN THE CULTURE WARS?

'What did you do in the great culture wars Grandad?'

'Well,' I say, resting my vape pipe on the side of my chair, 'I did a lot, my boy. I wrote articles. I fearlessly retweeted things I agreed with. I threw things at the radio when James O'Brien was on. It was the time of the Gammons versus the Snowflakes and it went on for years.'

'It sounds awful, Grandad. Were you scared?'

'Of course I was scared. We all were. The risks were high. You could get in a three-day argument with a journalist from the *Metro*. Worst of all, you could get quote tweeted by Piers Morgan. However, you put all that to the back of your mind, because you have to stand up for what you thought was right at the time.'

'And what did you think was right, Grandad? Were you Labour or Tory? Did you vote for Brexit?'

'Is that the time, son? Grandad needs to have his nap.'

Of all the wars to have served in, the culture wars are the least impressive. Especially because they carried with them no real prospect of personal risk. You might be one of the unlucky ones who gets 'cancelled' but for most people the only jeopardy was that your opinion did not find favour. Or perhaps you were subject to a 24-hour public mauling for a bunch of words you casually tossed into the ether while taking a dump. The bruising experience still wouldn't change your mind, though. You'd emerge the following day with your opinion conker well and truly intact.

It's hard to describe exactly what a 'culture war' is. In short, there are two teams made up of people whose views on most things can be usually be predicted. It starts with politics but fans out into a type, like one of those online personality tests. Someone who voted Leave may also get annoyed by the withdrawal of 'Rule Britannia!' from Last Night of the Proms and find Greta Thunberg a bit aggravating. Remainers, however, generally think Greta is awesome and that any criticism of Meghan and Harry is motivated by racism. Personally, I was very pro Meghan and Harry at the beginning but they became like one of those holiday couples you befriend: they're awesome for the first three days but by day four you're hiding behind bins desperately hoping to dine alone.

It's not even clear exactly when the culture wars started. Like the First World War (but also obviously not like it), you can look back to a number of skirmishes stretching well beyond the outbreak of fighting itself. One early example of the culture war was how the nation reflected on the 2012 Olympics in London.

Post-Brexit, the liberal Left began a strange habit of fetishising those two Olympic weeks as an example of a simpler time when the country had universally joined in a national jamboree which validated the principles of neoliberalism, globalism, as well as flash new dining facilities in the East End. Mo Farrah winning gold washed away any lingering questions about the issue of immigration. Danny Boyle's epic opening ceremony cleared up that the NHS was the single greatest thing that had ever happened. This was everybody's Olympics, despite the fact you'd have to remortgage to afford tickets for the dressage.

I was gigging around the country at the time, a long way from London and becoming acutely aware the euphoria wasn't reaching too far outside the M25. Naïvely, I opened a gig in Manchester with 'Are we all enjoying the Olympics?' The answer was met with resounding indifference (though I was in Manchester and that is a common response to most things).

I ventured further north and asked the same question in St Helens; the answer was a resounding 'No'. The third gig that week was in Dumfries (my agent at the time clearly hated me) where me even mentioning the Olympics brought a chorus of boos. I'm not saying no one outside London enjoyed the tournament, just that there was a gulf in perception. Not only was there indifference, there may also have been a touch of envy.

London, already seen as having its fair share of advantages, was swanning about on the world stage, a reminder of the unnatural degree to which attention and resources are skewed towards the capital. Very few other countries have a capital so far ahead of the next biggest city. London is the city equivalent of Google, which makes everywhere else a bit Ask Jeeves. If anything united the nation in 2012 it was the idea London was a bit up itself.

If the Olympics were the start of a cultural proxy war, Brexit was Germany invading Poland.

One of the most important knock-on consequences of the Leave vote was the purge-like way it vanquished the old binary lines of Left and Right. Labour Leavers found themselves being called 'racist' by Metropolitan pinkos. Tory Brexiteers were called 'traitors' by the kind of Cameroonians who'd just hired a gay au pair and liked to talk about it.

Two months after the Brexit vote, I was doing the Edinburgh festival. I had a political show called *Conswervative* (continuing the Norcott penchant for lazy names). The magnitude of the Leave vote compelled me to include a segment on the referendum. As you can imagine, the atmosphere in the venue was pretty tense most nights, so I saved up the reveal of my Leave vote until the end of the show. It was always a difficult moment. In truth, I didn't have many good jokes on the subject ('Europe's like a boy band, it's best to be first out. Let's be the Robbie Williams'). I was frequently heckled. I captured one incident on my phone (and it's still on YouTube if you're interested in getting a feel for the mood of the time).

That night, I'd started the section on voting Leave and was immediately called 'traitor' by a very posh-sounding bloke. It was a small room and I could see him. He was tall, skinny, wearing mustard chinos and a salmon coloured shirt. Because of the compact size of the room I could see the whites of his eyes; he was shaking with adrenaline. As a working-class male, it's sometimes hard to resist your normal reaction to such a blunt insult (give the bloke a dry slap) so, while I was being professional and trying to compose myself, an Australian woman, perhaps smelling blood, also chipped in.

'Why did you vote Leave?' she asked.

I tried to explain but she butted in, not accepting self-determination or sovereignty as legitimate reasons. I've had this kind of argument a lot since. I've worked out that 'Why did you vote Leave?' isn't always an actual question, it has huge invisible italics. What they really mean is '*Why* the *FUCK* did *you* vote *Leav*e?' They're trying to work out if you're an idiot, racist or a patriotic billionaire. In some ways, life would've been easier if people had actually just said 'idiot' or 'are you racist?' Back in the punch-drunk summer of 2016, I was still naïve enough to think we could talk it through.

My Australian heckler responded to my point about the issues within the EU by saying, 'If there are problems you should stay and help sort it out.'

Not realising the irony, she neither stayed nor sorted it out and left the gig immediately. My middle-class Edinburgh Fringe audience, having seen far too much theatre, were unable to comprehend that real life could involve spontaneous irony and were convinced she was a 'plant'. A suspicion not helped when, moments later, she came back in the room because her girlfriend, who she'd automatically presumed would follow her out, hadn't.

Then, being posh, she ruined the whole thing by apologising.

That one-month run at the Fringe underlined an issue that would dog the debate for years. There I was, a person who'd voted in line with most of the country, standing on stage each night being regarded like some sort of exotic and dangerous bird.

'Come see the lesser-spotted Brexitty working-class Tory. MARVEL as he shares his niche ideas also held by 52 per cent of Britain.'

I found that run of shows very hard throughout, not just because of the political dimension. In 2013 and 2015, I'd dipped my toe in the political water but for this show I'd divebombed and found the laughs were at the shallow end.

It was undoubtedly the least funny show I'd ever taken to the Edinburgh Festival, so naturally – given the peculiar attitude towards comedy at the Fringe – it was also my best reviewed. Now, that may sound paradoxical but trust me, there is a very strange relationship with laughter and good reviews at the Fringe these days. It's become so painfully middle-class that belly laughs can be viewed as a bit crass. Shows taking 'risks' tend to be rewarded. I thought not being funny was already a pretty big risk but it turns out many modern critics want more now, preferably personal anguish and a dead parent (in which case they might like this book).

All well and good but the festival still remains the engine room for emerging TV comedy talent. What is rewarded at the Fringe is unlikely to play out as well with a mass audience. Maybe a schism like that makes total sense during a culture war. If the Labour Party could lose touch with the working classes, why wouldn't comedy do something as careless as moving away from laughter?

During 2018 and 2019, when the whole Brexit process seemed in crisis, a lot was written about how the referendum vote could possibly be undone. However, in the period immediately after the vote, as anger and recriminations flew about, hardly anyone seemed to think that process could be halted. The early marches for the EU seemed more like a protracted wake than any real force for reconsideration. People seemed less focused on staying in the EU and more exercised by meeting Eddie Izzard and hitting their Fitbit target.

That sense was aided and abetted by the two main parties holding fairly similar sounding policies on Europe. Corbyn was adamant that freedom of movement must end, which implicitly also meant exiting the single market. Labour spoke nebulously of *a* customs union rather than *the* customs union. Keir Starmer devised his ingenious 'six tests for Brexit', which sounded like a plot McGuffin in a fantasy film. These were early forerunners for Labour's semantic straitjackets and prevarication on Brexit.

My engagement with the culture war had, up until this point, been largely under the cloak of anonymity. Sure, I had a few followers and fans but knowledge of me was mainly confined to the industry. That all changed when I was asked to do *Question Time* in early 2017. I'd seen comedians on the show before and they seemed to be on a bit of a hiding to nothing. They either got slated for not being funny, or, if they did manage to squeeze a laugh out of the *Question Time* crowd, it switched to, 'Why's he even *on* a political show?' I had some sympathy with that view, however the chance to be on it felt like taking on an extreme sport. Something I'd kick myself for if I didn't give it a go.

I spoke with the producer beforehand. She advised me not to try too many obvious attempts at humour before adding that she'd seen me live, which didn't do wonders for my confidence. I don't know what she thought I was planning. Walking out there like an old-fashioned Northern club comic going, 'Now then, now then, now then. What do you call two Lib Dems in a bath? All of them!' However, the producer seemed definite about her advice so I took it.

That episode was to be filmed in East London. The panel was SNP MP Angus Robertson, Conservative James Cleverly and journalist Susie Boniface (Fleet Street Fox). I would be sitting next to Labour's Diane Abbott. On *Question Time.* In Whitechapel, more or less her home turf. It felt like playing Liverpool at Anfield, midweek and under lights.

I'd tried to block out my growing nerves until the night before when I was getting ready to do a gig to a handful of people in the East Midlands. I was sitting in a substandard curry house close to the venue. *Question Time* tweeted the line-up for the following night's show and I was totally unprepared for the torrent of shit that would unleash.

I won't bore you with all the insults but there were several tropes which I found really interesting. As a lot of people hadn't heard of me, let alone heard me speak, many rushed to judgement about the kind of person I was. The presumption was largely that I was a typical posh Tory boy. The best of which was the extremely wide of the mark, 'Why don't you go back to managing your property portfolio, you prick?' I was annoyed at the complacent presumption about my class and simultaneously pissed off that I hadn't amassed the kind of wealth the guy imagined I had.

Some comments made me laugh, though: 'Why's he on *Question Time*? He comes across as the kind of bloke who'd know where to order a skip.'

I also got lots of people putting inverted commas around 'comedian'. No other profession gets this. Probably for the best; if you saw that around the name of your 'doctor', you'd have second thoughts.

The next day, I was sitting in a coffee shop over the road from the church the show would be recorded in. It was early 2017 and Theresa May was visiting the US for her first meeting with newly inaugurated President Trump. In the wake of his Muslim travel ban, the Left were fizzing with the idea that she should boycott the trip. I said to myself, sarcastically, under my breath, 'Maybe right now isn't a great time to boycott your biggest strategic ally.' The simple pragmatism of it made me laugh so I decided that if it came up I'd pitch this revolutionary idea of not slamming the door in the face of the world's greatest superpower.

Taking my seat in front of the audience, I was nervous. Comedy audiences are never easy but at least when you walk on they're usually looking to laugh and be entertained. The *Question Time* crowd on the other hand is already a bit furious as they enter the venue. The very reason they are there is to feel fury. Even when they clap, their hands sound like angry pistols. Everything about the show is gladiatorial. It also goes out at the worst possible time of day, 10.30pm, just before sleep. It's like putting Red Bull in Ovaltine; you could very easily stray onto the upper cut of people's late-night angst.

I was extremely nervous, not least to meet the great man Sir David Dimbleby. But he put me at ease. The bloke just exudes a special something. I was amused to find he treated the recordings like a gig.

'The London shows,' he advised me, 'these audiences don't laugh much but get up to Birmingham and beyond and you get way more out of them.'

I'd never really thought about it, but he was like me: on a circuit, gigging 40 weeks of the year.

Diane Abbott arrived. I introduced myself to her and she said, 'Ah, you're that Tory comedian,' And nothing else. At least she didn't put air quotes around comedian.

I managed to get settled in my seat on the panel, then the music started. I don't know what it is about the music from TV shows you've known your whole life but it *does* something. Not only is the *Question Time* music dramatic and hectic, it's also the signature sound of a programme you've watched for a long time. Hearing it in the studio felt like a bizarre portal had opened up between me and my younger self and I'd fallen into the television.

How had I blagged this? My impostor syndrome was lacing itself with performance anxiety and the gravity of the situation. I looked down and had already drunk my whole jug of water in the time it took them to mic up Diane Abbott. I'd have asked for some of hers but she didn't look in the mood for sharing. I can't explain the internal monologue that runs through your brain when you're appearing on a show like that, especially on your debut. You're trying to take it in but the whole time your inner doubt isn't just talking to you, it's shouting, louder than anything the panel or audience are saying.

'WHAT'S HAPPENING? . . . IS DIMBLEBY COMING TO ME? . . . NO, HE ISN'T. . . WHAT'S THAT BLOKE SAYING? . . . I HOPE HE DOESN'T COME TO ME NOW BECAUSE I DON'T KNOW WHAT THAT BLOKE JUST SAID . . .WHAT IF HE ASKS ME A GENERAL KNOWLEDGE QUESTION . . . IT AIN'T *MASTERMIND*, GEOFF! . . . FUCK'S SAKE . . .'

Eventually I was brought into the discussion about May visiting Trump. I curried favour with a couple of lighthearted gags about how I'd butter up the Donald before suggesting maybe the only way you could speak truth to power was by having a dialogue with power in the first place.

Then I heard it, the thing I didn't realise I'd been wanting my whole life, the *Question Time* round of applause. This was it, validation. All those people who'd called me dumb, all those reviewers, *now* they'd see. I'm getting claps on *Question Time* AND I'm muckers with Dimbleby . . .

In the middle of this narcissistic reverie I was suddenly aware my new mate Dave had come back to me a bit quicker than I expected with another question. Some bright spark in the audience had posed an absolute riddle of a question, saying that while we mocked Trump for wanting to build a wall, with the immigration controls due from Brexit, why *not* a wall? What's the difference?

It was a brilliant piece of semantic rhetoric where he'd placed any Brexit voter a lot closer to Trump than seemed comfortable. I was only driftingly aware of what he said so let me transcribe in full my pathetic attempt at an answer (someone helpfully uploaded it to YouTube under the heading 'Geoff Norcott bombs on *Question Time*').

Sir David Dimbleby: Geoff Norcott, what's so impossible about a wall?

Me: Well . . . well . . . well . . . the impossibility of ever building it. As I've already said, there may be some fences [I hadn't already said that]. It's like when you dilute any idea 'there may be some fences' [again, referring to something I hadn't said]. I think . . . and I'm sure we'll get on to this . . . the idea . . . [pauses, then, remembering how politicians wriggle out of a tight spot, decides to answer a question I posed myself] I'm someone who voted Leave . . .'

I'd gone from total self-validation to being on the ropes in less than a minute. Thankfully, that early ride on the

Question Time rollercoaster put me in a better place for the rest of the recording, not least when Diane Abbott, for the third time, tried to trot out a line showing empathy and solidarity with Labour Leave voters in the north. This was a bit rich for me, as I was fully aware of some of her less than empathetic statements about Leave voters in aftermath of the EU Referendum.

I chipped in with, 'After the Leave vote itself, your view of some Leave voters wasn't exactly complimentary. You characterised it as a vote to see less brown people on the street.' I hadn't planned to say this, I'd just had enough of the hypocrisy of a Labour party who were belatedly and expediently reaching out to their former heartlands. The audience clapped again and Dimbleby's eyes lit up like a bloke going, 'Hello! It's kicking off.'

I was ready for a set-to but Diane surprised me by shutting down and I continued onto another point.

Before I knew it, it was over.

We all had a drink and some pizza afterwards, it was all quite conciliatory, though I got the distinct impression from Diane Abbott that she wasn't willing to shake hands and move on. She wanted to reconcile with Leave voters but not the one standing in front of her.

I'd survived the gig but had also put my head above the parapet. As a comic, a political discussion show is an odd way to make your debut with the nation. It had been said for a long time that right-wing comedy was impossible. That right-wing comedians were unfunny and hateful.

Well, I'd got a few laughs from a notoriously tricky crowd and hadn't been cancelled in the process. I'd picked up a few fans but had also made my way onto the radar of a few enemies too.

At the time of writing, I've done *Question Time* on four occasions. The most recent appearance was the antithesis of everything that had gone before. It was two days before Britain formally left the EU and I went 'tooled up' for yet another big row but the recording couldn't have been further from a fight.

The Buxton crowd, probably like much of Britain, had talked about Brexit more than enough and the main thing they wanted to discuss now was trains. We did 40 of the 60 minutes on trains and I suspect that if many of us hadn't had trains to catch we would still be there now, talking about trains.

Given everything that happened with coronavirus it's a shame that the window of normal news was so short. Everybody deserved a much longer break from the heavy stuff. Since 2014, it's been incessant. The Scottish Independence referendum, a general election a year later, Brexit the year after and then the snap election of 2017. For anybody, too much. Any kids born in 2016 must wonder when their parents are going to lighten the fuck up.

By the time Theresa May called the snap election in 2017, to bolster her power base in the Commons and to get a majority that would help her make Brexit happen, there had already been indications that some of the usual class lines in party politics were beginning to dissolve. The Conservatives had made big gains in local elections and won metropolitan mayoral elections in formerly dependable areas like Tees Valley and the West Midlands. Meanwhile, the 'Corbyn problem' was already an issue on the doorstep for many working-class voters, it seemed. In a surprise twist of fate, blue-collar types weren't massively keen on voting for a staunch republican with little time for the military and a questionable history in relation to the IRA. In short, like many modern politicians on the Left, he just didn't seem to *like* Britain very much. In the States, both sides of the political divide drape themselves in the stars and stripes. In Britain, if you popped a Union Jack on the hard Left they'd shrug it off like they were being attacked by wasps.

Labour had, however, picked up support by offering to spend money, lots of it. The British public – so accustomed to choosing between different versions of austerity (like being offered the sexy choice of an array of consolidation loans) – were now being showered with cash and seemed flattered by it.

The Tories' one radical idea was that pensioners with money might contribute to their end-of-life care. Even if it was a progressive taxation at heart, that's not a vote winner. When you put 'Nanna pays for her own bed bath' against 'we'll abolish tuition fees' there was only going to be one winner, especially with the young.

Corbyn had all the youth on his side. I'll never forget the first time I saw a crowd at a music gig chanting 'Oh, Jeremy Corbyn'. The Left lapped it up, although it occurred to me that, historically, the public chanting politicians' names doesn't always end well. The event was Wirral Live 2017 and the clip went viral quickly. I decided to watch the whole thing. It wasn't just the chanting that bothered me, it was what elicited it: a sub sixth-form debating forum address from Corbyn, in which he envisaged a society where people could play sport and learn music (as though all those things weren't already possible), ending with a rhetorical binary choice: 'Or do you want selective education and fox hunting?'

It marked out one of the problems with Corbyn and the start of a growing issue on the Left: rabble-rousing populism masquerading as a social conscience. It also underlined his simplistic approach to politics.

'What do kids like?'

Music.

'What do they not like?'

Fox hunting.

He was one step from forming a band called 'Spit on your Fascist Bloodhound'.

My relationship with the Labour party had clearly changed. While my shift away from them in 2010 had been fairly pragmatic, I now considered them the 'other side'. I guess it's inevitable when you keep getting called a Tory bastard – you end up thinking, 'Fuck it, I'll be one.' I couldn't bear the constant repitching of the same old battle of good versus evil. It seemed fundamentally immature to view politics in this way. To the Left, it was always Jedi versus Sith, where, surprise, surprise, they always got to be Luke Skywalker and I was always Darth Vader.

Eventually, the much mooted 'youthquake' was overstated. Despite it being one of the most crucial elections in a generation, despite them being pitched to like never before, the uptick in turnout among the young was only 2.5 per cent. Typical millennials, couldn't even be arsed to turn up to their own statistic.

I've always had an issue with the idea you need to make politics accessible to the young. Why? Its 'relevance' couldn't be clearer. There was so much at stake in the 2017 election that you couldn't blame politics, or even the Left, for not creating a greater turnout. The apathy of the young was something for which only they could take responsibility. They might argue that none of the parties had anything to offer them but Corbyn's goodie bag for young adults in 2017 was considerable. Even if it wasn't, politics isn't like choosing an outfit. You don't end up with something that totally suits you. It's all about that essential compromise between the least shit of two options.

I said earlier that in 1997, when I voted Labour, it was the only time I've walked into the polling booth with political conviction. In 2017, my assessment was that the

Tories were a better option to be in office. I didn't think they had run a good campaign but it was an easy choice compared to Labour under Corbyn. I could see the shift towards identity politics happening and felt that, if given power, the Parliamentary Labour Party would renege on their stated position to honour Brexit. Any conviction I had about where I put my cross this time was all personal. I wasn't voting so much for what I was for, but what I was against. I put a cross next to the Conservative candidate but I might as well have written 'fuck off'.

It seemed like Labour increasingly wanted everybody to identify as something so I decided to identify as Mr Fuck-off Man. Fuck off labelling me, fuck off taking the working-class vote for granted, fuck off telling the 52 per cent they were racist, fuck off making excuses for laying wreaths on the graves of terrorists, fuck off back to Islington and preach to the converted. This was a culture war and I was battle hardened.

When the exit poll was published, I experienced something I hadn't for a while: not being on the winning side in an election. The Tories had lost 13 seats while Labour had gained 30. It wasn't a win for the Left but a serious bloody nose for the Tories.

The narrative legacy of the 2017 election was that Corbyn had scored a great success but he'd done it against the worst political campaign in living memory. There's nothing worse than losing a fight you picked and Theresa May, for all the empathy she might have evoked, seemed like a horse who'd not only thrown its rider at the finish line but had also started moonwalking in the other direction.

With the focus on Corbyn's surprise showing, it went largely unnoticed that the Tories had increased their share of the vote too. It had gone up from 36.9 in 2015 to 42.4. Though Theresa May's anxious demeanour suggested less 'Iron Lady' and more 'lady behind with her ironing', the party's vote share was up there with Thatcher in her prime in 1987. There was also a sign of things to come in Labour heartlands when Conservative candidate Ben Bradley won a seat in the staunch ex-mining town of Mansfield. Labour had done well generally but carried forward an unstable coalition of voters: those who trusted that they were serious about getting Brexit done and those who thought they could manoeuvre to reverse it.

As 2017 wore on, a sense of political stalemate set in. The Tories were neutered in parliament. The Left had briefly fallen into line behind Corbyn (but if you listened closely, his MPs who'd tried to oust him less than a year previously were saying 'hear, hear' through gritted teeth).

In April 2017, I'd been in the pilot for a TV show called *The Mash Report*. Against expectation, it got commissioned and I was in the debut episode which aired in July. As a right-winger I had to concede the irony: a straight, white, middle-aged man had somehow taken advantage of a diversity quota. The BBC had become aware of its under-served political audience and were starting to realise that diversity of race, gender and sexual orientation might also mean 52 per cent of the country's opinions might need a place at the table too. There had been no right-of-centre comics for a generation, meanwhile BBC 6 Music had employed three left-wing presenters called Russell.

I looked at the audience coming in to watch us record the debut episode of *The Mash Report* and they seemed every bit the left-leaning metropolitan crowds I'd seen working on TV shows as a writer, if not more so. Consequently, at the start of my segment, I decided to ask, 'Any Tories in?' As catchphrases go, it's not up there with the greats but the pause and silence were funny. It suited me, if I was going to swim against the tide I wanted people to know it. Doing this kind of comedy on telly would be like Dad jumping in that swimming pool fully clothed and swimming with one arm.

I was in the minority among the cast too. Not the only Tory, but one of very few. During auditions, I'd felt like the only kid who hadn't worn an outfit for World Book Day. The producer of the show was a guy called Chris Stott. Despite being very liberal, fairly left-wing and hating Brexit, he also has the strange tendency among his class toward flagellating himself for being part of the soppy liberal elite; he genuinely loves avocado but also understood why I found that funny. Chris was encouraging me to push the envelope as far as I wanted to.

Not that I had to push it far for the audience to react like I'd said something controversial. In this context, all I had to do to was articulate widely held opinions. That middle-class protests are a bit wanky. That men and women are a bit different. That cancel culture at universities was getting out of hand. They were just common reactions to life and politics but played out as edgy in the studio. In one piece on masculinity, we watched a very limp advert for the army. An older-looking squaddie opened a package from his missus, pulled out a teabag, sniffed it and got emotional. I made the very reasonable point, 'A bloke that cries sniffing a teabag can hardly be relied upon to torch a village.'

Actually, maybe the controversy was warranted for that one.

I enjoyed being on the show. When you stripped away all the context, TV and politics, I was just a comic in front of an audience, trying to make them laugh, something I'd been doing since 2001. In truth, being the odd one out didn't even worry me too much. Gigging all around Britain is a reassuring reminder that most people are grown-ups. The vast majority of people can laugh at things they don't agree with. In many ways that's the best kind of laugh: a reluctant one, like the comedy equivalent of a tricky par-five.

People often ask if satire is more difficult coming from the Right, especially since, during the period I've been doing it, the Right has held the balance of power in both

Britain and the US. I'll often be challenged to 'do a right-wing joke' – the implication being that I should somehow get laughter out of my centre-right politics. The truth is that no one can do this on Left or Right. Comedy is always about the people and ideas you disagree with. No left-wing comic has ever brought the house down with their love of comprehensive education; instead they take the piss out of private schools.

And no left-wing comic can make a genuine joke about the success of socialism because apparently the real version hasn't been tried yet.

I have three simple rules for what makes satire possible. I call them the 'three Hs'. Do you detect hypocrisy, hyperbole or hysteria? If any of these exist, you have a target. The culture wars and Brexit threw up plenty of examples. Take the 'People's Vote' marches for starters. The name itself was an awful own goal with its implication that the Brexit referendum wasn't by the people. The idea that loads of liberals having a day out in London with chopped kale power salads and terrible chants in some way spoke for the country was laughable.

Then there was the 'Wooferendum', when metropolitan liberals chose to express their displeasure with flags, banners and expensive dogs. I don't know quite how taking your Bichon Frise for a walk around Hyde Park could impact on democracy but they seemed to think it would help. Did they seriously think that a working-class Brexit voter in Sunderland might see that on the news, turn to his missus and say, 'That beagle looks genuinely sad, love, what have we done?'

The Remain movement was dogged throughout by a sense of hysteria. There were the headlines that took reasonable concerns over the impact of a no-deal Brexit and spun them out into all manner of fanciful dystopian outcomes. The most extreme of which was the *Evening Standard* who ran with a headline claiming Brexit could cause a rise in diseases, 'INCLUDING A SPIKE IN GONORRHEA'. A no-deal Brexit was a legitimate thing to worry about but sometimes the more extreme claims pulled focus from the legitimate ones.

During this time, it was easy to poke fun at the culture Remain had become. On social media, I saw videos of people on coaches re-wording hymns to praise the EU instead of God. It was odd that the marches were so well attended and yet never seemed to kick off. I guess if you have a nice life you wouldn't jeopardise it by getting a criminal record. When the working classes protest, things tend to happen. In the poll-tax riots, the government looked out of the window and thought, 'This could kick off.' During the EU marches, the main chance of civil unrest was if Browns were found to be using shop-bought hollandaise. I'm not saying the marchers didn't care about Britain leaving the EU but you'd have thought that at some point *someone* would've at least knocked a copper's helmet off.

The comedic holy grail of 'punching up' is way more subjective than it's made to seem. It depends where you see power lying. Power could be said to lie within Westminster but the cultural establishment have their own form of influence and control. The problem for the Left has been that every time they lose an election, they either have a hissy fit or double down on their dominance in matters of art and culture. I've distilled it down into a new theory I'm calling 'Norcott's Law'. Just like me, it's incredibly basic:

RIGHT WINS ELECTION > LEFT DOUBLES DOWN ON CULTURE > RIGHT WINS ELECTION > AND SO ON . . .

It was noticeable since the Brexit vote the revisionism of British history and culture was ticking over a lot faster. Totemic figures and ideas of Britishness came under frequent and sustained attack, particularly from millennials. Great poems like 'If' were painted over at university campuses while Churchill's statue had more offensive graffiti than a men's toilets at a railway station.

These combatants were originally called 'social justice warriors', which then became 'snowflakes', but were quickly rebranded as 'woke' – an aggressive, fast-paced form of hyper-liberalism which makes very little sense once you get off social media. If you haven't come across the word, a 'woke' person might for example believe in the existence of hundreds of genders rather than two. They might say things like 'Men can have periods.' These are viewpoints that the rest of society may come around to in time but, because they're hothoused online, where discourse can move much more swiftly, the gulf between these views and what the rest of society thinks grows wider by the day. That speed of progress also means that by the time this book is published they will be probably be called something else.

It used to be a cliché of *Daily Mail* readers to dismiss political correctness by saying, 'Well, I can't keep up with all the new words.' But by 2017, people really couldn't (even as I write this, 'BAME', a relatively recent replacement for 'ethnic minorities', is under review).

In 2018, I became aware that the artist formerly known as 'LGBT' started expanding. First to 'LGBTQ' then 'LGBTQIA+'. People seemed to be adding letters and symbols all the time. It was in danger of looking like a Wi-Fi password. I found this odd for a number of reasons. Firstly, I'd always thought 'LGBT' rolled off the tongue. They also got the letters in the exact correct order. Any other arrangement wouldn't have sounded half as good.

'TBGL' would've sounded like a train driver's union.

'BLGT' would've sounded like a sandwich with guacamole it didn't really need.

But it wasn't just letters or semantics. The original four identities felt like an idea everyone could get their heads around. With any advance in social justice, it's always useful to wonder if you could explain it easily to an older relative. I could easily describe a lesbian, gay, bisexual or transgender person. 'Queer' was not so easy, especially as it hadn't been long since I'd openly chastised my mum for using that exact word.

During these years, it also became common to openly mock the idea of St George's Day. The same people who would wish the Irish well on St Patrick's Day or celebrate religious holidays like Eid were quick to pour scorn on the idea that anyone should celebrate England or Englishness. It wasn't just their hypocrisy, the mockery became horribly clichéd, as their default move was always to point out that St George 'wasn't actually from England, he was from Palestine/Assyria/Westeros'.

It didn't need pointing out. The moment you hear a story involving a dragon it suggests some degree of mythical bollockery. I don't think anyone was sitting in a Wetherspoons thinking St George came from Telford. The point of St George's Day for me was to simply acknowledge that England was a good place to live: prosperous, liberal and democratic, in a relative global sense. The mockery of St George's undoubtedly mythical origins seemed to have undertones: 'We don't want you to celebrate this day. However, we're aware we can't say that so we'll resort to shitting on it from a great height.' Yet another wedge between everyday working-class people and the liberal Left.

Simultaneously, it became all too easy for this brand of politics to seem frivolous or performative. Students graffitiing over statues of old white poets, campus societies no-platforming totemic beacons of free speech –

it seemed to be like an arms race of one-upmanship (or up-personship) as to who could hold the most radical thought. Instead of getting high on drugs, students were getting high on the idea you could call clapping a 'micro-aggression'. The problem for the political Left was that they became synonymous with these risk-averse and wacky schools of thought. Millions of working-class Labour voters suddenly found themselves lining up in the same cultural trenches as Owen Jones and didn't feel like it suited them.

If you don't know Owen Jones, as I once told him, he's the 'grand poobah of wokeists' (which to his credit he laughed at). With his satchel and beta-male aesthetic, Owen is typical of the movement in that he might look low status but is extremely smart in using social media to create significant influence. He gets a fair bit of stick but Owen only has a profile because he represents a genuine constituency – the kind of left-wingers who would join a picket line but only if the line was sufficiently diverse and the thing they were picketing was a statue.

Looking back now, it seems odd that this branch of the Left felt so spurred on to promote what was essentially pressure-group politics. It's hard to work out where the encouragement came from. The first mistake was the reaction to the 2017 election. Whatever Corbyn had achieved, it was still a loss. The closest modern Britain had been to socialism was coming second by 60 seats. The Left, however, felt that their mastery over social media was like British naval superiority in the early part of the last century. They could win any war so long as their memes and emotive viral clips had a sea to sail on.

This idea of social media's power to assist left-wing social-justice causes was given a further boost as a consequence of the #MeToo movement, when many women shared stories of sexual harassment, on a previously unheard-of scale. I was raised by a straight-talking mother and had a close relationship with my sister who would speak to me frankly about these things. Early on, I was aware of early that creepy blokes were a sad reality of life.

In terms of media exposure, #MeToo was a huge phenomenon. Social media gives a certain anonymity and strength in numbers, so women felt emboldened to share anything from excessive 'flirting' to experiences of rape. The experience was powerful and sobering. It felt like the male 'brand', which had been faltering for a while, was now teetering on the brink.

The #MeToo discourse also fed into a questioning of gender identities, an idea I'd last heard get traction at Goldsmiths. 'Gender is a construct' the lads would say, in a desperate attempt to cop off.

#MeToo was an important moment but it quickly morphed into something else and wasn't helped by companies trying to hop on the feminist bandwagon to make a few quid. One of the most ill-judged of these was Gillette's advert in early 2019 exhorting men to 'do better'. The advert references #MeToo early on and goes on to show clips from news reports about sexual harassment. It includes clips of men leering at women. This is Gillette, the same company who not so long ago had their slogan emblazoned on cheerleader's arses and spent decades telling us that if our jaw couldn't slice open a watermelon we weren't real men. The problem wasn't just that they were woefully late to the party in terms of addressing #MeToo issues, but how often do you insult the client as a way of selling products to them? It was alienating to see a row of deadbeat dads flipping burgers like Stepford husbands.

Women also have clichéd insults you could throw at them. However, you wouldn't see Dove adopting a slogan like 'Women, let's be honest, we could get ready quicker.' Or L'Oréal showing a woman starting an argument just for the thrill of winning it.

Maybe Gillette thought that, as most women are the purchaser of grooming products for men, lining up on 'their' side would appeal to them. This disregards another characteristic of the wider populace: the vast majority of women are not in relationships with sexual assaulters and don't want to think of their partners, dads, brothers or sons in that way. Gillette weren't alone in this new wave of corporate virtue signalling. Everywhere you looked, companies were aligning themselves with sexy causes or trying to 'parent' their clients.

I ended up getting quite defensive about masculinity. Looking back, it might have been because I had just created one of these toxic male things in the form of my son. This is not to say I was averse to the idea of a new dialogue around ideas like consent. Even with my mother's frankness, the scale of sexual assault revealed during #MeToo had been an eye opener. But the debate seemed light on practicalities; how and when would I have the consent conversation with my son? At what point in sexual congress would I advise him to ask the question? At every stage? Or all agreed up front? The more I thought about the idea, it seemed a conversation worth having, but dangerous to simplify.

Of course, it was good to talk about masculinity but did we need a huge corporate entity like Gillette to take the lead? Even if their new male model did look like a quarterback who could also make pasta from scratch. And why was Gillette throwing around pejoratives at the same time I was being asked to be ever more careful around stereotypes?

The whole principle of the Left for many years had been to not use pejorative language or negative stereotypes against large groups of people. Yet suddenly it was open season on specific enemies, white men especially. Some of the points about white men in power were legitimate, but few bothered to make the distinction between power holders and the powerless. For me, the concept of universal male privilege was too broad and it got people's backs up. Biological sex being the most common distinction between humans, the idea accorded exactly half of the planet with privilege. It's not that on balance men don't experience benefits but it's very difficult to understand how a female middle-class professional from London could have less going for them than an 18-year-old panel beater from Wigan. In *Fleabag*, I'd rather be Phoebe Waller-Bridge than the bloke who rebalances her tyres.

In 2018, we saw the popularisation of a new word, 'gammon'. If you haven't come across it, the word describes the kind of angry-looking men in late middle-age that you'd see on *Question Time* asking questions about who'd have the balls to deploy nuclear missiles. Usually right-wing, possibly UKIP once upon a time.

It was interesting in that it was a word not only specific to one race, it was also age and gender specific. It deployed three of the 'isms' at once. I was surprised at how freely it was taken up by people I worked with in the liberal bubble. I didn't think it was as bad as the racial slurs against people of colour, I just didn't think it was very helpful. The Left seemed to be developing a habit of climbing to the moral high-ground then diving off it face first.

More and more, the sense was growing that, with the backing of a radical group called Momentum, the Labour party were in thrall to the aggressive band of young revolutionaries we were increasingly seeing on news discussion shows. The party had for several years boasted of its huge membership but party membership is like penis size: it's not what you've got, it's how you use it.

At conference after conference, the Labour party showed an interest in identity issues which far outstripped that of the nation at large. Not to mention Palestine. That's not to say the situation in the West Bank shouldn't be high up any foreign policy agenda but the membership seemed to fly the Palestinian flag like a badge of honour. They were so invested you'd have thought the West Bank was just outside of Warrington. The more Momentum types funded the party, the more the party had to throw them red meat in the form of policy.

Previously, we always used to know where we stood with political party funding. The Tories were funded by evil businessmen; Labour were bankrolled by 1970s-style trade unions and the Lib Dems were funded by the Campaign for Real Ale, probably. But now Labour had two disparate entities exerting influence on them. On the one hand, some old-fashioned unions and on the other a membership with liberal values from the year 3000. It hasn't ended with the departure of Corbyn. Keir Starmer may well be clever and sanguine but he's just one man while the parliamentary party and wider activists are still frequently miles out of step with the rest of the country. At the height of the coronavirus crisis, Shadow Minister Dawn Butler announced on Twitter she was doing research on micro-aggressions on WhatsApp groups. Not exactly a key priority in Dudley North.

All too often, the Left acted in real life the way it used to be represented in parody. I watched a *Young Ones* episode recently. It was hard to believe Rik Mayall's badge-wearing Marxist character was over 30 years old. He seemed like exactly the sort of bloke who'd now be talking about 'defunding the police' and declaring 'Language is a form of oppression'. The trouble is, Rik from *The Young Ones* is alive and well, still wearing the same badges and still running the local Labour party up and down the country.

The tone of the woke Left seemed so obviously alienating to the general public that it begged the question 'Do they even *want* to win power?' And maybe moving the focus from actual political power wasn't so daft after all. With no chance of winning in Scotland, Labour's odds of an overall majority are low. Perhaps the young Left is happy to become a largely cause-based movement. Winning general elections is hard but getting the odd company to withdraw a product or a studio to re-cast a film is a win you can experience more than once every five years.

Meanwhile, Corbyn's northern working-class vote was being further rattled by the increasing influence of metropolitan EU flag wavers like Starmer. Caught in a pincer movement between the Labour heartlands and a fear of losing votes to the Lib Dems, Corbyn finally caved in to the pressure to openly support a second referendum. The claim often made in Corbyn's defence was that he'd always been on the right side of history. In the case of Brexit, it was a couple of years down the line and he still hadn't picked a team. The policy was sometimes referred to as 'constructive ambiguity'. That could work if you were a young gay pop star trying to cultivate a female fanbase but not when the country was going through its biggest political and social upheaval since the Second World War.

The Lib Dems went one further and eventually supported a straight revocation of Article 50. Given Mum's views on democracy, she'd have been appalled at this position by the party she once helped raise funds for. She once said something about voting which always stuck with me: 'A vote is the only time we're all equal, son. That's why some of those bastards don't like it.'

As the first deadline to leave was extended, the Remain camp smelled blood. The Tory rebellion had become a constant state of convulsion within one wing of the party. Meanwhile, as the power vacuum at the heart of government widened, Theresa May fell into it. I felt sorry for her but that was probably a sign she should go. Pity is reserved for people in a hopeless situation. Prime ministers should leave office to either cheers or boos, not the nation tilting its head and saying, 'Bless'.

In the absence of a mandate at the heart of government, other things temporarily occupied that space. Andrew Adonis, Gina Miller, bigger and bigger marches. An e-petition reportedly signed by 6 million people. (The exact same politicians who implied Russian interference now seemed to think democracy could be shaped by people with multiple Gmail addresses.) We then had 'indicative votes', a bold move where backbenchers would set the agenda and break the deadlock. They then proceeded to not vote *for* anything. It was sad for backbenchers really, this was their moment, but if anything it compounded the inertia and made a strong case for benevolent dictatorships.

Whether Brexit happened came to stand for more than just the vote, it seemed to test the very capacity of the public to set the political tempo of the nation.

The curious effect of the culture war was that issues in no way intrinsically linked to Britain leaving the EU became battlegrounds on which to fight proxy wars. There was no specific reason why Remainers were more likely to be vegan but they certainly seemed to be. There was also no reason why climate-change denial should be mixed up with a mistrust of the EU but Brexiteers seemed far more likely to look on the bright side of barbecue weather in November.

Brexit had somehow gone beyond politics and bias and revealed that the UK predominantly had two political 'blood types' which guided everything they stood for.

In my own way, I got involved in identity politics when I made the documentary *How the Middle Classes Ruined Britain*, which aired in July 2019. During the making of the show, we went to ex-mining towns in the East Midlands and the attitude to Labour was not just changing, it was palpably hostile. As Labour were lurching towards a second referendum, it had shone a light on the overall brand of the party and the disconnect had become a gulf. There were Labour MPs like Caroline Flint and Gloria De Piero who 'got it' but too many were resting on the lazy assumption that Labour was 'in the blood', despite large swathes having already shown themselves to be willing to take a radical choice at the ballot box in 2016.

Being the BBC, the show was made almost exclusively by very nice middle-class people. Every once in a while, you have a cultural moment which sums up that divide. We were filming in Ashfield for the day and had set up at the local Asda. The producer, Christian – a lovely bloke and brilliant at his job – asked the cashier at the café if we could run a tab. I wish I could describe to you the look on her face. He might as well have asked her for *patatas bravas*.

The point of my documentary was simple, to shine a light on the growing hypocrisy among the very class of people whose politics tended to preach virtue. I was already aware of the issue of deception and sharp elbows in the race for places at good schools. The same couples who poured scorn on the idea of private and grammar schools were frequently renting flats opposite the academy they wanted to send their kids to. Or, arguably more dishonest still, a huge number were attending church to get their kids into a good faith school. The devil may have the best tunes but it seems like God had all the best schools.

Though I didn't just want to highlight middle-class hypocrisy, I wanted to highlight my own. However, I often get a degree of unconscious bias from middle-class people where they presume any contradictions weren't factored in but just me being dumb. It's a problem when you speak and look like a plumber; people will often miss any attempt you make at nuance or irony. At a recording session for the Radio 4 show *The News Quiz* in early 2020 on the day Britain left the EU, I asked the brilliant Anand Menon, a professor of European politics and foreign affairs at King's College in London, a question about the European Union. I then interrupted and caught myself, before commenting, 'Surprise, surprise, Leave voter ignores expert.'

It didn't get any laughs.

Thirty seconds later, the notoriously pro-EU host repeated the exact same joke and got a round of applause. I laughed to myself. It must be how women feel in meetings when they float a good idea to silence then some braying twat called Gavin says the exact same thing and gets a payrise.

For me, perhaps the most surprising thing to come out of the documentary was finding that assortative mating – people coupling up outside of their social class – was actually reducing. In a time when prejudice about mixed-race relationships is on its way out, we are actually going backwards in terms of variance between couples based on class. Think about it, think about your own circle of friends – how many of them have settled with someone from a noticeably different social class? And your bloke simply being northern doesn't count. It turns out people from the north can be posh too (trust me, I'm as surprised as you are).

Assortative mating is one of the quickest ways to redistribute wealth. I may be over-simplifying but if you call yourself a socialist, then marry someone from a council estate. Go on. I dare you. Bring Darren back to meet Mother and Father. Feel the tension as he wipes his hand on the back of his mouth and asks where the 'shitter' is. Relax as Darren looks at his tuna niçoise salad and asks for salad cream. What fun as Darren agrees with your parents that the police should be defunded, then they might stop knocking on his fucking door at 3am. But you love him, right? These are just cultural differences, man, it's all part of life's beautiful rainbow.

How the Middle Classes Ruined Britain got a violently different reaction. In *The Times* alone it was reviewed five times, from a very good review to a terrible one and everything in between. As the reviews kept coming in, I was in constant contact with my PR guy, Julian. Julian has been with me since the start and done a cracking job promoting a comic whose opinions he didn't always agree with. I was talking about the bad review I'd read in *The Times* and trying to be philosophical about it. He was sympathetic and pointed out how many decent reviews there had been and that the show in total had been watched 1.5 million times, very good for a one-off documentary.

Then he added, referring to the review he thought we were both discussing, 'Camilla is just one reviewer.'

'Camilla?' I enquired, 'I was talking about the one by Hugo Rifkind.'

There was a pregnant pause.

'Maybe stay offline for a couple of days, Geoff.'

I won't lie, the process of that show going to air took it out of me. Not just because of the programme, it was also around the exact same time as the ten-year anniversary of my mum passing and the five-year anniversary of the little girl my wife and I never got to meet. I'm normally quite resilient but it all felt like a bit too much. Not just the bad reactions, the good ones too. The criticism and praise were mangling my head.

Once I came out the other side of that period, however, something had changed. Getting past those two sad anniversaries felt like a milestone. The wild spectrum of reaction to the documentary had acted like aversion therapy. The country's different factions were still at each other's throats but I felt different. I still had strong opinions, I still felt moved to comment and duke it out with the best of them, but the motivation wasn't coming from the same place any more. Life had reminded me it was much bigger than politics.

There was something circular about these two great lumps of grief I had to revisit that helped me understand my own views better and those of other people. Anger is rarely an isolated emotion. It now seemed clear to me that our politics are not the clear-headed interpretation of the world we hope them to be. Our views are hunches built on ever-sliding tectonic plates of experience, prejudice and our own bullshit. They are subject to bias. Bias isn't something that just happens in curmudgeonly middle-age, it's building from the moment you're born. The problem is, by the time you're 40 you've forgotten a lot of what formed it in the first place. You just think you've conveniently ended up right, about everything.

How many men drinking red wine and tweeting at *Question Time* are really angry with whatever Tory or Labour frontbencher they've reeled out that night?

Did anyone really give a shit about the actual customs union? I mean *really*?

That novelist from the eighteenth century you got cancelled. Did you really care? Or was he on a website hit-list and cultural decolonisation had all become a bit like Pokemon Go?

How many left-wingers really think Tories are guilty of state-sponsored murder? (In fact, Lefties, don't answer that.)

Writing this book has confirmed to me that my Conservatism is pretty fixed. My core political engine room is driven by a belief in personal responsibility, a small state, a lean benefits system and low taxes where possible. But is my personal political constitution in any way objective? Maybe I believe in personal responsibility because when Mum left Dad she opted to leave him with the house and make her own way. Maybe I believe in a small state because when it did get really big my country was hopelessly exposed to the global credit crunch. Is it possible I favour lean benefits because I'd seen so many people never return to work because it didn't make financial sense to do so?

And perhaps I believed in lower taxes because . . . well, look, I just like keeping most of my money, OK? At least I admit it.

Knowing about this kind of powerful subconscious political bias doesn't change those hunches and convictions as they arise, but it's given me cause to reflect on them. Maybe I don't think Keir Starmer is a class charlatan. It might just be a projection of fears regarding my own gentrification (between you and me, I have known the taste of brioche).

With a bit of perspective, I also saw that a lot of my political comedy hadn't entirely been an attack on the Left. Whether it was welcome or not, I was often trying to give advice. Lefties might scoff at that idea but, looking back over a lot of the TV slots I did and articles I wrote during that time, it was obvious that one part of it was me saying, 'Do you realise how people like me see people like you?' In some ways, speaking up for the kind of Labour party my dad was once proud to be a part of.

These reflections felt liberating as 2019 drew to a close and the election approached. A lot of people around me seemed to think Corbyn might pull off a miracle. However, they were the same people who thought Miliband would win, Remain would walk it and that a buffoon like Boris Johnson would never be Prime Minister.

Maybe the mistake was to call all this a culture 'war'. Most of the debates represented skirmishes. Politics remains the true battleground to meaningfully improve people's lives and the Left felt as far from victory as they'd ever been. They'd had me at one point, like they'd had my father before. But, however you framed it, I couldn't see them getting me back, not for a long time.

EPILOGUE

As the 2019 *Alternative Election* finally wound down in time to hand over to the morning breakfast shows, I got in a taxi away from Riverside TV studios. A lot had changed. It wasn't just that having a working government felt more secure than the hung parliament of the previous two years. I felt different. I still had the opinions, was still up for the debate, but I no longer had the rage. Similarly, when it came to the people I'd lost, I still had the memories but not so much of the sadness.

Politically, it was very simple in the end. I wanted a government that would spend more on public services, but not loads more. I also felt the issue of leaving the EU couldn't be avoided. It was wrong to talk about a second referendum before the first was implemented. Any party looking to do so was condemning Britain to more years of uncertainty and, by this point, it felt like uncertainty had become more damaging than Brexit itself.

Boris did his best to make me reconsider. Despite all the promises of how good he was on his feet it never seemed to materialise in the live debates. However, if I could still vote Conservative after seeing the party's leader duck interviews, steal mobile phones and get caught hiding in a fridge, then maybe there really was no turning back.

It wasn't even so clear cut on the goodies/baddies front this time. The Tories had shown clumsy insensitivity around Grenfell and arguably fared even worse over Windrush. The Labour party, however, was mired in anti-Semitism. Just like the expenses scandal, they'd welched on one of their own USPs.

The final vote in this chapter of my political life was exactly as it should always be in a democracy: a choice between the least shit of two options.

As I was on the final part of my journey back to the hotel, many of my fellow right-wingers were gleefully re-tweeting the moment on Channel 4 when the exit poll came out. They were enjoying the audience's shock at something so utterly predictable. The crowd's reaction did have a certain comic appeal but I wasn't in the mood for trolling. As a country, that kind of thing didn't seem to be getting us anywhere.

Politically, I knew where I wanted to go. A dynamic country unafraid to speak up for itself. An inclusive social dialogue which makes sense to everyone and not just the culture warriors thrashing it out online. An acceptance of Right and Left as two competing ideas for a better society, where arguments have to be won rather than steamrollered with simplistic notions of good guys and villains.

I watched that Channel 4 clip again recently and spotted something different this time. Just as the TV pollster was telling us about the huge landslide of Tory seats, he had to make a quick summary before handing over to the next segment.

'So,' he said looking at swathes of blue on the map, 'we are in for ten years of Boris . . .' and stared meaningfully at the camera, '. . . barring a national emergency.'

'OK mate,' I'd thought to myself, it wasn't like we were on the brink of a global pandemic.'

Maybe you're still wondering whether I ever got around to telling my dad I was a Tory before he died.

Thankfully I did.

I came clean in the autumn of 2013 after he watched me perform at the Edinburgh Fringe. In the show, I spent a good 15 minutes talking about my swing to the right. I met up with him in a bar shortly after.

'Good show, son,' he said, passing me a pint. 'That Tory thing is a good angle.'

I stopped in my tracks. This was supposed to be my political 'coming out' and he'd completely missed the point. I realised then that, just like my evasive answers of 2005 and 2010, I could skirt around the issue and pretend it was indeed just an angle – but I was ready to be honest.

'It's not an angle, Dad. I voted for them last time. If there was an election tomorrow I'd do it again.'

His eyes narrowed. He looked on the verge of anger. I breathed in. I could handle being at odds with my old man, it wouldn't be the first time, but so late on in his life and having closed so much difficult ground between us, I didn't want to become estranged over something as silly as politics.

Interestingly, earlier that day he'd corrected me on a crucial bit of family history. My grandparents had only been able to buy their house because of Thatcher's right-to-buy. Despite them both working, it hadn't been on the cards until those big discounts were introduced by Thatcher in 1980. I started to think about Dad's union work versus the glint he got in his eye whenever we spoke about money. I thought about the fact that, despite the mishaps, my family were always knocking at the door of social mobility. The Norcotts might not have voted Conservative before but it turned out we might have *been* that way for quite some time. Had me and the old man finally found ourselves on the same page?

His long intake of breath eventually finished. Something in him seemed to give. Finally, Dad exhaled and said, 'I've been going a bit that way myself of late.'

I nodded and studied his face hard, as ever, never entirely sure of what was coming next.

'Mind you, I don't think I could ever *vote* for the bastards.'

ACKNOWLEDGEMENTS

Firstly, I have to thank my wife, the love of my life, Emma. As any partner of a creative type will know, these kinds of projects take up a lot of (to use a political buzzword) 'bandwidth'. When she might want to talk about real-life issues, the first words to come out of my mouth could be, 'I think I've worked out where to put that story about the cowboy competition.' She expects me to do well, which makes one of us.

Also, my son. The majority of this book was written in lockdown. It was a great relief to be able to come out of my office and wrestle with him or talk about *Star Wars*. Without his magical presence in my life, a lot of the personal challenges of the last few years would've been even harder to look back on.

I give thanks to my sister. Who was kind enough to let me talk in detail about our family life, but who also did that wonderful big-sister thing of always having an eye on me. The lovely family she has made of Stephen, Rhoderic and Beatrice are something I'm thankful for on many levels.

I thank my stepdad Roe, for being a parent to me

without ever stepping on my father's toes. And his daughters, my new sisters, Sarah and Lorraine, who were kind enough to share a good man and add to our family in so many ways.

As a relatively small clan, we are always look on the look-out for new recruits. The Moore family helped make my childhood better and taste nicer. Thank to you to Joan, Mrs Moore, Mike, Peter and William and all the partners and kids.

Also, the entire Edmonds family. In particular Sarah, Jake and Joe. Though Mick isn't around any more, his hard graft and cheerful demeanour is an example I'm always trying to emulate. His sons are a credit to him.

I've also been lucky enough to have a close friend like Matt, and seeing him find happiness has been a recent life highlight.

Thanks to my agent Sophie and to Jake, who took this book on. They've both taken creative risks in worlds that are used to doing things a certain way when it comes to comedy. Their support, backing and guidance has been invaluable.

And thanks again to my mum and dad. If I did my job properly, you'd either want to go drinking with them or, at the very least, have a heated debate.

Wimbledon, the eighties (ish)

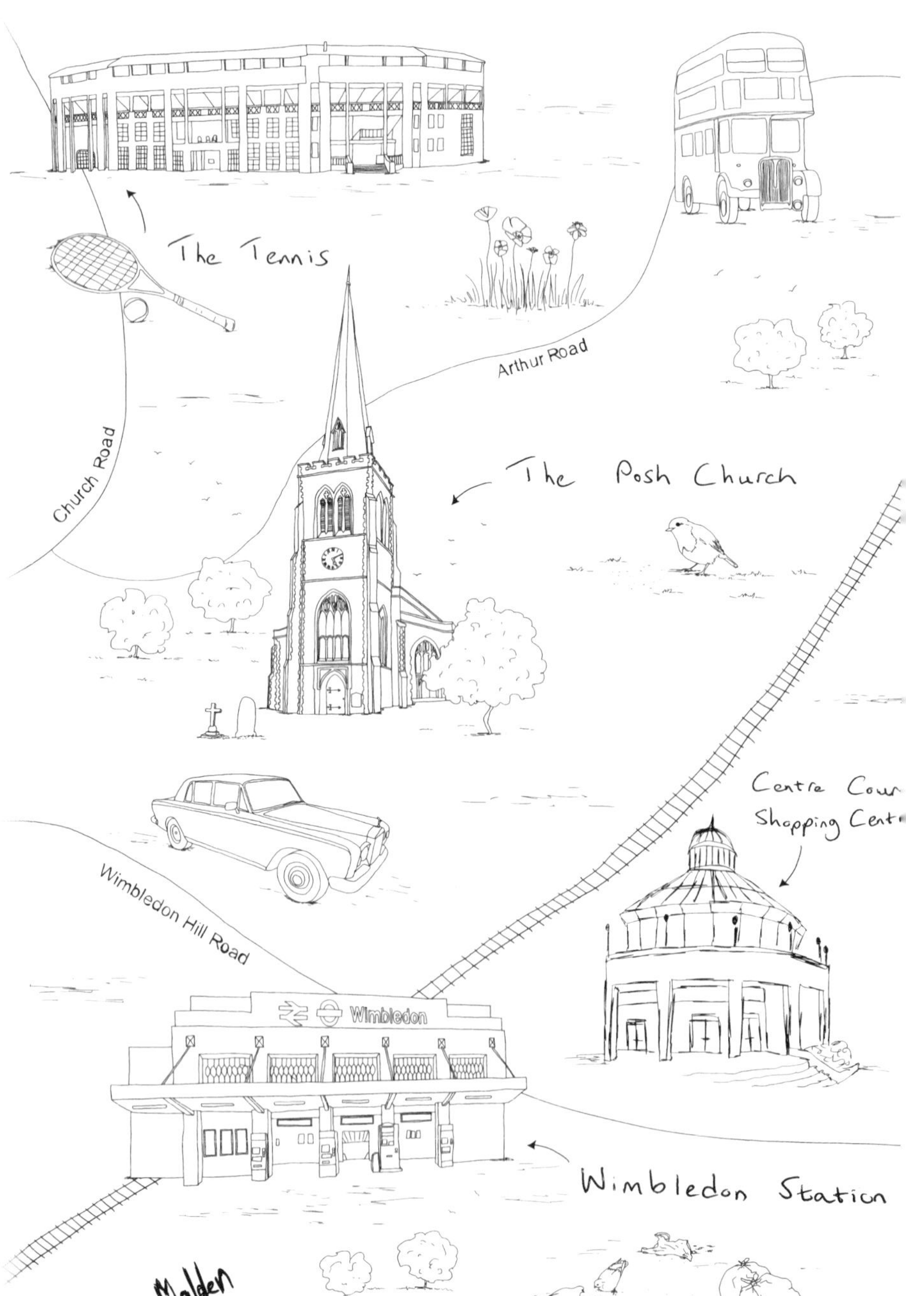